Science Fair Projects For Dummies®

Cheat Sheet

Project idea checklist

When you come up with an idea, ask yourself these questions to decide whether the project is doable:

- Do I enjoy this topic?
- Do my parents and teacher approve?
- What's the estimated total cost?
- Can my family afford it?
- Do I have the knowledge to do this project?
- Is there enough information available?
- What supplies do I need (and where can I find them)?
- Can I finish by the due date?
- Is it safe?
- Is it too controversial?
- Do I know anyone who can help me with my project?
- Does my idea follow the rules for student science projects?
- Where can I find the necessary forms?

Tips for writing a good research paper

Writing a research paper involves finding and organizing information, and then drafting and polishing your paper. Here's how the process works:

- Gather all the information you need from books, magazines, the Internet, government publications, and interviews.
- Keep track of the sources of all your facts.
- Organize information by grouping related facts together.
- Use this simple formula for your writing the paper:
  - Tell them what you're going to say.
  - Say it.
  - Tell them what you just said.
- Outline your paper by determining your main headings and grouping related facts under each heading.
- Write a first draft of your paper using your own words (so that you don't plagiarize anyone else's work).
- Format the bibliography.
- Review, edit, and revise the paper.
- Ask someone else to read it over.
- Check your spelling.
- Create your final copy.

Building a great display

Before going to the science fair, you need to create a backboard display that attracts attention. Here's how:

- Check the science fair size requirements before you design the backboard.
- Make a sketch of your layout to make sure that all your material will fit on the backboard.
- Glue all material *firmly* on the backboard.
- Combine complementary colors that enhance your project.
- Put titles in larger fonts so they're readable from a distance.
- Add texture to emphasize your display.
- Add drawings and photographs to make the display more interesting.
- Summarize your project hypothesis, materials, procedures, results, and conclusions — you don't need to tell the whole story.

For Dummies: Bestselling Book Series for Beginners

Science Fair Projects For Dummies®

Cheat Sheet

The scientific method (in a nutshell)

Here's a quick look at the parts of the scientific method:

- **Question or Problem:** What your project will accomplish or solve. In other words, why you're doing the project.

- **Hypothesis:** What you think your project will prove — it's stronger than an opinion, but weaker than a fact.

- **Subject:** What you'll test or build during your project.

- **Variables:** Factors that you'll change or evaluate in order to test the hypothesis. Variables are most often used in experiments, rather than engineering, computer, or research projects.

  The different kinds of variables are:

  - **Experimental (independent) variable.** What you purposely change during your project in order to test your hypothesis.

  - **Measured (dependent) variable.** The change you'll evaluate and measure, which occurs when you apply the experimental variable.

  - **Controlled variable (control).** The factors that must be the same for all samples in your experiment — every time that you do your experiment — in order to ensure that your results are valid.

- **Experimental group:** A number of identical subjects to which you apply the experimental variable.

- **Control group:** A group of subjects that's identical to the experimental groups, except that no variables are applied.

- **Results:** The facts and figures that show what happened during the project. They can be represented in charts or graphs.

- **Conclusions:** The conclusions compare the results to the hypothesis to determine if the project proved the hypothesis.

What happens at the science fair

When you're all done, it's time for the fair. Here's a thumbnail sketch of what goes on:

- **Setup.** Your project will be checked to make sure that it follows the rules, and then you'll be given a display location.

- **Judging.** Scientists and engineers who are volunteer judges will look at the projects in their fields and interview the students responsible for the work.

- **Awards ceremony.** Usually, a public announcement of the winners is made in each category, along with professional society awards and sweepstakes awards.

- **Fun.** You get to meet other students, see different projects, and enjoy whatever activities are planned for exhibitors.

For Dummies: Bestselling Book Series for Beginners

Science Fair Projects

FOR

DUMMIES®

by Maxine Levaren

Wiley Publishing, Inc.

Science Fair Projects For Dummies®

Published by
Wiley Publishing, Inc.
111 River Street
Hoboken, NJ 07030
www.wiley.com

For general information on our other products and services or to obtain technical support, please contact our Customer Care Department within the U.S. at 800-762-2974, outside the U.S. at 317-572-3993, or fax 317-572-4002.

Wiley also publishes its books in a variety of electronic formats. Some content that appears in print may not be available in electronic books.

Library of Congress Control Number: 2002110317

ISBN: 978-0-7645-5460-5

Manufactured in the United States of America

10 9 8 7 6

Wiley Publishing, Inc. is a trademark of Wiley Publishing, Inc.

About the Author

Maxine Levaren, is a Jill of all trades, who's worked as a writer, teacher, software developer, personal success coach, and consultant (not necessarily in that order).

In a former life, she was a science fair mom and cheerleader for a project involving 30 mice (back when working with live animals was easier). That experience paved the way for her career as an author of science fair project books. Maxine has also published works on computers and travel and lifestyle issues. She lives in San Diego with Senji and Bandit, her two dogs.

Dedication

To my mom, Jean Haren.

Author's Acknowledgments

Bravo to all the exhibitors at the Greater San Diego Science and Engineering Fair, who gave me so many great projects to choose from. Most especially, I want to give a big hand to the students who graciously allowed me to use their projects in this book.

Thanks also to my agent, Matt Wagner at Waterside Productions, who played matchmaker between Wiley Publishing, Inc. and me. Kudos to the editors at Wiley: Tracy Boggier who helped birth this project and Allyson Grove who nurtured it throughout its development. And a special vote of gratitude to Shirley Parrish, Director of the Management Committee of the Greater San Diego Science and Engineering Fair, who served as technical editor for this book, keeping me on the scientific straight and narrow.

Appreciation to my supporters and fans, Kathie Wickstrand Gahen, my coach, and Patricia Dibsie, fellow writer, best friend, and "partner in crime."

Loving thanks to my awesome sons, Michael Bruce Iritz and Stuart Allen Iritz, whose science fair projects got me started on this path.

Publisher's Acknowledgments

We're proud of this book; please send us your comments through our Dummies online registration form located at www.dummies.com/register/.

Some of the people who helped bring this book to market include the following:

Acquisitions, Editorial, and Media Development

Project Editor: Allyson Grove

Acquisitions Editor: Tracy Boggier

Copy Editors: Robert Annis, Chad R. Sievers

Technical Editor: Shirley Parrish

Senior Permissions Editor: Carmen Krikorian

Editorial Assistant: Carol Strickland

Cartoons: Rich Tennant, www.the5thwave.com

Composition Services

Project Coordinator: Nancee Reeves

Layout and Graphics: Carrie Foster, Kristin McMullan, Erin Zeltner

Proofreaders: Laura Albert, Andy Hollandbeck, Aptara

Indexer: Aptara

Publishing and Editorial for Consumer Dummies

> **Diane Graves Steele,** Vice President and Publisher, Consumer Dummies

> **Joyce Pepple,** Acquisitions Director, Consumer Dummies

> **Kristin A. Cocks,** Product Development Director, Consumer Dummies

> **Michael Spring,** Vice President and Publisher, Travel

> **Brice Gosnell,** Publishing Director, Travel

> **Suzanne Jannetta,** Editorial Director, Travel

Publishing for Technology Dummies

> **Andy Cummings,** Vice President and Publisher, Dummies Technology/General User

Composition Services

> **Gerry Fahey,** Vice President of Production Services

> **Debbie Stailey,** Director of Composition Services

Contents at a Glance

Table of Contents

Introduction

●●●

*Y*ikes! I have to do a science project! If you've never done one before, but have heard horror stories about them, you're probably dreading the whole thing. Contrary to popular belief, doing a science project isn't the 21st century equivalent of medieval torture. True, you may be required to do some hard work, and you may feel at times like you can never get through it, but you'll survive, without any visible scars.

In fact, help is on the way. Welcome to *Science Fair Projects For Dummies,* where you find out everything you can possibly want to know about doing a science fair project (but were afraid to ask). In this book, I plan to demystify the whole process and make it easy and fun for you.

The good news is that you already have a lot of the abilities that you need. Do you like to write? The research paper gives you a place to show off your way with words. If you're an artist in the making, you can have fun creating an attractive project display. If you're persistent, never giving up until you find the answer, research is made for you. And if you're crazy about details, lists, and statistics, I know you can keep excellent, precise records.

About This Book

This book is designed to be a no-nonsense, easy-to-follow guide to doing a successful science fair project and hopefully, having some fun in the process. Rather than discussing only projects that involve experiments, I include three other types of projects, including:

- ✔ Computer projects that either develop programs to solve a particular problem or analyze system performance.

- ✔ Engineering projects that design and build new devices or test existing devices to compare and analyze performance.

- ✔ Research projects that collect data, either by surveying a specific population or researching current sources, and that mathematically analyze and compare the information.

How to Use This Book

You don't need to read this book from cover to cover to get the most out of it (although you can if you want to). As with all *For Dummies* books, you can skip around to the topics that interest you most. However, to get an idea of the entire science project experience, check out Chapter 1, which provides a complete overview.

Then, feel free to scan the Table of Contents to find the information that you need. In each chapter, you can find a step-by-step approach to the easiest, most effective way to get the job done. I also cover information that can help you anticipate, avoid, and, if necessary, deal with any bumps in the road. One quick note: Part VI is a little different from the other parts of the book; it describes actual projects in a variety of categories and in varying degrees of difficulty.

Conventions Used in This Book

The following conventions are used throughout the text to make things consistent and easy to understand.

- New terms appear in *italic* and are closely followed by an easy-to-understand definition.

- **Boldface** is used to highlight the action parts of the numbered steps. You can see a lot of boldfaced steps in Part VI where I list sample projects done at a California science fair.

Foolish Assumptions

In order to include all the information you need, I make a few assumptions about you, the reader. For example,

- You're a student. Even though your parents (who are your biggest fans and support system) may read parts of this book, I'm mainly talking to you.

- This is your first or second project, so you want a simple approach that you can follow.

- Science, medicine, engineering, and computers aren't necessarily your favorite subjects, but doing a science project may lead you to a career in advanced science or medicine.

✔ You're ready, willing, and able to have a great science fair project experience.

✔ You want to have fun.

How This Book Is Organized

Science Fair Projects For Dummies is organized so that you can easily access all the information that you need. The chapters are in the same sequence as the activities that you may perform while doing your project, but you don't have to read them in order — when you want some information, just turn to the part that you need.

Here's the breakdown.

Part I: A Magical Mystery Tour of Science Fair Projects

Part I talks about how and why science fairs started, and briefly explains what's involved in doing a science project, from soup (finding a topic) to nuts (exhibiting at a science fair). I also talk about why doing a science fair project is a good thing, and how you can make the process manageable, educational, and fun. Yeah, I said fun!

Part II: Choosing a Project and Getting Started

Part II deals with what may be the most important part of any science project — finding the best project idea for you. Because you live with your science project for several months, you need to be sure to choose a topic that you like. So, I explain in detail the types of projects you can do and the official International Science and Engineering Fair (ISEF) categories.

In addition, to make sure that your project idea is feasible, I show you how to give your idea the "acid test" for safety, affordability, and "do-ability" given your time and resources.

Finally, in this part, I show you where to locate information (research) and after you find it, how to take notes. When you're done with the research, you organize your facts, outline your report, and write a clear, informative research paper. So, I give you a step-by-step guide on how to do just that.

Part III: The Nitty-Gritty: Stepping Through the Project

Part III deals with the heart of the matter — designing and executing your project. To be successful, you need to plan and organize your time, so I give you some tools to help you meet all your deadlines.

No matter what topic you choose, you need to understand and apply the *scientific method.* This involves asking a question that your project plans to answer and making an educated guess about what you think the answer is. For certain types of projects, you need to define *variables* and *controls,* which are the factors that remain constant or are changed. You may also need to establish *experimental* and *control groups,* which are subjects that are tested and observed during the project. If this all seems confusing, it isn't after you check out Chapter 8, where I describe the elements of the scientific method and demonstrate how this applies to different types of projects.

Then, I show you how and where to get your materials, including how to plan, describe, and document any "home builts." I also demonstrate how to design your procedures, and carry out your project. Perhaps most important, I explain how to effectively document everything that happens during the project. And finally, I escort you to the end of the road — assembling and analyzing your results and, based on those results, drawing your conclusion.

Part IV: Show and Tell

By the time you get here, you've put in many hours and done a lot of hard work. In Part IV, I show you how to present your project so that it gets a lot of favorable attention.

For starters, I talk about how to assemble your science fair notebook. And then, for all you artistic types, I talk about getting out the scissors and glue to create an attractive and informative display.

Part V: The Finals: Knowing What to Expect at the Fair

You did it! Your project is finished! In Part V, I talk about how to set up your project at the science fair, how to endure (and enjoy) the judging sessions, and how to graciously accept any awards that you may receive.

Part VI: Some Superb Science Project Picks

This part describes actual student projects that competed in the Greater San Diego Science and Engineering Fair in 2002.

Part VII: The Part of Tens

This section contains some valuable information that you need, but that doesn't fit in anywhere else — project ideas to avoid, great Web sites to visit, fun things to do while you're exhibiting at a science fair, tips for parents, and several science fair essentials.

Icons Used in This Book

Several icons appear in the margins of the book to highlight important information. Here's a quick rundown about what they mean.

The bull's eye marks information that can make your life easier while you're working on your project. Pay close attention to them.

This icon indicates something you need to keep in mind in order to have a successful project.

Text with this icon alerts you to a common mistake that can trip you up.

Text marked with the ringing alarm clock gives you information that you can use now to make life easier later.

The True Story icon indicates projects or examples from actual science fairs.

Part I
A Magical Mystery Tour of Science Fair Projects

The 5th Wave   By Rich Tennant

"You can take that old jar for your science project, I'm sure I have some baking soda you can borrow, and let's see, where's that old particle accelerator of mine... here it is, in the pantry."

In this part . . .

*1*f you're here, you've decided to do a science fair project (or perhaps your teacher decided for you). Either
way, the whole thing can be easier if you know a bit more.
In Part I, I give you a bird's eye view of the entire process
and summarize everything you need to know to carry out
a great science project. I also tell you how doing a project
can help you in your educational career.

Doing a science project is perhaps the biggest job you've
had so far in school, so dig in and read about how much
fun it can be!

Chapter 1

Science Fair Projects 101: Discovering What They're All About

You don't have to be a rocket scientist (or even a brain surgeon) to do a successful and fun science fair project, especially if you read this book.

You may be dreading the entire experience, remembering the horror stories that your older siblings or cousins told you about finishing their projects at 3 a.m., only five hours before the project was due. Or you may be looking forward to sinking your teeth into your science project, confident that your project will result in a great discovery.

No matter how you're feeling now, I guarantee that you'll be stronger, smarter, and more self-confident when you're done.

But to gain that strength, courage, and confidence, you have to make a commitment to do the best project you possibly can. I know that's kind of hard without knowing what you're in for, so in this chapter I give you a preview of coming attractions, so you can see what a science fair project is all about and how *Science Fair Projects For Dummies* can give you all the help you need.

Explaining What's Involved in a Science Fair

A *science fair* is an exhibition where students display scientific experiments, computer programs or systems, or engineering designs and tests that they've created. Each project in the fair demonstrates that the students understand the scientific method (see Chapter 8) and can apply it, while having an independent, hands-on learning experience.

Science fairs grew out of teachers' desire to advance interest in scientific knowledge. When the Russians launched Sputnik, the world's first artificial space satellite in 1957, many Americans became anxious to encourage students to study the sciences so as not to fall behind other nations in scientific research.

With the support of businesses, universities and research facilities, government agencies, and other organizations, science fairs have grown from many small school exhibitions into one huge international science and engineering fair (oddly enough, it's called the International Science and Engineering Fair [ISEF]), where students from all over the world show off their work and compete for recognition and valuable prizes. (In fact, if you're curious, Chapter 15 has more details about the types of prizes you can win.)

The purpose of a science fair is to help you (the student) find out more about a specific topic. Don't think that you need to choose a difficult or complex project to impress the judges. Selecting a project that you can understand, doing it by yourself, and explaining it to the judges at the fair is better.

Here are a few more reminders as you begin working on a project and preparing to display it at a fair:

- ✔ **Don't compare your progress with others.** If you're a seventh grader doing your first project, don't compare yourself to a twelfth grader who's worked on the same topic for five or six years, and won several awards along the way.

- ✔ **At first, compete only with yourself to do the best project that you can.** Later, when you go to the science fair, you can size up the competition.

Figure 1-1 shows a chart of the activities involved in doing a science fair project.

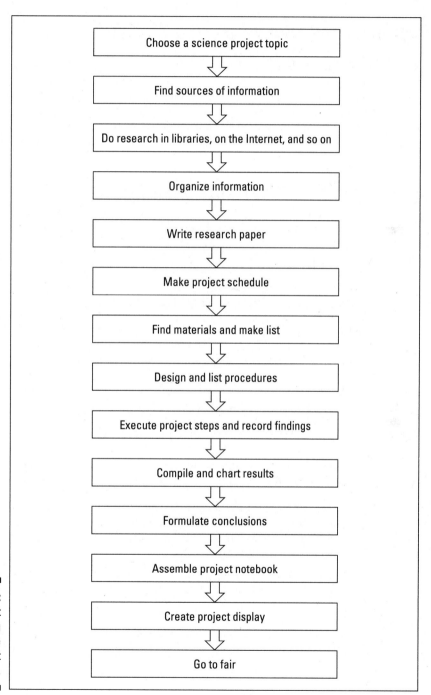

Figure 1-1:
A flowchart
showing
science
project
activities.

Finding the Best Project for You

Science fair projects can range from the simplest experiment to a complex project that involves experimentation, observation, and advanced mathematical calculations.

Where you fall on that scale, naturally depends on your prior knowledge of science, particularly in the subject matter you are dealing with.

Identifying the different types of projects

You can choose from several different types of projects. Chapter 3 has a full explanation, but here's a quick breakdown:

- In an *experiment,* you conduct a test to prove that a certain assumption is true.
- With a *computer science* project, you do one of the following:
    - Develop one or more computer programs to perform a specific task.
    - Test and analyze computer performance.
- In an *engineering* project, you do one of the following:
    - Design and build a new device that performs a specific function.
    - Test and analyze the performance and capabilities of an existing device.
- With a *research* project, you gather data, either by doing research or conducting surveys, and then mathematically analyze that data.

Choosing among the categories

Science fair projects are also broken down into a number of categories in the biological and physical sciences. In Chapter 3, I list the official ISEF categories, and give examples of the types of projects in each category.

Making the project suit you

A science project can be a great experience if you're working on something that's interesting and fun. Just ask someone whom computers fascinate whether she'd like to spend four months developing some new software. I'm sure that the answer would be a resounding yes!

So, it really doesn't matter whether you choose botany, physics, or computer science — the winning formula is selecting something that you like, that you have the skills to do, and that stretches your abilities. Check out Chapter 4 for some hints on how to find a project that suits you to a "T".

Looking at other students' past projects is another good way to see what types of things may appeal to you. This activity may also show you what's involved in doing your own project. If you'd like to see some actual projects, flip back to Chapters 16, 17, and 18.

Investigating and Reporting Background Information

Science is all about discovery, but before you can break new ground, you have to understand what went on previously. That's a fancy way of saying that science projects involve doing research — lots of research.

Research, research, research

If you haven't done much research before, you have to figure out where to find all the information you need about your topic. From there, you can pick out the facts that directly apply to your topic and then organize them in preparation to write your research paper.

As far as where to find information, the sky's pretty much the limit. At first, most students rely on their school or local libraries, but some find that they need books at a central library or a university library. The Internet also contains a wealth of information. Don't think that this resource is unavailable to you if you don't have your own computer — these days, you can get computer access in most schools and libraries.

Another source of information is the U.S. government. Uncle Sam is the country's largest publisher — you can get almost anything you need from the government if you know where to look. Finally, an overlooked way to get information is by talking to experts in the field. For example, if you're doing a project about dental health, an interview with your dentist can be a fabulous source of information. Chapter 5 runs down all the basics of doing research for a science project, so head there to get more details.

Tackling your paper

After doing all your research, you need to write your paper. Your research paper's main objective is to summarize what you've found out about your topic. In fact, the information in your paper serves as a springboard for the project that you'll be doing, because whatever you find out during the project builds on what you discover when writing your research paper.

Many people can give you advice about how best to do your paper. Parents or older siblings who've written a research paper before can be great sources of help (and are probably more than willing to give advice).

Plus, I'm sure that you already have valuable information about writing, especially if you've had to write essays in English class. But, if you still need a few pointers, check out Chapter 6 to get the inside scoop on how to write a great research paper.

Doing Your Project

Actually doing your project is the heart of the matter — what you did before is just preparation.

Starting with the scientific method

Because the objective of doing a project is finding out how science really works, understanding and applying the scientific method (see Chapter 8) is crucial. How you use the scientific method varies depending on whether you're doing an experiment, writing a computer program, building or testing a device, or researching and tabulating data.

Briefly, the *scientific method* consists of stating a problem or asking a question, and then making an educated guess about the answer or solution, which is called the *hypothesis*. Most experiments manage *subjects* (things to be tested), arranged in *experimental groups* (subjects with changes applied) and *control groups* (subjects with no changes applied). *Variables* are the conditions that are changed and measured; *controls* are the factors that remain constant.

If you're doing a computer science, engineering, or research project, you may not use variables and controls in your project, because variables and controls apply to projects where you're testing the effects of one substance or condition upon another.

Organizing your materials and procedures

An integral part of your project is a list of all the materials that you use. Hopefully, you've given the material list some thought early on, especially if you have to order some of your supplies and equipment.

Most of you can buy or borrow what you need. Some of you, however, may have to build your own equipment. The needed materials can be the actual subject of an engineering project (building a better mousetrap?), or it can be something that you need in order to conduct your experiment, such as a distilling device that will *desalinate* (remove salts and other chemicals) water, or a rack to hold your experiment. In any event, whether you bought, borrowed, or built your supplies, you need to make a list that "shows your stuff." Chapter 9 gives you more details about listing your materials.

Next, you need to explain your procedures, showing exactly how you plan to do the project. You may use a narrative, but procedures are typically compiled in a sequential, numbered list. That method makes it easier for you to follow and simpler for a teacher or a judge to understand what you're doing. Again, Chapter 9 provides more info about presenting your procedures.

 The size of your procedures list really has no relation to how good your project will be — it all depends on what you're doing. For example, one experiment may involve just three simple steps repeated every day for three weeks, where another project may involve a great number of setup steps.

Keeping good records and noting irregularities

Whenever you work on your project, you need to keep timely, accurate, and complete records of everything that happens. Record keeping is especially important if you're working on an experiment where you make observations and measurements each day. Think of it as keeping a diary (except that instead of writing about what your friends said, you are recording what happened with your project).

Keep notes about other, unusual things that may happen in the course of your project (for example, if a gust of wind knocks over the rack of samples in the back yard), because these events may affect the results, and influence your conclusions. Keeping good documentation ensures that all your hard work gives you workable results. Don't worry if your project didn't work as you expected. More importantly, you need to have reliable proof of what occurred.

Compiling results and conclusions

Because your records will be letter-perfect (of course), you'll have no problem getting your results. But, in order to make the data meaningful, you have to arrange it in a clear and intelligible way.

This may involve doing some calculations, such as taking an average, arranging the data into tables, or graphing the measurements that you've collected. Chapter 10 explains more about how to do these things.

In your conclusions, you analyze and interpret your project's results. What does that mean? You get to compare the actual results to the hypothesis, your prediction of what would happen. Did you guess correctly? Either your results proved the hypothesis or they did not support your theory. In any event, if you use the scientific method, you'll have a successful project.

Putting Your Best Foot Forward: Presenting Your Work

When you get to this point, you probably think you're all done, but two important pieces remain — the notebook and the display. These two items ensure that your hard work and dedication don't go unnoticed.

In the science project world, your display is what you use to get attention. Think of it as a billboard or a TV spot that advertises your project. You want to entice your audience — the science fair judges — to take a closer look at your work. To do that, the display has to be attractive and easy to understand. Use color, texture, and design to illustrate your project to its best advantage. Check out Chapter 12 for more tips on creating an effective display.

After you've piqued their interest, you need to have something of substance to show the judges — your science project notebook. This notebook contains your research, materials and procedure lists, logs, results, and conclusions, as well as any required forms and applications. Chapter 11 covers how to prepare your project notebook.

Your display and notebook show your project to the world!

Exhibiting at the Science Fair

After you transport your project to the science fair, an official directs you to a spot where you can exhibit your project with others in your category. At that time, you can set up your backboard and notebook, arrange any project material that you want to display, and plug in anything electrical.

Knowing what the judges are looking for (creativity, scientific thought, thoroughness, skill, and clarity) can help you through the entire course of the project, as well as judging day. You can stand there while the judges walk past your display, look through your notebook, and (gasp!) ask you questions about your project. By this time, your display and notebook are "done deals" — the best thing you can do for yourself at this point is to know your subject, relax, smile, and answer the questions. See Chapter 14 for more info about judging at the science fair.

After the judging is done, meet and talk to other students who are exhibiting at the fair — you have a great opportunity to get new ideas and make new friends. If special activities have been arranged for exhibitors, take advantage of every last one!

Nearly every science fair I've attended has had an awards ceremony, where awards, ribbons, and prizes are given. Go, root for your classmates, and celebrate a job well done!

Chapter 2

Getting the Skinny on Science Fair Projects (And How They Can Help You)

*I*n this chapter, you may expect me to give you a lecture about why science projects are good for you and how they can be learning experiences that build self-discipline. Well, that's all true, but I promise to keep the lecture as painless as possible.

You probably remember some of the big firsts in your life, such as riding your bike without training wheels or cooking your first meal solo. Now, recall the feeling of pride and accomplishment you got when you did those things. You get that same feeling when you finish your science project, too. (Actually, that feeling comes just after the big sigh of relief you take when the project is finally finished!)

This chapter takes a closer look at why doing a science fair project has such a positive impact on your educational experiences, now and in the future.

Identifying the Benefits of a Science Fair Project

Do you like science? Are you good at it? You won't know unless you try, right?

Although you've probably taken science courses before, you probably haven't done hands-on science, working independently. When you do a science experiment in class, the materials come from the supply closet and your teacher or a textbook spells out the procedures. However, when you're working on a science fair project, you call the shots. You decide what your project is about, research your topic, write a paper, and design and execute a project plan. (Of course, your teacher and/or parents are great resources along the way, but you're really the captain of the science project ship.)

Besides allowing you to assert your independence, doing a science project also has some more practical benefits. For example, you can

- Collaborate with scientists and engineers
- Hone your mathematical skills
- Improve your writing skills
- Try out new computer hardware and software
- Find out how to keep good, accurate records
- Use power tools and build your own equipment
- Work safely with equipment
- Create artistic displays
- Give oral presentations
- Receive awards, prizes, and rewards (always a favorite)
- Have something really cool to put on a college or job application

Simplifying the Task: Breaking Your Project into Manageable Pieces

A science project is fun, provided you keep the experience stress-free. (This includes keeping your parents stress-free, too!)

Your science project is likely the largest, longest assignment you've ever gotten, even harder than building the model of the George Washington or Golden Gate Bridge (depending on which coast you're on). So, the best thing you can do is make the science project look less overwhelming.

To make the project less overwhelming, I recommend the following:

1. **Divide your science project into a number of mini-assignments, each of which has to be done before you can start the next one.**

2. **Look at each mini-assignment as a separate task, if possible.** This step will help you to concentrate on one step at a time, without worrying about what's going to happen next.

If your project is required, your teacher may provide some intermediate deadlines for you. But, if your project isn't required, break it down yourself. Follow this list to create your schedule:

✔ Find a topic idea (see Chapter 4)

✔ Do project research (see Chapter 5)

✔ Write a research paper (see Chapter 6)

✔ Submit a question and hypothesis (see Chapter 8)

✔ Submit your materials list and procedures (see Chapter 9)

✔ Compile results and conclusions (see Chapter 10)

✔ Prepare your notebook and display (see Chapters 11 and 12)

Estimate the amount of time needed to finish each task. When you have a realistic estimate, lay it out on a calendar or a timeline. For information about using calendars, timelines, and to-do lists, check out Chapter 7.

If you're like most people, your time estimates may tend to be a bit optimistic. However, your "guesstimates" can be more accurate and workable if you think about the things that can go wrong, such as losing a computer file, and add some time for those glitches and delays.

Getting the Most from Your Science Project

Besides the practical benefits mentioned earlier in the chapter, one of the most important things you can take away from doing a science project is your grade. That's pretty obvious, but if your project is required, you don't pass science if you don't finish it. (In some schools, your English teacher also gives you a grade on your research paper.)

But your grade is only one motivation for seeing the project through. The rest of this section takes a look at some other takeaways from doing a successful project.

Broadening your knowledge

When you do a science project, you're not just working on science. You're actually doing math, art, writing, and maybe even computer science. (You can also find out about psychology, history, or anthropology, depending on your project.) So, why not use the project as a great opportunity to discover new information on various topics — or even to start a brand new interest?

Finding your hidden talents

Even if you don't picture yourself as a budding scientist, you may find that you have other talents that can help you during the project and beyond.

For example, if you're a good writer, the research paper should be no problem. Fancy yourself an artist? You'll love creating an awesome display. Delight in knowing every statistic about your favorite baseball player? That means you probably love details, lists, and numbers — so you'll keep an excellent log of your experiment.

These talents (and the self-esteem boost you get from discovering them) can help you when considering future career options. Who knows — you may be the next Stephen King or Picasso just waiting in the wings!

Discovering new things about yourself

When you do a science project, you find out something about yourself that you never knew before. Besides discovering what things you like (and dis-like), you also can find out how you like to work.

For example, some people are loners, preferring to work independently — only asking for help when desperate. Others want a support team that's as close as the next room. Some people are really great when they follow a schedule and keep on track. Others do their best work when their deadline is right around the corner. You may be extremely neat and organized, or your desk may look like a combat zone. You have more than one way to be successful, but after you've done your science project, you can understand how you like to work.

In addition, you may find out how it feels to take a risk. A science project involves predicting the answer to a question, and accepting the results, even if your prediction was wrong.

Finally, you can find out how to follow a trail to the end despite all the twists and turns along the way. And, you can bet your project will have its share of twists and turns!

Getting a head start on the future

In the course of doing your science project, you may come up with an idea for next year's project (no groaning, please). I know it may seem a bit too early to think of next year now, when you've barely started this year's work, but if you find a topic that fascinates you, it can lead you to projects throughout your middle and high school years. It can also inspire a lifelong passion, and maybe even lead to a career in science.

Enjoying yourself no matter what

To get the most out of the whole experience (and possibly a good grade, too), go into it wholeheartedly. Make up your mind to enjoy it, and have fun, even during the hard times.

If I can give you one piece of advice (okay, four pieces of advice) about doing a successful science project, they are:

- ✔ Immerse yourself in the experience.
- ✔ Do your best.
- ✔ Go with the flow.
- ✔ Have fun.

Chapter 3

Tackling and Categorizing Your Projects

*A*ll branches of science aim to discover new information, but not all discoveries happen in a lab. Although doing an experiment is likely the first idea that jumps to your mind when thinking about a science project, other ways to do an effective project do exist.

For example, you can do a research project where you collect and analyze data, or if you love computers, you can write a computer program or analyze computer performance. Are you an inventor in the making? Check out the possibilities for doing an engineering project.

In this chapter, I show you how each type of project is constructed. I also list the official Intel International Science and Engineering Fair (ISEF) categories, and describe some project titles in each one. By the way, if you want to know more about ISEF, check out Chapter 4.

Exploring Four Ways to Do a Science Project

The object of all science is to answer a question or solve a problem. This idea also holds true for all science projects. Another thing all projects have in common is a *hypothesis,* which is an educated guess about the results and conclusions of a project.

However, the type of procedure and the kind of data collected differ depending on the type of project.

Performing an experiment

An *experiment* is where you perform a procedure, according to the scientific method, in order to see whether a stated hypothesis is true.

To find out how to develop a hypothesis and use the scientific method, see Chapter 8. To discover how to design and follow an experimental procedure, see Chapter 9.

Table 3-1 shows an example of an experiment about plant growth. Table 3-2 offers an example of an experiment that tests students' memory after doing exercise.

Table 3-1	**Project That Involves an Experiment with Plants**		
Question	*Hypothesis*	*Procedure*	*Data Collected*
How much drainage is best for plant growth?	Plants with the most drainage will grow the best.	Grow plants with no drainage, two drainage holes, and four drainage holes.	Size of plants in each group

Table 3-2	**Project That Tests Students' Memory after Doing Aerobic Exercise**		
Question	*Hypothesis*	*Procedure*	*Data Collected*
Is memory better or worse after doing exercise?	Students' memory will improve after doing aerobic exercise.	Give memory tests to two groups of students, one group who has done no exercise and one who has done aerobics.	Scores on memory tests

Conducting research

In a research project, you gather information, analyze it, graph it, apply mathematical calculations, and describe what the data shows.

Doing a research project isn't the same as writing a research paper. To have an effective research project, you must collect all the data and do the analysis yourself.

Table 3-3, for example, shows a project that collects and analyzes data about earthquakes.

Table 3-3	Project That Compares Earthquakes and Solar Activity		
Question	*Hypothesis*	*Procedure*	*Data Collected*
Are there more earthquakes when there's more solar activity?	When there is more solar activity, there will be more high-magnitude earthquakes.	Collect 50 years' worth of data on solar activity and earthquake magnitude.	Correlation coefficient (a statistical test that measures how current trends follow actual past values)

Building or testing a device

You can do an engineering project in one of two ways. You can

- ✔ Devise something new that solves a specific problem, build it, and test it. (No doubt, this step appeals to budding inventors.)
- ✔ Test and compare existing devices or substances.

Table 3-4 shows an engineering project that develops a new device, and Table 3-5 summarizes a project that tests and compares the durability of concrete.

Table 3-4	Project That Creates a Remote Control Fireplace Damper		
Question	*Hypothesis*	*Procedure*	*Data Collected*
If I forget to open the fireplace damper before I build a fire, can I open it with a remote control?	I can build a fireplace damper that can be operated by remote control.	I will use an automatic garage door opener and adapt it to a fireplace damper. I will install it in my fireplace and conduct at least 50 tests to make sure that it works.	What happened during each of the 50 tests of the remote control device

Table 3-5	Project That Tests and Compares the Strength of Concrete, Depending on the Amount of Water Added		
Question	*Hypothesis*	*Procedure*	*Data Collected*
Does the amount of water affect the strength of concrete?	Adding too much water will make concrete weaker.	Make four batches of concrete with different amounts of water in the solution. Let the concrete dry, and then drop weights on the concrete until it breaks.	Weight required to break each concrete sample

Developing a computer program

Your project can design, code, and test one or more computer programs that solve a specified problem. In this type of project, you always say in your hypothesis that you can solve the problem — you gotta believe! Table 3-6, for example, summarizes a computer project that responds to a user's native language.

Table 3-6	Project That Displays Screen Information in Several Languages		
Question	*Hypothesis*	*Procedure*	*Data Collected*
Can I create a system that displays screen information in the user's language?	I can develop a computer program that will display screen information in English and Spanish.	Design system, write pseudocode, install language dictionaries, code programs, test programs, and conduct user tests.	Information on whether users like the program

Running Down the Official ISEF Project Categories

Many categories of projects compete in science fairs. They cover all scientific and engineering disciplines, ranging from botany to zoology and everything in between. If you already have an idea for your project, check out the list of categories in this section to see where yours belongs. On the other hand, if you're still totally clueless, investigating the categories may give you a few good ideas.

In this section, I describe each category and also give examples of projects that have been exhibited in the category. Sounds simple right? Often it is, but sometimes confusion arises because the project can go in one or more places.

For example, if you're testing water purity, does the project belong in chemistry or environmental science? Does a project about eating disorders fit in behavioral and social sciences or medicine and health? As much as possible, I try to clarify it for you, but your science teacher is your best guide. The sidebar, "Yikes! Where did my project go?" later in this chapter, also provides a few more details.

Note: When you see the words Phase II, Phase III, or something similar in a project title, it means that the project is a continuation of a prior year's work.

Biological sciences

All the *biological sciences* look at the world of living things. Just as everything on earth is made up of atoms, every living thing is made up of cells. A living thing can be a single cell organism, such as an amoeba, or it can have billions of cells, such as a tree or a human being. Most cells have similar components — after all, "parts are parts."

Behavioral and social sciences

Why do people do what they do? Projects in the *behavioral and social sciences* category examine psychology, sociology, anthropology, archaeology, *ethnology* (the science of human cultures), linguistics, learned or instinctive animal behavior, learning, perception, urban problems, reading problems, public opinion surveys, and educational testing.

Examples of behavioral and social science projects are:

- ✔ Ethics and teens: Is it possible to detect troubled youth?
- ✔ Leading polls: Can rewording sentences influence survey results?
- ✔ Multitasking: Productive or disruptive?
- ✔ The way of the warrior: Effect of traditional martial arts training on aggressiveness
- ✔ Effects of race and gender on personal space
- ✔ Investigating the accuracy of eyewitness testimony
- ✔ The eyes have it: Visual perception in children with and without dyslexia, Phase II
- ✔ Relationships between weight, locus of control, gender, weight satisfaction, and self-esteem
- ✔ Slim hope: Eating disorders in teenage girls
- ✔ How confidence affects math scores

Biochemistry

Okay, if all living things are composed of cells, what are cells made of? Cells are made of molecules, which consist of chemical compounds. And that's *biochemistry* — the chemistry of biological organisms.

Biochemistry projects deal with the chemistry of life processes, including molecular biology and genetics, enzymes, photosynthesis, blood chemistry, protein chemistry, food chemistry, and hormones.

Some examples of biochemistry projects are:

- ✔ Cholesterol analysis of various poultry species

- ✔ Bacterial comparison of organic and pasteurized milk

- ✔ A second look at antioxidants: How vitamin E affects the life span of *Drosophila melanogaster*

- ✔ Urbanization of coastal waters: Concocting hormonal chaos

- ✔ Establishing evolutionary relationships of Oklahoma Native Americans through mitochondrial DNA analysis

- ✔ Verifying the origin of gourmet coffee beans

- ✔ Stress tests

- ✔ Sperm say NO: Measuring for levels of nitric oxide in sperm samples

- ✔ Effect of soil types on the decomposition rate of buried apples

- ✔ What's the effect of various concentrations of aloe vera gel on the regeneration of planaria?

Botany

Botany is the study of all kinds of plant life. Projects that deal with agriculture, *agronomy* (the study of soil relating to soil management and crop production), horticulture, forestry, plant biorhythms, anatomy, *taxonomy* (the classification of organisms), physiology, pathology, *hydroponics* (the study of plants grown in nutrient solution), *algology*, (the study of algae), or *mycology* (the study of fungus) belong here.

Here's a list of some botany project titles:

- ✔ Effect of nutrient absence on the amount of DNA in plants: Two-year study

- ✔ Can the calcium level in plants be raised? Phase III

- ✔ Effects of microwave heating on seed germination

- ✔ A new breed of vegetation: Phase III

- ✔ Does centrifugal force affect plant growth?

- ✔ Finding relationships between proteins and food allergens

- ✔ Flammability of the needles and scales of seven species of western Montana conifers

- ✔ Plant growth regulators and seed dormancy

- ✔ Tissue culture on a genetically modified plant

- ✔ Effect of transplantation on the growth and development of population of prickly palm

Gerontology

Gerontology is the study of the aging process in living organisms. A fairly new ISEF category, gerontology isn't yet exhibited in all local and regional fairs. Most of the projects I list here can easily fit in the medicine and health or behavioral and social science categories, if necessary.

Here are some examples of gerontology projects:

- Effects of age on sensory memory
- Relationship between metabolic rate and life span
- Remembered and forgotten: Autobiographical memory
- Just say no to osteoporosis
- Assessment of risk factors contributing to falls in the elderly
- Influence of diet, dietary supplements, environmental factors, and vaccination on the development of bone cancer
- Reactions to distractions
- Arterial oxygen depletion during the onset of aerobic exercise: "The Shuldberg Effect" from youth to mature adult
- Are you aging before your time?
- Generation Y: Attitudes and perceptions toward the aging process

Medicine and health

The *medicine and health* field is concerned with diseases, health, and the healing of animals and humans.

Medicine, dentistry, pharmacology, veterinary medicine, pathology, ophthalmology, nutrition, sanitation, pediatrics, dermatology, allergies, speech and hearing, and optometry are good candidates for this category, as shown in the following list of titles:

- Macular degeneration and short wavelength macular thresholds
- Electromagnetic fields on human health
- Why are sharks resistant to cancer? The unique core structure of the shark P53 gene
- Comparison of citronella oil extracts as mosquito repellents
- Antibiotic production during fermentation of Ppi
- Diabetes: How different exercises affect blood sugar

✔ Try to hold your breath: What made you stop?

✔ Should you wear sunglasses while checking your e-mail?

✔ Organ donations

✔ Do cellular phone companies provide consumers with the facts about cellular phone radiation and its effect on humans?

Microbiology

Microbiology is the branch of biology that deals with microorganisms and their effects on other living organisms. This category includes bacteriology, *virology* (study of viruses and viral diseases), *protozoology* (study of *protozoan*, microscopic single-cell animals), fungal and bacterial genetics, and so on.

To put it in simple terms, microbiology projects deal with germs, as shown in the following list:

✔ Are you in danger of "Superbugs?"

✔ Antibiotic-resistant bacteria: How common are they?

✔ Counter cultures: Bacteria growth on kitchen countertops

✔ Microwave madness: Media hype or scientific fact?

✔ Quality tests of pasteurized raw milk

✔ Can common indoor mold produce hazardous airborne toxins?

✔ The "Darwinian Reversal" theory: What is an effective solution to antibiotic resistance through selection?

✔ Antibacterial action of raw and commercial Australian honeys

✔ Pathogenic bacteria on soft-drink cans: Are they harmful?

✔ Myth of T-cells

Zoology

The science of *zoology* includes all studies of animals, including genetics, *ornithology* (the study of birds), *ichthyology* (the study of fish), *herpetology*, (the study of reptiles and amphibians), *entomology* (the study of insects), animal ecology, anatomy, paleontology, cellular physiology, animal biorhythms, animal husbandry, *cytology* (the study of the formation, structure, and function of cells), *histology* (the study of the microscopic structure of animal and plant tissues), animal physiology, neurophysiology, and invertebrate biology.

The following are some sample zoology projects:

- Gerbil coat color genetics
- Microstructure of the shark's jaw
- Mutant flies and brain genes
- Feed versus milk quality and production
- Echolocating beluga whales
- Effect of colony size on resilience in ants
- Stereotypic behavior of captive giant panda
- Searching for the intelligent earthworm: Cognitive abilities of *Lumbricus terestris*
- Comparative habitat use by shore birds
- Effects of melatonin on the cellular processes in selected organisms

Physical sciences

Physical sciences, such as chemistry and physics, analyze and compare energy and nonliving matter. In terms of science projects, computer science, engineering, and mathematics are also physical sciences.

Chemistry

Chemistry deals with the composition, structure, properties, and reactions of different substances. Projects in this category include physical, inorganic, and organic chemistry (other than biochemistry), materials, plastics, fuels, pesticides, metallurgy, and soil chemistry. Projects that analyze fossils, fuels, vitamins, or crystals also belong in this category.

The following are some sample projects:

- How does changing the components of concrete affect its properties?
- Extract from catnip as mosquito repellent
- Interactive effect between iron and vitamin C in spinach
- Effect of pigment size on UV-related fading of paint: Phase II
- An anticancer tree?
- Creation of a high-performance polymer blend
- Concentration of nitrates in private water supplies

✔ Sunscreens: Analyzing active ingredients for UV absorption

✔ Converting carbon directly into electricity

✔ Application of eco-friendly natural dyes on natural fibers

Computer science

Computer science projects include the study and development of computer hardware, software engineering, Internet networking, communications, and graphics, including human interface. Simulations, virtual reality, or computations science (including data structures, encryption, coding, and information theory) are other topics in this category.

Check out some sample projects:

✔ Interpretation of tactile, vision, and hearing: A communication and feedback experience

✔ Little room for real messages: How spam clogs e-mail accounts

✔ Internet music composer with voice2note sound recognition system

✔ Advanced video animation compression

✔ Virtual flashcards

✔ An improved algorithm for meshing large and complex terrains

✔ MooBrick: An artificial intelligence conversation system

✔ Enhanced reality

✔ Project pathfinder: Development of a genetic navigation algorithm

✔ Modeling global warming

If you use your computer as a tool while doing your project but it isn't the subject of your project, then computer science isn't the proper category. For example, if you use the computer to make calculations for a research project, assign the project to the earth and space sciences category (see next section) instead of computer science.

Earth and space sciences

Earth and space sciences projects deal with soil, minerals, petroleum, weather, and the atmosphere. They cover topics in geology, geophysics, physical oceanography, meteorology, atmospheric physics, seismology, geography, *speleology* (the scientific study of caves), mineralogy, topography, optical astronomy, radio astronomy, and astrophysics. If you're analyzing the geological age of fossils, your project also belongs in this category.

Here are some other sample projects:

- Contemporary and ancient hot spring deposits
- Using the Doppler effect to discover extra-solar planets
- Mysteries of Mars: The search for the oldest terrain on Mars
- A new meteor shower during the Leonids
- Developing electron spin resonance (ESR) dating for sharks' teeth
- The salinity of Boggy Bayou: A trend analysis, Year VI
- Analysis of a previously unmapped region of Venus
- Coastal community risk from tsunami waves
- Do certain jet stream patterns affect tornado formation and location?
- Aircraft icing: Why does it happen?

Engineering

If you're doing a project that applies scientific methods to manufacturing and testing, then your project belongs in the *engineering* category. This category includes civil, mechanical, aeronautical, chemical, electrical, automotive, marine, and environmental engineering. Photography, sound, heating and refrigeration, transportation, power transmission and generation, electronics, communications, architecture, bioengineering, and lasers can also fit into this category.

Check out some sample project names:

- The design of a localized positioning system
- Construction of a fly-fishing reel with a belonging brake system
- Big array system: A new technology for directional hearing aids
- The most effective material for sleeping bag insulation under wet and dry conditions
- PCPU: "Pop Can Picker Upper" at your service
- Recycling waste products: Kiln dust, slag, and strength in concrete
- ZOOM: Closed circuit television to low vision people
- Development and testing of instrumentation to determine supersonic speeds
- Design of ergonomic desk for students with scoliosis and other conditions of the spinal cord
- Improved crossing for physically impaired pedestrians

Just because you design and build a device doesn't necessarily make it an engineering project. For example, if you had to design and construct a *still* (an apparatus to distill liquids) to do a project that tests methods of *desalinating* (removing salts or minerals) water, the project belongs in chemistry and not in engineering.

Environmental sciences

Any project that deals with the environment on land, in the air, or in the water belongs in the *environmental sciences* category. Environmental science projects deal with the sources and control of pollution, waste disposal, impact studies, environmental alteration (heat, light, irrigation, erosion, and so on), and ecology. This category also includes the effects of pollution on different organisms.

Take a look at some sample projects:

- Turbidity: Life in murky water
- Effects of runoff on water quality
- Cost-effective native plant roadside restoration
- Salinity of groundwater in the Algarve
- Bird populations as indicators of gulf coast environmental quality
- Fibre bag: An alternate for polybags
- Bioavailability: Will metals in sludge budge?
- Lethal lactic acid
- Phytoremediation: Can a plant clean up contaminated soil?
- What to do with the garbage?

Mathematics

The science of *mathematics* deals with logical, numerical, and algebraic principles and systems, including calculus, geometry, abstract algebra, number theory, statistics, complex analysis, probability, *topology* (history of a region influenced by its physical surface), logic, operations research, and other topics in pure and applied mathematics.

Here are a few titles of mathematics projects:

- Game theory models for Middle Eastern policy
- Pitch frequencies of Bach's No. 13 invention
- Design of custom integrated circuits via new algebraic method

- Barcodes: Reading between the lines
- Winter wonderland: A mathematical analysis of snowflakes
- Mathematical correlation of sound and light waves
- Geometric sequences
- Ideal systematic computerized game theory
- Pattern counting on chessboards
- The sound waves of music: A comparative mathematical analysis of different models of the flute and violin, Phase II

Physics

Physics is the science encompassing the theories, principles, and laws governing energy and the effect of energy on matter. Projects that deal with solid state, optics, acoustics, particle, nuclear, atomic, or plasma physics, superconductivity, fluid and gas dynamics, thermodynamics, semiconductors, magnetism, quantum mechanics, and biophysics belong in this category.

Some sample titles of physics projects are:

- Effects of electric fields on the growth of ice crystals
- Designing for heat resistance
- Temperature's influence in digital electronics
- Astroturf traction research
- The same pitch but a different sound
- Can sound be transmitted through a laser beam?
- Microwave energy as an auxiliary source of heat
- Heat transfer and mass change
- Low-cost plasma reactor
- Relationship between kinetic energy of a dropped object impacting water and height of its resulting wave

Local specialties

Some regional and local fairs have project categories that can't be entered at ISEF. Often, these categories are acceptable for the younger grades, which can't compete at the international level anyway.

Yikes! Where did my project go?

After your project is done, you may find that it doesn't wind up exactly where you thought it would. For example, one student did a project on dental adhesives and entered it in the medicine and health category. However, on the day of his school science fair, he couldn't find his project — his teacher reclassified it as an engineering project, because it was really about the properties of adhesives and not about orthodontia.

If a teacher or science fair official decides to change your category, they do it because they are experienced and know where your project belongs — trust that this move can show your work to its best advantage.

For example, the Greater San Diego Science and Engineering Fair features a *product testing/consumer science* category, which includes projects about quality control or comparison and analysis of product designs. It goes without saying (but I'll say it anyway) that a good product testing/consumer science project uses the scientific method or accepted engineering tests to obtain specific, measurable results.

Check out this list of product testing/consumer science project titles:

- How does ground surface affect a baseball's roll?
- Effects of knots on fishing line strength
- Do fabrics differ on how they absorb dye?
- Which backpacking stove boils water fastest?
- Which fish tank chemical produces the least evaporation?
- Effects of skin cleansers on bacillus cereus bacteria
- Will bottled water or filtered water prevent water stains?
- Effect of chemicals on pipe clogs
- Does washing affect flame-retardant fabrics?

If, eventually, you want to take a product testing/consumer science project to the next level, you have to reclassify it into one of the official ISEF categories. The most common homes for these projects are the chemistry, engineering, or physics categories.

Part II

Choosing a Project and Getting Started

The 5th Wave   By Rich Tennant

ELLIOT MISTAKES HIS SON'S SCIENCE PROJECT NOTEBOOK FOR A DESSERT RECIPE

"Generally speaking, should a raspberry Clafoutis resemble an erupting volcano?"

In this part . . .

In Part II, I discuss the different project types and categories. I help you pick the perfect project — the one that's an ideal match for your interests, abilities, resources, and environment. Because science is all about making new discoveries, I also show you where to detect, collect, and select all the information you need to find about your topic, including tips on how to use libraries, the Internet, government publications, and experts in the field.

After you gather your information, you need to write a research paper. This part gives you all the tips, tricks, and shortcuts to use, as well as pitfalls to avoid to make this process as painless as possible. If I've done my job right, you may actually have some fun!

Chapter 4

What's the Big Idea? Finding a Project Topic

*T*he most important ingredient to a successful science fair project is finding the right project idea.

What's the right idea? Something that captures your imagination and keeps you interested and motivated. Ideally, the right idea isn't so difficult that it frustrates and discourages you, but also the idea is challenging enough to stretch your abilities and creativity.

Several first-timers told me that finding a good topic was the hardest part of the entire science fair experience. But a good idea really isn't that hard to find if you know where to look.

In this chapter, I explain all the ways you can find a great idea for your project, and then help you figure out if your idea is possible.

Using What You're Studying in Class (And Not Just Science Class!)

Of course, your first thought may be to get a project idea from your science class. From astronomy to photosynthesis, what you're currently studying can be the springboard to a great project topic. Besides, brainstorming for ideas in science class gives you a built-in source of help and information, because your teacher is right there with you.

But, be sure to do your project on a topic that you already know a little something about. Although learning is one of the main objectives of your science project, now is a really bad time to take a crash course in calculus if elementary algebra is giving you a lot of grief.

Your other classes can also inspire you with a science project idea.

Even your social studies classes, which may seem completely opposite from physical sciences, may get your gray cells going. For example, a class discussion on subliminal advertising led to an animal behavior experiment that measured the effect of sound on a mouse's appetite. History courses that deal with prehistory may lead to a project dealing with fossils or dating ancient artifacts.

If you want to combine physical and social sciences, the environment is a great source of ideas for many students (just go to any science fair to see what I mean!). And of course, looking at the way people interact in any classroom, gym, or video arcade can lead to a behavioral science project idea.

Getting Inspiration from Media Sources

Every year, people become more saturated by all types of media, from newspapers and magazines to movies, music, TV, and yes, the Internet.

If you look and listen carefully, you can find loads of project ideas there, such as:

- ✓ **The written word:** You may find something that sparks your curiosity in a newspaper or magazine. Feature articles often discuss areas of science, especially those that are important in your city or state. Weekly news magazines deal with the areas of health, aerospace, the environment, and other scientific fields, particularly when new problems, discoveries, or theories are presented.

✔ **The virtual word:** Everyone knows that the Internet contains all kinds of information, both good and bad. While surfing the Web, you may just come across things you wonder are true (or not) or things that motivate you to find out more information. The great thing about getting an idea from the Internet is that at the same time, you can probably find sources of information you need for your project.

✔ **The visual world:** Movies or television shows, even if they're fiction, can give you ideas for a science project. For example, several years ago, a TV movie about the effects of a nuclear holocaust inspired several projects about children's reactions to the film.

TV has such a great influence — and I'm not just talking about the shows! Take a look at the project catalog of a major city's science fair and see how many projects are designed to either prove or disprove the advertised claims. For example, one project tested how long three different battery brands lasted, because they all claimed to last the longest.

Other common projects at science fairs focus on the media's influence on people's lives. For example, many projects examine the effect of watching TV on test scores or concentration. Even more frequent are projects dealing with the effects of rock music (with or without suggestive lyrics), MTV, or video games on heart rate, grades, or a variety of other measurable factors.

When you become inspired by something you see on TV, give it a reality check, as I describe in the section, "Applying the Acid Test: Can I Really Do This Project?" later in this chapter. Doing so keeps you from taking on something that's beyond your ability, time, or resources.

Cultivating Ideas from Current Events and Issues

Current events can generate great science project ideas.

For example, the news, both good and bad, can inspire a project topic. Likewise, environmental issues and medical research are popular sources of project ideas, as are people's reactions to world events or the psychological impact of such events.

Inevitably, science fairs of 2002 featured projects dealing with people's reactions to the terrorist attacks on September 11. For example, one student did a project that researched which emotions students felt most strongly after the attack.

Other projects with a focus on current issues dealt with cell phones. Is it safe to use one while you drive? Which phone has the best reception? Do cell phones emit dangerous levels of radiation? Similarly, other safety issues, such as the bacteria present in food or the danger of running red lights, also inspired science projects.

Many students utilize environmental and conservation issues to find project ideas too. A large area of concern is the energy shortage. For example, at a recent Greater San Diego Science and Engineering Fair, several projects explored alternative energy sources, from fruits to horse manure. Other projects looked at ways to retain heat as a way to save energy. Still other projects tested natural, nontoxic methods of eradicating weeds or insect pests, and then compared them to the chemical variety.

Often, local issues are springboards to project ideas. Look at a West Coast science fair, and you may see projects about ocean water and sea life. In San Diego, projects may deal with the local air and water pollution, controlling erosion, or fire-retardant plants to grow in Southern California canyons. A science fair in Louisiana or East Texas may feature projects that are concerned with plant and animal life in the bayous, and students in the Appalachian region may have projects that deal with the effects of coal mining on the environment.

Doing Your Own Thing: Parlaying Personal Interests

To have a successful project, choose a project that can be fun. Sounds simple, but it's true. You may wonder how to do that, but the answer is right in front of you.

Look at your surroundings, your interests, and your concerns, and you may find the perfect project!

Sports, games, and hobbies

Those of you who are team players, committed fans, or fierce competitors will find great project ideas from the world of sports. Some projects deal with the statistical side of sports, such as whether the home-field advantage makes a difference in team sports.

Other sports-related projects may deal with how to play the game, for example, analyzing the best angle for taking a shot on a goal. However, the majority of these projects, which you may find mainly in the engineering and physics categories, test different types of sporting of sporting equipment, including:

- ✔ Curvature of a baseball
- ✔ Tennis ball bounce
- ✔ Swimsuit drag
- ✔ Aerodynamic skateboards, surfboards, and scooters
- ✔ Slide of a hockey puck

Check out Chapter 17 to see projects that test baseball bats and golf balls.

If your interests run more toward games than sports, you may want to focus your project on the odds of winning games of chance. Looking at the probability of getting a certain throw of the dice or beating the house can give you a really good mathematics project.

If you enjoy paper airplanes, loads of engineering and physics projects analyze speed, lift, and distance. Radio-controlled cars and planes are also great subjects for science projects.

However, if you're into more sedentary or solitary pursuits, don't despair — you, too, can find a project idea. Students have developed computer programs to play chess, create origami, or randomly compose music.

Everyday life

You may want to do your project about some everyday products.

Science project time has turned many homes into consumer testing labs. New and improved? Whiter and brighter? How about those nutritional facts? Science isn't just about the discoveries of tomorrow, but also about everyday life, the here and now.

Bet you didn't know how helpful your house (or apartment) can be when trying to find a project idea. Start in the kitchen, where personal interests and science come together. For example, you can find lots of project ideas in food, such as the amount of sugar, fats, or acid. Going a step further, you can look at how to ripen fruit faster or keep food fresher longer. You can also examine how you cook your food. For example, one project analyzed how much aluminum and iron is absorbed from pots and pans into food.

Moving out of the kitchen and into the workshop, you can find project ideas looking at rust resistance, paint durability, glue strength, and insulation effectiveness. In the bathroom, you find even more ideas, for example, how long soap bubbles last, which whitener makes your teeth the whitest, and which deodorant works best. Continue your home-and-garden tour to find out about flame-retardant fabrics, paper towel absorbency, and whether washable markers are really washable.

School and social life

Problems affecting teenagers can inspire many projects.

For example, in the past, projects have centered on the effects of using alcohol, drugs, and tobacco. These days, however, the use of drugs or alcohol is prohibited at many science fairs.

If you want a project where you gather people's opinions via a survey, you may opt for a project that deals with relationships, with family, friends, or dating. As much as people strive to be gender neutral, gender issues are still a very popular source of project ideas. In 2002, many projects explored gender differences in attitudes, sports, memory, phobias, and performance on various tests.

The desire to look and feel good also provides a good source of project ideas.

Some of these topics go back to food — the effects of sugar and fat in your diet, the effect of smell on taste, or the chemical analysis of different foods. Other projects in this area focus on exercise, including its effect on heart rate, memory, problem-solving skills or lung capacity.

Talking to Friends and Family

Friends and family can be great sources of project ideas, too.

Sometimes someone's profession can hold the key. For example, one student whose dad investigates accidents for the motor vehicle department did a project to determine whether cars follow each other too closely. Having a parent who's a scientist or a doctor has inspired lots of project ideas — after all, what could be better than having an in-house mentor and adviser?

Even if you don't get a project idea from your parents or another adult, your connection to these people can still have some benefits. A statistician, a computer programmer, a writer, or an artist can offer some great advice and assistance while you're working on the project.

Your family members' hobbies and interests can also give you ideas. If Dad's a gardener, a botany project is probably a natural for you, and if Mom's a golfer, you may want to do comparative tests of clubs or balls. Other students get project ideas because they want to understand the problems that family members have. For example, if a grandparent uses a cane or a walker, you may want to find out how much it really helps him or her.

When you talk to friends and family, they may get so enthusiastic about what you're planning to do that they not only offer assistance, but also try to force you to adopt their project idea as well. Before you decide though, make sure that the project is something that you want to do and are capable of doing. Help and guidance are great, but you are doing the project, not your parents, friends, or relatives. If you're uncertain about what to do, talk to your teacher to get an objective opinion.

If you travel with your family, you may get some ideas from trips you've taken. One student, traveling through Palm Springs, California, saw several different types of windmills used to generate electricity. She wondered about the advantages and disadvantages of the different types of wind turbines. From this curiosity, her project, which tested and evaluated different types of windmills, was born.

Another student, on a cross-country trip with his family one summer, had an advantage — he already knew that he had to do a science project the next fall! He wanted to do a project about erosion, so he collected soil samples from various locations so that he could find out which soil eroded fastest.

Building on a Previous Project

Exhibiting at the International Science and Engineering Fair (ISEF) is, for many students, the culmination of a lot of work. (See the sidebar, "The grand-daddy of science fairs" in this chapter for more about ISEF.) A required first project turns into a consuming interest, which becomes a project that gets more polished and professional each year.

The granddaddy of science fairs

The Intel International Science and Engineering Fair (ISEF) is the world's largest science fair.

For 53 years, high school students, teachers, corporate executives, and government officials from all over the world have gathered to celebrate and reward scientific inquiry. Although Intel is ISEF's main sponsor, many other corporations and institutions fund the fair and donate student awards and prizes.

The ISEF, which is held in a different city each year, also sponsors local and regional fairs throughout the world. The local fairs, which comply with ISEF rules and guidelines, send their first-place award winners to exhibit their work at the international fair.

Consider these two examples:

- ✔ A student did a computer science project that translated programming commands into Spanish and Tagalog. It started as a simple seventh grade project. By ninth grade, he won a place at ISEF.

- ✔ Another student started with an experiment on the effects of caffeine and dopamine on frogs. Then, after seeing a TV special on Parkinson's disease, he adapted his idea to the effects of caffeine on Parkinson's symptoms. Six years later, his work, supported by the National Parkinson's Foundation, won an award at ISEF.

If you look at a catalog from a previous science fair, you can also get lots of ideas. These catalogs list all the projects, arranged by category, along with the name and school of each exhibitor.

One of the first things you notice is that some categories have a lot more projects than others, especially in the younger grades. I think that the most important reason for this relates to the science classes the students are currently taking. Another reason is that in certain categories, more possibilities exist for projects that directly relate to the students' lives, for example behavioral and social sciences, computers, or medical science.

You may have an easier time finding a project idea in a popular category, but keep in mind that many other students are thinking the same thing. And more projects make for more competition!

Applying the Acid Test: Can I Really Do This Project?

Some students have some huge, noble objectives for their science projects, but to be successful, you must have a project that you can research, plan, and execute, according to your abilities and the time available. So this section helps you take a critical look at your Number 1 project idea to see whether it fits.

Is it within my abilities?

One mistake that several students make is biting off more than they can chew.

Remember that as much as you want to, you're not going to find a cure for the common cold doing a four-month eighth grade science project. You may, however, find one small aspect of that topic that you can do, for example, testing which over-the-counter cold medicine kills the most bacteria.

Ask whether you have enough knowledge and experience to do this particular project. Have you covered any of this material in your science, math, or computer classes? Have you done anything like this before? A "no" answer to these questions doesn't automatically rule out your idea, but if you find butterflies fluttering in your stomach at the very thought of doing the project, the project probably isn't going to work.

One more thing: Even if you have an expert in your family, remember that this is your project, not your Mom's or Dad's.

Do I have enough time?

Usually, you have three to four months to do your entire science project, and that includes doing your research and preparing the project notebook and display. Figure out if the project has anything you need that either takes more time than you have, or relies on factors outside your control.

For example, a project that requires a certain amount of rainfall may be unsuccessful in a drought year, and a botany experiment that uses a slow-growing shrub probably means that you should choose a different shrub.

Can I afford it?

A successful project doesn't require a lot of money. In fact, some very complex and successful projects have been done for very little money.

But I do recommend figuring out how much money you need to do your work. Before you make a final decision on a project idea, figure out how much everything's going to cost, from the materials for your experiment to the art supplies for your display.

If you're somewhat clueless about prices, ask your parents if they know how much things cost (and also whether they'd like to help with project expenses). You can also use the Internet to get prices of the equipment that you need.

To help you estimate your project costs, make a budget, like the one in Table 4-1.

When you make up your budget, try to include as many things as possible. For example, if you need to get containers, tools, or art supplies, be sure to put them on your list. Many students say that their projects ended up costing more than they thought, mainly because they forgot to add the supplies for the project display into the budget. (To find out about what you need for your display, check out Chapter 12.)

Table 4-1   Budget for a Project to Build an Air-cushioned Vehicle

Supplies Needed	Source	Cost
Four-inch circle of particle board	Hardware store	$8.00
One 1.2-horsepower shop vacuum	Uncle Ed	Free
Pipe connection	Hardware store	$2.00
One roll duct tape	Dad's workshop	Free
Staple gun and staples	Dad's workshop	Free
Drill	Dad's workshop	Free
Saw	Dad's workshop	Free
Scissors	Mom	Free
Coffee can	Mom	Free

Supplies Needed	Source	Cost
Shower curtain	Discount store	$6.00
Nuts, bolts, and washers	Dad's workshop	Free
Backboard	Office superstore	$15.00
Colored paper	Office superstore	$12.00
Printer cartridge	Office superstore	$30.00
Three-ring binder	Office superstore	$4.00
Total		$77.00

Estimating your budget may also get you thinking about how to get what you need without buying it (honestly, that is!). You don't need access to a million-dollar computer or a state-of-the art laboratory to do a thorough and creative experiment.

For example, you may use the equipment on high school and university campuses when classes aren't in session. Using such equipment lets you do a project that you otherwise may not be able to afford.

If you think you may need facilities of this type, make the arrangements early. For more information about getting equipment for your project, see Chapter 9.

Do my parents and teacher approve?

Because you may be doing a great deal of your project at home, make sure that your idea is okay with your parents by asking them some questions, such as:

- Do they mind that the guest room is full of my stuff for the next three months?
- Can I keep the E. coli bacteria in the food containers?
- Is it okay to let lettuce rot in the refrigerator?
- Do they mind jars of worms, ants, and fruit flies in the bathroom (or worse yet, the kitchen)?

Also, check with your parents to see how far they can commit to the project in terms of time, money, transportation, and the ability to keep siblings and pets away from the project. If your parents' level of commitment has to be limited, see if you can assume more responsibility for your project. For example, check out the bus schedules for routes to the central library. You can also close the door to your room to make sure that little children and animals can't disturb your project.

If you're required to do a science project, your teacher likely wants to see a statement of your project idea by a certain date. He or she looks at whether your idea is feasible and whether it can be considered a true science project.

Best performance in a supporting role goes to . . .

Parents. The truth is that your support can be crucial in the success of a science fair project. So, I address how you can be involved without doing the science project yourself!

You're probably reading this book because your son or daughter is going to do a science project. Some students are absolutely dreading their science project while others are interested in science and look forward to doing their projects and competing in the science fair. Possibly the most intimidating step about doing a science project is the amount of time and effort that it will take.

Unfortunately, you may not know how to best help your children, especially if you've never done a project yourself. But you don't need to be a scientist to help. The most important things you can give are encouragement and moral support.

However, you can also take some specific steps.

✔ You can help your child organize the different tasks he or she needs to do and make sure that he or she stays on schedule.

✔ You can help your child to find resources. He or she may need your help to navigate the libraries, stores, and Internet sites he or she needs to check out.

✔ You can help your child find a space of his or her own to do the project.

✔ And surprise, you probably need to do the driving. From library to mall to laboratory, your child needs transportation to get everything he or she needs for the project.

The one thing that your child doesn't need is for you to do the project. If you do the project for your child, you are depriving him or her of a valuable experience, and besides, teachers and judges can often spot when an adult has done the work.

Whether or not your child decides on a scientific career, the experience of doing a project has lasting benefits.

One young man, who worked on several science projects in junior and senior high school, was faced with a large sociology project during his freshman year in college. Most of his classmates were in a panic, but he was quite calm. "It's just another science project," he said.

For example, if your project idea is simply to build a model without doing any testing or analysis, your teacher may veto it and send you back to the drawing board.

If you look at science fair programs from previous years, you can notice that certain project categories are very popular, and certain projects are often repeated. You don't necessarily need to find something completely original, but if you want to use an idea that's been done often, try to find a new twist — remember that teachers and judges get bored, too!

Is it safe?

If you're planning to use chemicals or electricity in your project, you need to make sure that you can use them safely.

Ask yourself these questions:

✔ For projects involving electricity:

- Is battery power adequate (in other words, can I avoid using house current)?

- If I'm going to use house current, is the wiring okay?

- Can I avoid overloading circuits?

- Do I know how to properly insulate and ground everything?

- Do I need an electrician in order to conduct the project safely?

- Do I need to have an electrical inspector or the local power company check my work?

- Do I need transformers or converters (for example, do I need to convert 110 to 220)?

- Will my experiment cause a blackout in my neighborhood? (This sounds pretty wild, but I got your attention, right? Electricity is powerful, but it can also be hazardous — be safe!)

✔ For projects involving chemicals:

- Do I need special permits to get any of the substances?

- Are these chemicals (or a combination of chemicals) flammable or toxic?

- Do I need approval from any authorities (such as the EPA) to do my experiment?

- Do I need special containers to store these chemicals?

- Do I need protective gear, such as goggles, aprons, or gloves?

If you answer "yes" to some of these questions — and that makes you feel overwhelmed — you may want to reconsider your project idea. However, if you still want to do the project despite answering "yes" to some of these questions, see if you can line up some adult supervision to make sure that your project is safe. In fact, I recommend finding out if this type of help is available before you begin.

Is there enough information available?

Determining whether you can find enough information to do a project is also very important.

Also remember the time element — anything's available if you have enough time to find it, but you have only a few months to finish your project.

Before deciding on a project idea answer these questions:

- ✔ Is the information that I need readily available to me?
- ✔ Where can I find the information?
- ✔ If the information isn't available locally, where is it, and how long will it take to get?
- ✔ Will I need to pay for my information? (You usually have to pay for government pamphlets.)
- ✔ If I need special books, can I check them out of the library or must I use them there?
- ✔ Will I need professional advice? Specifically, from whom? Is he or she willing and able to help?

See Chapter 5 for more details on where to find information for your project.

Does it follow the rules for student science projects?

Science Service, which runs the International Science and Engineering Fair (ISEF), has developed a list of rules that help to ensure the safety of students and the well-being of any specimens used in experiments.

Years ago, doing a science project using live *vertebrate* specimens (animals with a backbone or spinal column such as reptiles, birds, and mammals) was quite easy. However, the rules have changed, due to a greater public consciousness about animal rights and the responsibilities of animal care.

Doing such a project can be rewarding and lots of fun, but take a close look at what you need to do.

For example,

- ✔ Find out all that you can about the specimens, including their reproductive cycles and gestation periods (especially if your project involves both males and females, which is probably not the best idea).

- ✔ Find out how much room the specimens will require. Some animals, such as mice react badly to overcrowding and sometimes resort to cannibalism to fix the problem.

- ✔ Find out about the care and feeding of the animals, including food and water, but also cleaning the cages. Consider whether you're willing to take complete responsibility for animal care — your parents may or may not be willing to help with these chores.

Any project using live vertebrates will be closely scrutinized. Therefore, you must have an expert certify that you provided adequate care for the animals and that your experiment didn't harm them in any way. You have to fill out forms showing that you used the proper procedures. If officials harbor any suspicion, they can prevent you from exhibiting at a science fair.

If you can't make this kind of commitment but still want to work with animals, consider using *invertebrates* (animals without a backbone or spinal column).

Some sample projects in this area would be:

- ✔ Which sugar substance do ants prefer?
- ✔ Which wattage light attracts more moths?

You can also do a project that uses live vertebrates, but doesn't involve potential harmful substances or procedures, such as feeding them unusual substances or depriving them of light.

Projects that record an animal's reactions can be excellent choices, for example:

- ✔ What did my cat hear?
- ✔ Dogs: Lefties or righties?

For any project that involves live vertebrates, you need to submit official forms ensuring that you followed the proper rules and procedures. Ask your teacher or check your fair's official Web site to get copies of the forms that you need. You can also check out Chapter 11 for more information about official certifications and forms.

ISEF also has a number of rules concerning *recombinant DNA* (created by combining genes from two or more species), controlled substances, chemicals, bacteria, and tissue samples.

If you plan to use any of these, you should check the ISEF rules as well as rules for your local science fair. You can look at the ISEF rules on the Internet at www.sciserv.org/isef, or you can order a copy from Science Service, 1718 N. Street N.W., Washington, DC 20036.

Chapter 5

Getting the 4-1-1:
Information Please!

*A*fter you decide on your topic, the first major part of your science fair project is doing research.

Before you begin, you may want to know why you need to do research at all. First (and maybe most importantly), the research is required. To have a successful project, you need to understand what's known about your topic. This research can help when you form your question and hypothesis, which I talk about in Chapter 8.

Second, just like other things, research is good for you. Of course, some of you may find that doing research is a lot more fun than other things that are "good for you" (like eating peas, for example). Your science project research may be the first of many fact-finding missions that you undertake, so now is a good time to build your detective skills. For example, you may look at one book that doesn't have anything you need, but it leads you to a magazine or a Web site where you find exactly what you're looking for.

When you do research, you need to take notes on the facts that apply to your project. You also need to keep track of where you find each piece of information, so that when you finally write your paper, as I talk about in Chapter 6, you can give credit where credit is due.

Depending on your project topic, you may also want (or need) to find a *mentor,* or coach, who can guide you to the information and other resources that can help you. This chapter helps you with all those things. So grab your magnifying glass, detective!

Following the Trail: Finding the Info You Need

You can find information in many places, and not just the traditional ones. In fact, your school or community library is only one option. Beyond that, you can gather information from all over the world, via e-mail or snail mail, from the U.S. government, private companies, and even universities.

To help you to zero in on the best places, in this section I give you the low-down, one place at a time.

Hitting the library

Despite the variety of choices, for many of you, libraries are still the best — and maybe the only — place to do your research.

Searching for information in books

Today, most catalog systems are online, but smaller libraries may still have card catalog systems. (See the sidebar, "Doing it the old-fashioned way: The card catalog and other manual methods" in this chapter for more info.)

If your library has an online catalog, you can use it to find whatever's available throughout your *library system* (most often found in larger cities that have one central library and a number of neighborhood branches). You can search by author and title if you know what book you want. Most often, though, you know only what subjects you want to search for. That means you need to do a *keyword search*.

For example, if you want to find information about earthquakes, you can enter the word *earthquake* as your keyword. However, if you want more information, you may also enter *tectonics*. To take it further, you can enter *seismograph* and *aftershocks*. Actually, you can enter all these keywords to get a wider range of sources.

Sometimes a keyword search turns up more sources than you ever have the time or inclination to look at. (That may seem hard to believe if you've ever had trouble finding enough information about a topic!)

To deal with all the search results, you need to narrow the search. In the previous earthquake example, for instance, you can narrow your keyword search by only requesting information on earthquakes between 1950 and 2000.

Doing it the old-fashioned way: The card catalog and other manual methods

Because some library systems have only recent sources in their online systems, you may need to use the card catalog to find older sources. Also, if you're working in a small library, the card catalog may be your only "search engine."

Most local branch libraries often have card catalogs that use the Dewey Decimal System, but others libraries may use the Library of Congress method to catalog books. Both methods can guide you to the areas of the library where you can find materials dealing with your subject. If you need to use the card catalog and don't know how, ask the librarian to help you.

Some libraries also use a *microfilm* (a roll of film that contains reduced-size images) or *microfiche* (a sheet that contains a number of microfilm images) catalog, which is organized in much the same way as a card catalog and usually shows everything available in the library system.

Your search result is a list of publications, which includes the name of the book or article, the author, the publisher, and the publication date. If you're lucky, you can find a number of the sources available in your local library now. You may also find that some of the books you need are currently circulating (yeah, everyone's working on their projects at the same time!). If a book is out, simply request that the library notify you when it comes in.

You may also find out that the book you want is in the library system, but at another branch. Many library systems can borrow the book from the other branch and send it to your local library. If your library doesn't offer this service, you need to travel to the other branches. Eventually, you probably wind up at the library's main branch to get all the information you need.

If the book you want is available, have a quick look to see if it really has what you need. First, check the copyright date to see whether the material is out-of-date. In some fields, information becomes obsolete very quickly (but in other fields, an older book may be as useful as one published last month). Looking at the table of contents, index, and appendixes can also give you a good idea of what's inside.

If the book still looks like a good resource, read a few pages to make sure that you can understand the material. Someone's PhD dissertation on genetic engineering may use terms that you're totally unfamiliar with, and contain more information than you can ever need for your first science project. If the book has what you need, in language you can understand, get out your library card, and take the book home.

Some of the books that you want to use are reference materials, which means you have to use them at the library. If you don't have time to take notes on all the reference material you found (Mom's waiting for you!), you can make photocopies of important information.

The library's photocopiers aren't free. Bring enough money to make all the copies you need. At many libraries, you can also buy a copier card, which saves you the trouble of carrying all that change with you.

Searching other sources

Don't limit your research to books.

You can find lots of information in newspapers and popular magazines, such as *Newsweek, Time, The Wall Street Journal, The New York Times,* and *Readers Digest.* Popular science magazines, such as *Science Digest, National Geographic, Today's Health,* or *Psychology Today* are also good resources. Recent issues probably are available in hard copy, but you may need to read older articles online or on microfiche.

If you want more specialized information, you can also check into professional or scientific journals. *The Readers Guide to Periodic Literature* is the ultimate guide to magazines and journals. Need help using this resource? Ask your librarian.

If you can't find what you need at the public library, try your local college or university library. Often, they have materials that a public library doesn't have. The librarians and assistants who work at the library are usually glad to help you. In most cases, you can use their materials (and sometimes even their databases) on-site.

If a college or university library has good information for your project, see if you can buy a library card. At San Diego State University, for example, an annual library card, which costs $60, allows you to check out up to five books at a time. To find out more about the requirements, rules, and regulations at a particular university library, check with the individual library's main desk.

If you're trying to decide whether the library card is worth the money, think about the other classes you're taking and if the information at the university library may be helpful for those, too.

Asking Uncle Sam

You may not have known this fact, but the largest publisher in the country is the U.S. federal government. In fact, the *Catalog of United States Government*

Publications, which you can find either online or at the library, points you to all the government publications, regardless of branch or agency.

Searching this catalog is pretty easy. Simply enter your keyword(s), and you get a list of sources, including the title of the work, publisher, copyright date, and details about where to actually locate the information.

When searching online, you may get lucky and find a direct link that allows you to access the data via the Web. Notice I said "may" get lucky. If that's not the case, take note of the source's title and stock number and order it from the Government Printing Office (GPO) at www.access.gpo.gov.

Make sure, however, that the materials you want are available for delivery. If you're ordering through the Web site, only the publications with an "Add to Cart" notation are in stock. If the item you need is out of stock or out of print, contact the GPO to find out when it's available. At that point, you have to decide if you have enough time to wait for it.

Another strategy is to look directly to the U.S. government departments and agencies that publish material on your topic. But you may find many more sources than you think. For example, if you need information about nutrition, you can find it in Congressional records and publications from the Agriculture, Forestry and Health, and Education and Welfare departments. Do you need to know about earthquakes? The Naval Research Laboratory, Smithsonian Institution, and National Geophysical Data Center all have information for you. You simply need to find what you want and use it for your project.

Surfing the Internet

Anyone who's spent any time on the Internet knows that it's a great source of information. The fact is that you can find almost anything you need online. To take advantage of what the Web has to offer, you need to be careful and disciplined. (Okay, I know that being careful and disciplined may not sound like fun, but just imagine how much time you'll have to play games when your science project is done.)

One way to get started on the Web is to look at one of the online encyclopedias, which can give you some of the basic facts that you need and then guide you to other sources. You use this encyclopedia in much the same way you use the old 26-volume set.

Another great tool is a site such as Ask Jeeves (www.askjeeves.com), which allows you to put in a keyword or ask a question. The site then gives you a list of sites that refer to your subject.

You can also search using Yahoo! (www.yahoo.com), Google (www.google.com), or whatever other search engine you prefer. Of course, the most direct way is to type in the address of the site that you want (if you know the address, that is).

To make sure that the information you find is reliable, take a good look at who's sponsoring the site. For example, check to see that the site isn't simply a way for someone to present his or her opinions. If you're doing a project on the earth's rotation and gravitational pull, you don't want to include information from the Flat Earth Society! Often, though, questionable information isn't that obvious, so when in doubt, check with your teacher.

If you decide that you've found a great site with useful information, enter the site in your list of "favorites". That way, when you want to revisit the site, you don't have to go through the search again. When adding the site to your favorites list, make sure that you give it a meaningful name, which actually tells you something about the site.

And finally, a word about using your Internet time wisely. I've used this technique myself, even while writing this book. When I finish a certain number of pages, or have been working for a specific period of time, I allow myself to play one game, and then immediately go back to my writing or research. That way, I get my work done, but still don't feel deprived. Try it — it works!

Interviewing the experts

The written (or electronic) word is an excellent source of information, but sometimes talking to a real person helps to make the data come alive. For example, if you're doing a project on the effectiveness of different types of insulation, a conversation with someone who assesses energy efficiency can help you focus on the benefits of your project.

If you know someone who's an expert in the field that you're researching for your project, ask him or her for an interview. Most of the time, people are happy to share their knowledge with someone who wants to find out about their field.

If you don't know anyone to interview, try asking friends, relatives, and teachers if they know anyone you can talk to. You can also check the phone book or the Internet to find a professional organization — several groups have educational committees, and they may be able to hook you up with a good resource. You can also call the appropriate department at a college or university to ask whether it has anyone available to talk with you.

The following list explains a few things that you can do to make an interview fun and productive.

- **When you ask for the interview, be polite and courteous.** Ask how much time the person has and make the appointment at the expert's convenience.

- **Whether you're doing the interview in person, on the phone, or over the Internet, be on time.** If you're detained or need to cancel, make sure to call ahead as soon as possible.

- **Have a list of questions ready and a space to write down the answers.** If you don't understand an answer, politely ask for clarification. (And be sure to have enough paper and pencils handy. A mini-tape recorder is a very useful tool as well.)

- **If the expert seems to run on (which would leave you no time to finish the interview), politely thank him or her and then move on to your next question.**

- **Keep an eye on the time.** Don't overstay your welcome.

- **When you leave, be sure to say thank you.** Follow up with a thank-you note or e-mail.

- **Write down the name of the person and the date of the interview.** You need it for your bibliography later.

Tracking and Crediting Sources

Because every fact that you use during your research comes from somewhere, you have to record each of your sources carefully.

For all sources, write down the author and title and also include the following information for these specific sources:

- Books
  - Publication date
  - Publisher
  - Publication location
- Magazines
  - Title of the article
  - Name of the magazine
  - Date published

✔ Government sources

> You can find many types of government sources, for example, the minutes of an actual session or a government publication. However, all references must include

- Name of agency

- Date published

✔ Internet sites

- Name of site

- URL address

- Author (if stated)

- Publication date (if available)

Give each source an *identification key,* which is just a letter or number. When you go on to actually take notes, you can just record the identification key with each fact, instead of all the information about the source.

Jotting down where you found the resource is also a good idea. That way, if you need to go back and look at the book, magazine, or Web site again, you know how and where to find it.

Check out the following examples of how to record your resources. (***Note:* A** and **B** are the identification keys for these two sources.)

✔ **A.** Jane Goodall, *In The Shadow Of Man,* Houghton Mifflin Company, New York, 1971 (San Diego Public Library, Tierrasanta Branch)

✔ **B.** Desmond Morris, *The Human Zoo,* McGraw-Hill, New York, 1969 (San Diego Public Library, Carmel Valley Branch)

You use this information to create the bibliography and footnotes of your research paper. Carefully identifying your sources helps you to avoid *plagiarism*, which is using someone else's ideas or words without giving him or her credit (see Chapter 6 for more info).

Writing It Down: Note-taking 101

When researching your project, you're dealing with so many facts that trying to commit them all to memory can be a mistake (unless, of course, you have a photographic memory, but that's pretty rare!). So, the first step is to choose the facts that relate to your project and then write them down.

You want to have extra information than not enough, so that's why note-taking is so important.

Interpreting your research

Make sure that you understand the facts that you write down. However, don't necessarily ignore any confusing facts. If, despite being a bit puzzled, you think the information may be important, highlight it and remember to ask someone to help you interpret the data.

You may also find the same fact repeated in several books, periodicals, and Web sites. That's okay — again, better to have it twice than not at all.

What if you find information that disagrees with facts you already found? That's okay, too, because it shows that some disagreement or controversy about the information exists. This controversy may be something you want to talk about in your paper.

Be sure to record the identification key (see the previous section for details), plus the page number where you found the information, with each fact.

Using your own words

The best way to take notes is to write down each fact in your own words. This way, when the time comes to write your paper (don't worry, I don't go there until Chapter 6), the information is easier to understand, because you wrote it.

Having the information in your own words also helps you to avoid plagiarism. However, if you think you're going to need to use the information word for word, write it down exactly, with quotation marks around it.

Here's how you can take a paraphrased note and a note that's an exact quotation.

  ✔ **Paraphrased:** She made an exciting discovery when she realized that the chimpanzees were using grass stems as tools to get termites from the mound. **A,** page 51-52.
  ✔ **Exact quote:** "Most exciting of all, on several occasions they picked small leafy twigs and prepared them for use by stripping off the leaves. This was the first recorded example of a wild animal not merely *using* an object as a tool, but actually modifying an object and thus showing the crude beginnings of tool*making*." **A,** page 53.

Choosing the best method

If you're going to manage your information manually (not on the computer), your best bet is to use index cards to take notes.

Index cards make it easier to sort and group the facts when you're ready to create your outline. If, however, you're going to enter all your information into a computer, you can use index cards, notepaper, the backs of old envelopes or fast food receipts, because you are using your software to organize it.

Regardless of whether you use cards, notepaper, or anything else, try to write as legibly as possible. Personally, I find nothing more frustrating than being unable to read my own handwriting!

Finding a Mentor

If you think it may help to have someone guide you through the maze of doing a science project, you're right.

A mentor, can point you to resources that you may never find in a library, and be a great help when you have questions or when things aren't working as planned.

When you look at a project that a student has worked on from simple beginnings in seventh grade through an advanced twelfth-grade project, you probably discover that somewhere along the way, he or she found a mentor. The mentor may have helped the student find an internship at a laboratory, where he or she worked on the experiment with guidance and other supervision.

So, where to find this exceptional guide, guru, or coach? Here are some ideas:

- ✔ If you've done any interviews, perhaps one of the people that you've talked to is willing to be your adviser.

- ✔ If you live near a university, you may try calling one of the departments to see if a graduate student there wants to help you.

- ✔ If neither of those ideas works, you can ask your science teacher if he or she has any suggestions on someone who may want to act as your mentor.

Chapter 6

Writing Your Background Research Paper

· ·

In This Chapter

▶ Keeping the parts of your paper simple

▶ Creating an outline

▶ Writing the first draft

▶ Editing and revising your draft

▶ Preparing the final copy

· ·

No matter what type of project you do, a background research paper is required. This chapter gives you the short, sweet, and complete guide on how to prepare your paper. Even if you never do another science project, odds are that you'll need to do research and write about it again, so consider this chapter a great tool. And writing and researching doesn't end when you finish school — just ask your adult friends and relatives whether they've ever had to write a report for their bosses! I bet you'll hear a chorus of answers in the affirmative.

Anyway, writing your paper isn't as bad as it seems. And like every other part of this undertaking called a science project, this task is a lot easier if you take it in small steps.

Following the ABCs: The Anatomy of a Research Paper

Before you actually begin planning your paper, make sure you know what your teacher requires. Sometimes, he or she wants one or two pages summarizing what you discovered from your research, while others require a ten-page paper complete with bibliography and footnotes. (I explain these items in the section, "Roughing It: Preparing Your First Draft" a little later in the chapter.)

Any time that you need to convey information to someone, whether that information is in a speech, presentation, report, research paper, or even this book, you can organize it in a simple way:

1. **Tell them what you're going to say.**

2. **Say it.**

3. **Tell them what you just said.**

The "them" I talk about may be teachers, fellow students, judges, and so on depending on your individual circumstance. Just consider who your particular audience is and fill in the blank.

If you're thinking that this method seems simple (and a bit repetitive), you're right, but it works.

Telling them what you're going to say

The first element in telling them what you're going to say is your title. A good title is short and concisely describes what's in your paper. For example, "Using a Seismograph in the Study of Plate Tectonics," is too long and complicated. "Predicting Earthquakes" gives the same information in fewer words.

Next, use your first paragraph to say (in just a few sentences) what your paper's about. For example, in a five-paragraph paper about earthquakes, an opening paragraph may be:

> When seeing the amount of destruction that a major earthquake can cause, it's important to try to predict earthquake activity, so that we can prepare and maybe prevent death and damage. Currently, we can measure earthquakes using seismographs. However, the science of plate tectonics is making great strides in the ability to anticipate "the big one."

This paragraph lets your reader know what points you plan to cover in the rest of the paper.

Saying it

After the opening paragraph comes the main part of your paper (and, in fact, what the rest of this chapter is all about). Here, you use the data that you gathered to explain your topic, in a logical and orderly fashion. For example, the middle three paragraphs in the paper about earthquakes may cover what causes earthquakes, how seismographs measure earthquakes, and what new discoveries in the science of plate tectonics mean.

Telling them what you just said

The final paragraph gives a summary of what your paper was all about. For example, in a paper about earthquakes, you may find something like the following:

> Analyzing earthquake activity by using seismographic data from previous years gives us a pattern of earthquake frequency and magnitude. Recent advances in plate tectonics will one day allow us to predict earthquakes and prevent their devastation.

Yep, you're right, that sounds a lot like the first paragraph, because it recaps the information you just presented.

Outlining Your Ideas

Before you can tell them what you're going to tell them, you need to make an outline. When you actually begin to write the paper, your outline keeps you on track, so that you can present your information in the proper sequence. However, before you can outline, you have to look at all your facts and group all related information together.

Making order from chaos: Sorting your notes

If you took notes on index cards, you need to separate them by subject.

You may want to spread them out on the floor or on a big table. Then, you can look through the cards to see which facts belong together. You can start this process by collecting the facts that define what your topic is about. Then, compile the data that describe the qualities or composition of the substance that you're discussing. Last, gather together all the facts that explain how the item is used.

For example, for a project on the effects of watering plants with gray (recycled) water, you can have these facts (courtesy of Kim D. Coder, Extension Forester, "Using Gray Water on the Landscape" University of Georgia, College of Agriculture and Environmental Studies, (`www.interests.caes.uga.edu/drought/articles/gwlands.htm`).

- ✔ Gray water is water that can be used twice.

- ✔ Gray water includes the discharge from kitchen sinks, dishwashers, bathtubs, showers, lavatories, and the household laundry.

- ✔ Using gray water can almost double water-use efficiency and provide a water source for landscape irrigation.

- ✔ Gray water doesn't include water from garbage disposals, toilets, or diaper water.

- ✔ Gray water contains high levels of grease.

- ✔ Gray water is warmer, by 10 to 15 degrees, than normal wastewater.

- ✔ Gray water contains a large amount of fibers and particles. Filters must remove these materials before gray water enters an irrigation system.

- ✔ Storing gray water is against health codes in many counties. Check with your local health department for additional information about using gray water at your address.

- ✔ Misused gray water can spread typhoid fever, dysentery, hepatitis, and other bacterial and viral problems.

- ✔ Disinfection is critical for gray water held more than three hours. Health hazards — especially with eye contact — are present in dissolved and suspended organic material and detergents.

When you sort and group the facts by topic, you'll find them in this sequence:

- ✔ Definition of gray water

  - Gray water is water that can be used twice.

  - Gray water includes the discharge from kitchen sinks, dishwashers, bathtubs, showers, lavatories, and the household laundry.

  - Gray water doesn't include water from garbage disposals, toilets, or diaper water.

- ✔ Characteristics of gray water

  - Gray water contains a large amount of fibers and particles. Filters must remove these materials before gray water enters an irrigation system.

- Gray water contains high levels of grease.
- Gray water is warmer, by 10 to 15 degrees, than normal wastewater.

✔ Warnings on the use of gray water

- Storing gray water is against health codes in many counties. Check with your local health department for additional information about using gray water at your address.
- Misused gray water can spread typhoid fever, dysentery, hepatitis, and other bacterial and viral problems.
- Disinfection is critical for gray water held more than three hours. Health hazards — especially with eye contact — are present in dissolved and suspended organic material and detergents.

✔ Using gray water can almost double water-use efficiency and provide a water source for landscape irrigation.

Notice that the list has an *orphan,* the last fact about the advantages of using gray water.

If you can't find logical homes for a few facts, don't try to force them into a particular topic. But don't get rid of them either. When you begin your experiment, you may have an "Aha!" moment, when you remember that lonely piece of information. Also, if you decide to do another project on the same topic, these facts can be the beginning of next year's research paper.

Come to think of it, that fact about the advantages of using gray water makes a great opening sentence for a research paper!

If you enter your facts into the computer, you can use the features of your software to organize the information. For more information about how to do this, see your software manual or check out *Excel 97 for Windows For Dummies* or *Excel 2000 For Dummies* (Wiley Publishing, Inc.).

Using the outline format

After you group and sort your information, those piles of cards on the floor or facts on the screen begin to make more sense. However, by using an outline, you need to arrange the facts in each group into a logical sequence. These sequenced facts become the basis of your first draft.

Subdividing topics correctly

Look at each group of facts and find the main theme or heading. Then, find the subtopics that go under the main headings. If an item is subdivided, it must contain at least two elements. Otherwise, the information should've been included in the division above.

For example, it would be incorrect to say:

    C. Health hazards

        1. Eye infection

Instead, you may say "Health hazards, including eye infection."

If you record your facts using a word processor, check out the automatic outlining feature. For example, Microsoft Word has a Bullets and Numbering item in the Format menu that allows you to select an outlining format. From that point, you can indent to get the outline level that you want. For more information about Word, check out *Word 2002 For Dummies* (Wiley Publishing, Inc.).

If you're not well acquainted with using outline form, take a look at the gray water facts (from the previous section) arranged in outline form:

    I. Definition

        A. Reusable water

            Recycled from "clean" water use

            Doesn't include wastewater

    II. Characteristics

        A. Grease content

        B. Fiber and particle content

        C. Temperature

    III. Cautions

        A. Storage regulations

        B. Disinfecting requirements

        C. Health hazards

Using sentences or fragments

When you create an outline, you can use either complete sentences or sentence fragments for the individual entries. But be consistent — pick one method and stick with it.

For a sentence outline, make each entry a complete sentence, for example, "Photosynthesis is the process of synthesizing sunlight." But, for a topic outline, make each entry a phrase with no punctuation at the end, for example "Photosynthesis — light transformation".

Coping with not enough or too much information

You probably know how long your paper needs to be, so check your outline to see if you have enough information. If not, back to the library (or the Internet) you go! But now you know exactly what you need to get.

On the other hand, if your outline has too many points to cover in the number of pages you're going to write, you have to shorten the outline.

You can do shorten your outline in two ways:

- ✔ Cut out some points, especially if they're not crucial to your paper.
- ✔ Reduce the number of facts that you discuss under each point.

If you doubt whether your outline is solid (or just need some reassurance), ask your teacher to take a look at it. And remember to always check that everything in your outline is spelled correctly.

Roughing It: Preparing Your First Draft

After you create a logical, organized outline, writing your first draft is a piece of cake. Not only do you know exactly where your words are going, but you've also broken your paper down into manageable, well-defined pieces. You don't necessarily have to write the whole thing in one sitting — you can draft one paragraph at a time!

Make your background research paper relevant to the problem that you plan to solve with your project. Also, remember to be as specific as possible — don't write a paper on general dentistry and good oral hygiene when your project is about wisdom teeth.

Taking it paragraph by paragraph

No matter how many paragraphs you plan to have in your paper, think of each paragraph as a minipaper, which has a beginning, middle, and an end. To help you develop each paragraph, or minipaper, answer these questions:

✔ What is the main idea of the paragraph?

✔ How can you state this idea in your topic sentence?

✔ How will you use your facts to explain, explore, describe, and support your idea in this paragraph?

Remember, though, that a paper isn't just a bunch of facts strung together. One way to make your paper sound really professional is to use transitions to go from one thought to another. For example, writing this way doesn't have a smooth transition:

> Gray water is recycled from sinks, dishwashers, bathtubs, showers, and washing machines. Gray water is not taken from garbage disposals, toilets, or diaper water.

However, your writing will be smoother if you add a transition, as follows:

> Gray water is clean recycled water, taken from sinks, dishwashers, bathtubs, showers, and washing machines. However, to ensure the safety of the water supply, gray water is not recycled from garbage disposals, toilets, or diaper water.

Your teachers, as well as science fair judges, are looking for continuity, creativity, and educated interpretation of the facts. Make your paper relate directly to your proposed project.

If you're a perfectionist, you can edit your words and sentences as you write them. The good news about being a perfectionist is that your first draft will be fairly polished, but the bad news is that the draft will take you a lot longer. Neither way is right or wrong; just realize that you'll spend the time either now or later.

Avoiding plagiarism

Imagine that you wrote an original story and had it published in your school newspaper. Then, a few months later, you see the story in a newspaper with someone else's byline. Obviously, someone took your creative work and passed it off as his or her own. *Plagiarism* is using someone else's words or ideas without acknowledging where they come from. Put simply, plagiarism is cheating!

Plagiarism of your research paper or science project is grounds for disqualification from a science fair. Plagiarism is also a serious academic infraction that's grounds for expulsion at the university level.

You can make sure you aren't plagiarizing any material in your paper several ways:

- ✔ If you use an author's exact words, put them in quotation marks, for example, as Robert W. Shaker says in his book entitled *Surviving Earthquakes,* "When an earthquake begins, get in a doorway or under a desk."
- ✔ If you don't use an exact quote but very closely paraphrase the author, you can say: In *Surviving Earthquakes,* Robert W. Shaker tells us in that the safest place to be is in a doorway or under a desk.

Unfortunately, deciding isn't always that simple or clear-cut. Is Shaker's advice common knowledge? Table 6-1, shown on the Online Writing Lab Web site, helps you to determine when you need to document your sources

Table 6-1	When to Document Sources
Need to Document	*No Need to Document*
When using or referring to somebody else's words or ideas from a magazine, book, newspaper, song, TV program, movie, Web page, computer program, letter, advertisement, or any other medium.	When you're writing your own experiences, observations, insights, thoughts, and conclusions about a subject.
When you use information gained through interviewing another person.	When you're using "common knowledge" — folklore, common sense observations, or shared information within your field of study or cultural group.
When you copy the exact words or a "unique phrase" from somewhere.	When you're compiling generally accepted facts.
When you reprint any diagrams, illustrations, charts, and pictures.	When you're writing your own experimental results.
When you use ideas that others have given you in conversations or over e-mail.	

Using footnotes

Years ago, research papers were peppered with footnotes. In fact, back in the dark ages when I was in college, professors required a minimum number of footnotes in a paper. Today, however, people have realized that lots of footnotes are distracting and make reading tedious. Therefore, use them sparingly.

Going back to the earthquake example from the previous section, you can put this statement in your paper: Get in a doorway or under a desk when an earthquake begins[1]. A footnote numbered 1, citing Shaker's book, would appear at the bottom of the page.

If you do use footnotes, you need to follow the specific, accepted format. For the first footnoted reference to a book:

[1]Robert W. Shaker, *Surviving Earthquakes,* (Los Angeles, American Tremor Association, 1971), p. 47

For subsequent references:

[4]Shaker, pp. 33-36

For a periodical:

[7]Seymour Seismo, "Evaluating Earthquakes," Tremors Today, October 1993, p. 54-57

Formatting the bibliography

When you finish your first draft, pull out the list of cards where you kept track of your sources, and format the *bibliography* (a list of all the sources that you used to get information for your research paper). As with footnotes, you need to follow a specific format, depending on the type of resource.

Books

The formatting for books depends on how many authors are involved. For example,

By single author

Lauber, Patricia, *Of Man and Mouse,* New York, Viking Press, 1971

By multiple authors

Anderson, Garron P., S. John Bennett, and Lawrence K. DeVries, *Analysis and Testing of Adhesive Bonds,* Long Beach, CA, Foster Publishing Co., 1971

Encyclopedias

The formatting for articles from encyclopedias depends on whether the article had an author. For example:

Selection without author

"Galena," Encyclopedia International, 1974

Selection with author

Roderick, Thomas H., "Gene," *Encyclopedia International*, 1974

Government or other institutional publication

Science Service, ABSTRACTS; 38th International Science and Engineering Fair, Washington, DC, 1987

Web sites

Different types of Web sites call for different types of bibliography entries, as follows:

Scholarly project

Victorian Women Writers Project. Ed. Perry Willett. Apr. 1997. Indiana U. 26 Apr. 1997 `www.indiana.edu/~letrs/vwwp/`

Professional site

Portuguese Language Page. University of Chicago. 1 May 1997 `http://humanities.uchicago.edu/romance/port/`

Personal site

Lancashire, Ian. Home page. 1 May 1997 `www.chass.utoronto.ca:8080/~ian/index.html`

Be careful when using "personal Internet sites" — they may express more opinion than facts.

Article in a reference database

"Fresco." Britannica Online. Vers. 97.1.1. Mar.1997. Encyclopaedia Britannica. 29 Mar. 1997 www.eb.com:180

Work from a subscription service

"Table Tennis." Compton's Encyclopedia Online, Vers. 2.0. 1997. America Online. 4 July 1998. www.aol.com, Keyword: Compton's

Polishing Up Your Paper: Creating a Final Copy

Your first draft is the rough-cut of your research paper. Although you're not bound by any rules about how many drafts to write, remember that each draft is an opportunity to correct, revise, rearrange, and reword the paper. How many drafts you write depends on how you like to work. For some people, the first draft is simply a way to get everything down on paper, without regard for correct usage or spelling. Other people like to have their first draft be as close to perfect as possible.

You may want to print your draft with double or triple spacing. This method gives you enough room to write in comments, ideas, or corrections when you're working on the final copy.

The best way to edit your drafts is to read and reread (and reread) your paper. As you do, ask yourself these questions:

- ✔ Does my introduction state what the paper and project are about?
- ✔ Does each paragraph have a main idea?
- ✔ Does each paragraph have at least two sentences?
- ✔ Does the entire paper flow (in other words, does each sentence lead into the next)?
- ✔ Is the entire paper clear, logical, and easy to read — does it make sense?
- ✔ Does your last paragraph summarize the paper (echoing the introduction)?

When you feel that your paper is the best that it can be, you're ready to create your final copy. If your drafts have been handwritten, use a typewriter or computer for the final draft. Even if your handwriting is good, your teacher will appreciate seeing typed copy, and it certainly makes a good impression on science fair judges.

Checking spelling and grammar

If your word processor includes a spell checker, run it each time you create a new draft. Whenever you add new material, you may be adding misspelled words or badly constructed sentences. Remember, though, that a spell checker won't catch everything. "Their are many species of antelope" looks fine to a spell checker. However, if you also have a grammar checker, it can tell you if you put the wrong "their" in there.

A grammar checker can also help you avoid other common mistakes, such as confusing the words "effect" and "affect" or "lie" and "lay."

Saying it another way: Using a thesaurus

Do you ever get tired of using the same word over and over? Are you totally bored with your research paper? You can use a thesaurus (either in print or online) to get a selection of alternate word choices. Using different words with the same meaning makes your prose look like it was written by a pro!

Getting a second or third pair of eyes

Take it from a writer: When you've looked at your words a number of times, you may miss the most glaring errors. You've seen the stuff so many times that the errors actually look correct. That's why having family and friends review your paper before you hand it in is a good idea. Request that they ask themselves the same questions listed earlier in this section. Although your reviewers may not be scientists or writers, they can find spelling errors, awkward grammar, or badly worded sentences that don't make sense.

Going through a final checklist

Regardless of how your paper was created (handwritten or typed), be sure of these things before handing it over to your teacher:

- ✔ Your margins are correct.
- ✔ Your text is double-spaced.
- ✔ Your paper is formatted according to your teachers' instructions.
- ✔ Your name is on your paper. (Seems obvious, but you can't believe how many people forget this step!)

Also, remember to include your footnotes and bibliography at the end of the report.

Staying on the safe side

When you finish with your research paper, make extra copies of everything before you turn it in. Making extra copies is your insurance policy in case your original gets lost or destroyed.

If your paper, your outline, and all your supporting facts are on the hard drive on your computer, copy everything (including the notes, bibliography, and footnotes, as well as the final research paper) to a disk or zip drive. One last note: Almost nothing's more frustrating than losing long hours of research and writing because of a power failure or a computer crash. So, always back up your computer files and save often.

Part III

The Nitty-Gritty: Stepping Through the Project

The 5th Wave   By Rich Tennant

"Paul, turn off your flashlight. I'm trying to start my science fair project."

In this part . . .

Here's where you actually get to conduct your project. But, before you begin, you need to lay out all the tasks you have to do and make a schedule for getting them done. In this part, I show you some tools that may help.

I also discuss how to use the scientific method correctly. The scientific method involves a number of steps, including stating your question and hypothesis; establishing variables and controls; and setting up experimental and control groups. You also need to list the materials and procedures for your project. I give you some strategies for doing that as well.

Finally, I talk about how to keep accurate records, which is essential to finding meaningful results and drawing your conclusions at the end of the project.

Chapter 7

Keeping Your Project on Track

. . . .

In This Chapter

▶ Planning your work ahead of time

▶ Making and keeping a schedule

▶ Meeting deadlines

. . . .

Doing a science fair project is a large undertaking that comprises many parts. For most of you, the project may span several months — perhaps from Columbus Day through Thanksgiving and on into the holiday break.

One of the hardest things about doing such a large assignment is knowing that you have so much time to finish it. Doing it tomorrow always looks like a good plan, especially when you have more urgent assignments to finish and more fun things to do.

But don't feel intimidated — it's feasible. The challenge is to keep all the elements going so that everything's done on time, without a last-minute mad dash designed to stress out parents, students, and teachers. And what is the trick to accomplishing that? Make a plan and stick to it. Read on, as I show you how to make the process (virtually) painless.

Deciding What to Do (And Putting It in Writing)

You may find it difficult to estimate and schedule your project until you know exactly what tasks you need to accomplish. In order to figure out how to do everything, look at the big-picture tasks involved, such as:

✔ Finding a topic (see Chapter 4)

✔ Getting in touch with people to interview (see Chapter 5)

✔ Doing research (see Chapter 5)

✔ Writing a research paper (see Chapter 6)

✔ Deciding on your hypothesis, variables, controls, and experimental and control groups (see Chapter 8)

✔ Obtaining your supplies (see Chapter 9)

✔ Listing your procedures (see Chapter 9)

✔ Doing the experiment (see Chapter 9)

✔ Analyzing results and conclusions (see Chapter 10)

✔ Finishing the project notebook and display (see Chapters 11 and 12)

Creating a to-do list

That may look like a to-do list, but you're not quite there yet. The items in the previous list are a little too broad to help you organize your time effectively. To do that, you have to break these big-picture tasks into small pieces that you can do in a short period of time.

Begin by thinking of all the tasks that you need to do to accomplish one item listed, such as doing research or writing a research paper. For example, doing research may include smaller tasks, such as checking the school library, visiting your local branch library, doing an Internet search for Web sites on your topic, ordering publications from the Government Printing Office, and taking notes. Likewise, writing the research paper may consist of organizing your facts, making an outline, creating the first draft, building the bibliography, and writing the final draft.

One really cool thing about having a to-do list full of items that you can finish quickly is that you get to check them off when you're done. I know that I get a real feeling of accomplishment when I can look at a huge list that seemed impossible at first and notice that I've crossed off half the items. Knowing what I've already accomplished also gives me incentive to do more, so I can cross off even more stuff!

Figure 7-1 shows an example of a to-do list for getting supplies. You can use this figure as a blueprint when you start making your to-do lists.

Designing a project log

Use a *project log* to document what you're doing at every stage of your project. Your teacher may require this log, but it can also be really useful if things don't go according to plan, and you need a way to prove that you've been doing everything that you possibly can.

Things To Do - Materials

X	Collect 10 one lb. soil samples
X	Buy 10 plastic storage trays
X	Punch 4 holes in each plastic storage tray
X	Collect 10 orange juice cans
X	Punch one hole in each can to create drip device
	Buy wood and nails to build storage rack
	Build storage rack to hold plastic trays and drip cans

Figure 7-1: Your to-do list shows the tasks you need to do and the tasks you already finished.

For the log to be helpful, start keeping it as soon as your teacher assigns the project (or as soon as you decide to do a project) and continue until you analyze your results and draw conclusions. You don't need to make entries every day, and your notes don't need to be perfect (they don't even need to be complete sentences). Just make sure that you document the highlights of your activities. For example, if you weigh your soil sample and record the results every day for two weeks, your project log entry may read "November 1– November 4 — Weigh soil samples and record results in my procedural log."

Figure 7-2 shows part of an expanded to-do list, which can be used as part of a good project log.

You can create and maintain your schedules and logs on the computer, using a word processing or spreadsheet program. Remember that although having them in your computer is great, the logs are the most useful if you print them out and put them where they can remind, motivate, and maybe even nag you to keep on track!

Creating a procedural log

You may also need to use a *procedural log,* which records what you do, and what you observe when you follow your procedures. This log doesn't cover the entire project, so it doesn't include tasks like doing research, writing a report, or creating a display.

Many teachers refer to this as an *experimental log.* However, because this book talks about projects that aren't experiments, such as writing a computer program or building a device, I call it a procedural log.

Collecting Materials **Month:** October

	Tasks	Due	Notes	Done?
1	Collect 10 one lb. soil samples	10/15	Collected on vacation going cross-country last summer	✓
2	Buy 10 plastic storage trays	10/15	Got on sale at swap meet	✓
3	Punch 4 holes in each plastic storage tray	10/20		✓
4	Collect 10 orange juice cans	10/23		✓
5	Punch one hole in each can to create drip device	10/23		✓
6	Buy wood and nails to build storage rack	10/30	I need to measure how much wood I'll need.	
7	Build storage rack to hold plastic trays and drip cans	10/30	Dad said he'll help me on Saturday.	

Figure 7-2: A more detailed to-do list shows more information and can be used as part of your project log.

Figure 7-3 shows an example of a procedural log for a botany experiment, where the plants are checked each week. The plants labeled A1, A2, and so on are in experimental Group A. The plants labeled B1, B2, and so on are in experimental Group B. (See Chapter 8 for information about experimental groups.)

Check out Figures 7-4 through 7-6 to see examples of procedural logs for different types of projects. Note that in Figure 7-5, you can omit the grams designation from each column, by noting in the column headings or in a note that all measurements are expressed in grams.

Date	Plant	Height (inches)	Notes
10/3	A1	0.25	
	A2	0.33	
	A3	0.50	
	A4	0.00	Plant died
	A5	0.45	
	A6	0.25	
	B1	0.60	
	B2	0.33	
	B3	0.25	
	B4	0.00	Plant died
	B5	0.00	Plant died
	B6	0.25	

Figure 7-3:
This procedural log shows the size of each plant measured on October 3.

Date	Activity	Observations	Notes
11/3	Finished pseudo code		
11/10	Finished coding		
11/15	Clean program compile	Had to resolve problems using alternate dictionaries	
12/10	Finished testing	Program can do translation in either direction	
12/18	J.B. tested program for usability	Worked but too slow	Modified code to run faster
12/27	S.P. tested program for usability	Liked program	
1/7	A.C. tested program for usability	Liked program	
1/14	M.L. tested program for usability	Liked program	

Figure 7-4:
This procedural log records observations for a computer science project.

Figure 7-5:
This procedural log records measurements for an engineering project, and allows space for notes and observations.

Model	Test 1	Test 2	Test 3	Notes & Observations
Beam	3414 grams	5650 grams	1100 grams	
Arch	2300 grams	3675 grams	1330 grams	
Truss	3450 grams	3231 grams	1150 grams	

Figure 7-6:
This procedural log lists data collected for a research project.

Year	6.0 Quakes	7.5 Quakes	Solar Activity *
1942	160	5	2
1943	175	3	3
1944	135	5	4
1945	93	5	5
1946	97	1	2
1947	105	4	6
1948	96	8	4
1949	124	5	1
1950	132	8	4
1951	64	5	3

* 1=low, 7=high

Establishing a Timetable for Yourself

If your project is required, the due dates are probably beyond your control, because your teacher has already given you some intermediate deadlines.

These deadlines may seem like a pain, but they can help you break the project up into the various activities you have to do and keep you motivated.

Handing in your work a little bit at a time is good for teachers, because it gives them time to look at everyone's work. A schedule with short-term deadlines also allows teachers to identify any problems with your project. It also gives you an opportunity to correct problems while they're still small. In fact, if the problems turn out to be larger than you expected, identifying them early gives you the chance to change course while you still have time to find other resources.

If your project isn't required, you may have to set up your own deadlines and schedules. Accomplishing this task is a bit trickier, because you have to estimate how long each task may take before you can set deadlines and schedules.

If this process of estimating how long something may take and then setting your own deadlines seems overwhelming, ask for help. Find another student who's already done a science project to give you advice. Other people you can ask are parents, siblings, or family friends — anyone who's done a large project of any type can give you some tips and hints.

Managing deadlines

Regardless of who sets the deadlines, a good way to keep track of them is to make your own *project calendar* and hang it on your wall, where it can constantly remind you of the tasks ahead. If you're really courageous, put it up on your refrigerator where your folks can see it — I'm sure they are more than willing to remind you when a deadline is coming up.

Figure 7-7 shows a monthly calendar that breaks down what needs to be done during a botany experiment.

Another tool you can use to help you make and keep a schedule is a *timeline*. Not only does a timeline show the deadline or the estimated completion date for a particular task, it also helps you keep track of your progress.

Check out Figure 7-8 for an example of a timeline for doing research and writing a paper.

November

Sunday	Monday	Tuesday	Wednesday	Thursday	Friday	Saturday
					1	✓2 Prepare 15 cups for planting
✓3 Plant radish seed in each cup and divide into 3 groups	4	✓5 Water plants	6	✓7 Water plants	8	✓9 Water plants
✓10 Measure and record size of each seedling	✓11 Water plants	12	✓13 Water plants	14	15 Water plants	16
17 Measure and record size of each seedling	18	19 Water plants	20	21 Water plants	22	23 Water plants
24 Measure and record size of each seedling	25 Water plants	26	27 Water plants	28	29 Water plants	30

Figure 7-7: Use a calendar like this to show and check off what you need to do during the month.

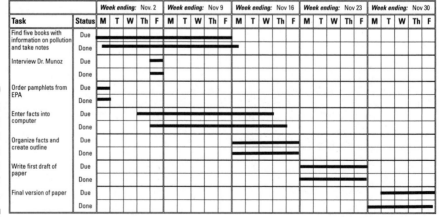

Figure 7-8: Use a timeline to compare your plan to your progress.

Making your schedule work for you

After you draw up a schedule on a project calendar, use it as a tool to help you manage the project. Use it to guide you, not to rule you. Even if your teacher assigned a final deadline, you make your schedule, so you can change the format or layout any time you want. If you find that when you begin following your procedure (see Chapter 9), your project calendar doesn't fit your needs, so change it! For example, if you don't have room for notes, create a new schedule, so that you can keep complete and accurate records.

Somewhere during the course of the project, if your project isn't going the way you planned, show your teacher your logs and schedules, and explain why you think the plan needs to be changed. He or she is glad to advise you and help work out the problem, but the task may be much easier with good documentation.

Remember that your schedule isn't meant to restrict your creativity, but to organize you for success. If your project (or your individual working style) doesn't seem to fit into any of the calendars or schedules I show you in this chapter, design your own. The bottom line: Choose and use whatever tool helps you to do your best.

Chapter 8

Getting to the Nuts and Bolts: The Scientific Method

. . . .

In This Chapter

▶ Coming up with a question and a hypothesis

▶ Determining the subject, variables, and controls

▶ Establishing experimental and control groups

. . . .

*T*o have a successful and effective science project, you must follow the scientific method. Basically, this method covers everything that you do, from researching your topic (see Chapter 5) to analyzing your results and drawing conclusions (see Chapter 10).

However, the heart of the scientific method is determining your project's objective, stated in your question and hypothesis, deciding what, if any variables and controls you plan to use, and what experimental and control groups you plan to set up.

Understanding a Method to the Scientific Madness

Science fair judges agree that the most important factor in rating your entire project is that you follow the scientific method correctly.

The *scientific method* is an organized way to conduct an experiment, including how to collect, measure, and document your data. The scientific method includes the *question* and *hypothesis,* which state your project's objective, the *variables* and *controls,* the factors that either change or remain constant during an experiment, and the *experimental* or *control groups,* which are the groups of subjects tested during the experiment.

Using the scientific method isn't a mystery — you just follow a series of steps while doing your project. Take a look.

1. **Ask the question that your project will answer.**

2. **State what you think will happen at the end of the project.** This statement is your *hypothesis.*

3. **If you're doing an experiment, think about how you're going to do it.** This step involves setting up *variables and controls,* and also the *experimental and control groups.* (I explain how to set up groups later in this chapter.)

   If you're doing a research, engineering, or computer project, you may not need variables, controls, or experimental and control groups.

4. **List the materials that you need.**

5. **Write down your procedures.**

6. **Follow your procedures exactly and record your findings immediately.** You must use a large enough number of samples and do your testing enough times to make sure that what happens isn't just a coincidence.

7. **When you're done, examine the results to see whether you notice any trends.**

8. **Draw your conclusions by deciding whether your results prove your hypothesis.**

The next few sections take a closer look at the different steps of the scientific method.

Stating the question and hypothesis

When you decide on your topic (see Chapter 4), you really decide to solve a particular problem with your science project. A project's purpose is to answer a question. This process isn't limited to science; if you ever take journalism, you find that the basis of every news story is the five Ws (and one H) — who, what, when, where, why, and how. If you think about it, your project is similar to a reporter's job.

The hypothesis, then, is your guess (educated guess, that is) at the answer to your question. I talk more about hypothesis in a minute.

Answering in the form of a question — it's not Double Jeopardy!

Just like on *Jeopardy!*, asking the right question is essential! For your science project, the right question must be specific. In fact, a good question identifies exactly what your project hopes to accomplish. Doing your project is much easier if you know exactly what you want to find out.

One of the most common mistakes that students make on their first project is to have too general of a question.

Check out Table 8-1 for some examples of questions that are too general and then reworded more specifically. Notice that the questions in the Too General column are vague and don't indicate the substances or quantities to be used. But the reworded versions in the Specific column are extremely limited in scope and clearly state what the project hopes to show.

Table 8-1   General Questions Reworded into Specific Questions

Too General	Specific
Does rock music have a bad effect on grades?	What is the difference in grades of students listening to rock music while doing homework?
Which wood absorbs the most water?	What is the difference in water absorption of five different types of wood?
What is the fastest swimsuit for competition?	Do different swimsuit fabrics create different amounts of drag in the water?

You can make general questions more specific in a few different ways. For example, if you're testing or surveying students, you can specify how many students you plan to survey and the students' ages. If you're testing several types of sporting equipment, you can specify what brands or types you plan to test. You get the idea!

If you're doing an engineering or computer science project, your question is to ask whether you can build or develop a particular device or program. For example, a question for a computer science project asks, "Can I design and code a BASIC program that allows a user to enter a program in either Spanish or Vietnamese?" For more information about how computer and engineering projects are different from experiments, see Chapter 3.

Making an educated guess: The hypothesis

After you ask the question, you may already have a good guess, or at least an opinion, on what you want to prove with your project. Decide that, and you have your hypothesis.

Before I go on, I need to define some terms. A *fact* is something that's been proven true, but an *opinion* is something you believe to be true. So, a hypothesis is stronger than an opinion and weaker than a fact. I guess you can call it a hunch, or an educated guess.

What makes your hypothesis stronger than your opinion is that you base it on facts that you already know or have discovered from doing your preliminary research (see Chapter 5). Even though your hypothesis may be only one or two sentences, it may be the most important few sentences you write, because everything you do from then on is aimed at testing that hypothesis.

Your hypothesis may also state why you're making this assumption, based on what you currently know. For example, in an experiment that tested the porosity of various types of Native American pottery, the hypothesis included the fact that cooking pottery is less porous than pottery used for storage, a fact found while the student was doing research

Table 8-2 gives examples of well-worded hypotheses that relate to the specific questions asked in Table 8-1.

Table 8-2	Comparing Questions and Hypotheses
Question	*Hypothesis*
What is the difference in grades of students listening to rock music while doing homework?	I believe that students who listen to rock music while doing homework will have lower scores than students who listen to classical music while doing homework.
What is the difference in water absorption of five different types of wood?	I believe that cherry wood will absorb more water than other types of wood.
Do different swimsuit fabrics create different amounts of drag in the water?	I believe that a metallic swimsuit fabric will have the least amount of drag because it is the sleekest material.

Notice that all the hypotheses begin with the words "I believe . . . " This shows that, so far, your hypothesis is only an unproved theory. When you actually do your experiment, build your device, write your program, or do your research, you want to try to prove your hypothesis. You can perform a series of tests or trials in order to prove your hypothesis. Then, you can observe, measure or weigh, and record what happens as a result.

Defining the subject, variables, and controls

Because the heart of your science project is the experiment itself, you need to carefully plan and execute it to be effective and successful.

When you do an experiment, you're testing a hypothesis to prove whether or not it's true. What you're testing is the *subject* of the experiment. The factors or substances that affect your subject or are measured during the experiment are called *variables,* and the things that remain constant throughout the experiment are *controls.*

Most engineering, computer science, and research projects don't use subjects, variables, and controls. Although you probably test your device or program to see if it works according to plan, you certainly don't compare it to something you build with the purpose of not working according to plan!

Subject

An experiment's goal is to test and examine how changes in the environment or condition affect a subject. For example, if you're measuring the growth of plants, the plants are the subjects of the experiment. Likewise, in a project about how far you can hit a baseball with different types of bats, the bats are the subjects of the experiment.

Variables

Most experiments use variables, which are items that are changed or evaluated in order to test the hypothesis. You can have two different kinds of variables:

- An *experimental* or *independent variable* is what you purposely change. To make your project easier to manage and document, you may only want to have only one independent variable.

- A *measured* or *dependent variable* is what you evaluate and measure. This change occurs because you applied the independent variable. Although you may have more than one dependent variable, for the sake of your sanity, limit the number of changes that you try to observe.

For example, in a project about the effect of court surfaces on tennis balls, the three types of courts are the experimental variables, and the measurement of how high the balls bounce is the dependent variable.

Controls

To make sure that your experiment is valid, you need to make sure that no unpredictable changes affect the experiment. *Controls,* or controlled variables, are the factors that must be the same for all samples in your experiment, every time that you do your experiment. Having controls is important, because if the conditions are different, you don't know what caused the results.

For example, if you're testing the effect of court surfaces on the height of tennis ball bounce, the controls are the brand and quality of tennis balls, the measuring tools, and the location, speed, and method of propelling the ball.

If these controls aren't identical, you can't prove whether differences in the groups are caused by the different court surfaces or by the differences in the tennis balls.

You can do an experiment without using any variables. For example, a project that tests the life of three brands of batteries won't use any variables. However, the project controls are the flashlights used to test the batteries and the length of each test.

Table 8-3 shows the subject, variables, and controls for the hypotheses discussed in Table 8-2.

Table 8-3	Examples of the Subject, Variables, and Controls for Various Experiments		
Hypothesis	*Subject*	*Variables*	*Controls*
I believe that students who listen to rock music will have lower scores than students who listen to classical music while doing homework.	Students	**Experimental:** Type of music **Measured:** Test scores achieved	Age of students, amount of studying time, test used
I believe that cherry wood will absorb more water than other types of wood.	Wood samples	**Experimental:** Type of wood **Measured:** Amount of water absorbed	Size of wood sample, amount of water available for absorption, absorption time
I believe that a metallic swimsuit fabric will have the least amount of drag.	Swimsuit fabrics	**Experimental:** Fabric samples **Measured:** Amount of drag produced	Amount of fabric used, device used to test amount of drag

Forming experimental and control groups

When you do an experiment, you look at what happens when you change something. For example, if you have two identical groups of objects, such as radish plants grown in the same pots with the same amount of water, light, and plant food, you don't gain any information by comparing the two groups, because they're exactly the same.

For the experiment to make any sense, you need to change something in one of the groups, such as giving plant food to one of the groups. While doing this experiment, you measure and record the size of the plants in each group, compare the two groups, and then decide whether the plant food had any effect on the size of the plants.

To make this comparison, you need to divide your subjects into at least two groups, the experimental group and the control group:

✔ The *experimental group* contains a number of subjects to which you apply the experimental variable. To make sure that your experiment is valid, apply these guidelines:

- The subjects in each experimental group need to be identical. For example, in a soil erosion project, start each experimental group with the same amount of soil.

- To prevent the project from becoming too complicated, restrict the number of variables and experimental groups. Make your project easier by limiting the factors you change.

✔ The *control group* is identical to the experimental groups, but with no variables applied. Other points to keep in mind are:

- Except for not applying the variable, the control group must be *exactly* like the other groups. Otherwise, you have no basis for comparison. For example, if you test the effect of adding crushed bone meal to the soil for growing tomato plants, your control group consists of a group of tomato plants that had nothing added to the soil.

- Have only one control group.

For a successful project, your experimental and control groups must be large enough to allow you to collect sufficient data to give reliable results and conclusions. I'm probably getting ahead of myself by talking about results and conclusions, but if you want to have a look about what that's all about, head over to Chapter 10.

Saying a quick word about results and conclusions

I know what you're thinking: I just said that I cover this topic in Chapter 10, so why am I still talking about it? I just can't resist giving you a few quick pointers right now.

Keep the following points in mind while you're planning your experiment, and your results and conclusions will make a lot more sense:

- **The more subjects you use, the more reliable your results are.** However, don't go overboard; use only as many subjects as you can reasonably manage. Another reason for having enough samples is to include a number of extras, "just in case." In case what? The dog ate it, the baby knocked it over, someone threw it away, or it just plain disappeared. Also, when dealing with plants, if you're planting seedlings, start with at least 50, and preferably more, to account for the fact that many won't sprout, or that seedlings may later die.

- **Do your experiment enough times to give conclusive results.** Statistically, you can draw no conclusions based on too few trials. You need a *minimum* of five trials to prove a hypothesis, and even five trials are conclusive only if they all give the same result. To be on the safe side, plan for a minimum of ten trials. For example, in a project that measures tennis ball bounce on different types of courts, you don't want to measure the bounce only once on each court. If you test each court ten or more times, your results are more meaningful, and your conclusions are more valid.

- **If you're doing a research project, look at as much data as you can to get enough information to make comparisons.** In some instances, you may be limited by how far back accurate records go. For example, if your project compares earthquake magnitude with solar activity, you don't want to use any data earlier than when measurements were scientifically taken and recorded. When using human responses to a survey or questionnaire, have enough to make sure that your results are representative.

  When you give out a survey, distribute many more than you need to make up for those who throw it away or don't have time to fill it out.

- **If you've developed a device or program for a computer or engineering project, you need to test it enough to make sure that it really works.** Almost anything can work once under the most ideal conditions, but if you've ever worked with new software, you know that glitches can often show up later.

Putting It All Together: The Scientific Method Up Close

If you've read the earlier sections, you understand the components of the scientific method, so now you can put it all together and see how these elements function in an experiment. Take a look at the series of tables in this section that summarizes the question, hypothesis, subject, variables, and controls for several different types of projects.

To begin, Table 8-4 summarizes a human behavior project with only one independent variable, dependent variables and controls, two experimental groups, and no control group.

Table 8-4	Project Summary — Long Live Rock & Roll?		
Hypothesis	*Subject*	*Variables & Controls*	*Experimental & Control Groups*
I believe that students who listen to rock music will have lower test scores than students who listen to classical music while doing homework.	Seventh and eighth graders	**Experimental:** Type of music **Measured:** Test scores **Controls:** Type of test given	**Experimental:** Students listening to rock music, students listening to classical music **Control:** None

For a computer science or engineering project, the hypothesis and subject may be the only part of the scientific method that you use. Table 8-5 shows a computer science project with no experimental or control groups, variables, or controls.

Table 8-5	Project Summary — The Art of Computing		
Hypothesis	*Subject*	*Variables & Controls*	*Experimental & Control Groups*
I believe that I can devise a computer program that will design origami patterns.	The origami computer program	None	None

You can successfully do a project with multiple experimental groups if you can either test or observe each group separately. For example, Table 8-6 shows a project where a student tested seven fabric samples. Because she was able to test one sample at a time, and then record her data before doing the next test, this project was manageable.

Table 8-6	Project Summary — In The Swim		
Hypothesis	**Subject**	**Variables & Controls**	**Experimental & Control Groups**
I believe that the metallic swimsuit fabric will create the least amount of drag.	The swimsuit fabrics	**Experimental:** None **Measured:** Amount of drag **Controls:** Amount of fabric used for each test, device used for each test	**Experimental:** Metallic lycra blend, denim lycra blend, striped lycra blend 1, striped lycra blend 2, patchwork lycra blend, spandex blend, microfiber blend **Control:** None

Likewise, Table 8-7 summarizes a project with eight experimental groups. Again, the student was able to manage the project because he submerged all the samples for an identical period and weighed each one at the appropriate time.

Table 8-7	Project Summary — Which Wood Would Be Best?		
Hypothesis	**Subject**	**Variables & Controls**	**Experimental & Control Groups**
I believe cherry will be the most absorbent type of wood tested.	Types of wood	**Experimental:** None **Measured:** Amount of water absorbed **Controls:** Amount of wood used for each test, device used for each test	**Experimental:** Cedar, cherry, douglas fir, mahogany, maple, oak, pine, poplar **Control:** None

Chapter 9

Over Here, Igor: Doing Your Project

. . . .

In This Chapter

▶ Getting the materials you need

▶ Planning and listing your procedures

▶ Executing your project

▶ Recording your findings

▶ Saving a doomed project

. . . .

Whether you choose your room, the kitchen table, or the garage, you now need to find a place to set up and do your science project.

To get started, you need to list and find (not necessarily in this order) whatever materials your project calls for. This can involve buying some pieces of equipment and building others. You also have to design and list your *procedures,* which are the logical, sequential steps you plan to follow. Finally, you need to write down your procedures so you don't forget an important step. While following those procedures, you'll make observations, take measurements, and maintain your procedural log (see Chapter 7).

It may sound like a lot, but in this chapter, I guide you through the whole operation, step by step.

Going on a Mission: Gathering Your Materials

No matter what your project is about, you have to use *materials* to get it done. From thinking through your project idea, you've probably already considered what you need, so now's the time to buy, beg, borrow, or build it.

Building some of your materials gives you a great opportunity to be creative with your project. Buying your materials is easy, especially if you're using fairly common items — in other words, items you can buy in most stores. (If you already know where (and how) to get all your materials, feel free to skip to the next section. But, for those of you who don't, read on!)

Shop 'til you drop

You can have a fabulous project using common items from any supermarket, home improvement emporium, drugstore, nursery, or general superstore.

However, if you need special equipment, such as an *ohmmeter* (an instrument that measures the resistance of a conductor in ohms) or a *refractometer* (an instrument that measures the refraction of light), or supplies, such as chemical or bacterial substances, you have to do some investigative work to track them down.

One option is to borrow the equipment or supplies from your school laboratory or from a local college or business, especially if you plan to use it during off-hours. But be careful — if anything breaks, you or your parents may be on the hook for the cost of replacements. If you have a mentor (see Chapter 5), you may already have access to the lab where he or she works.

If no one you know has what you need, you have to find out where to buy your supplies. Your science teacher may know. If not, your detective work continues. To make life simple, your best sources for live specimens, chemicals, or other equipment you may need, are local merchants. Check the Yellow Pages for chemicals, biological supplies, laboratory equipment, plant nurseries, and so on. If that doesn't work out for you, do an Internet search to find your resources.

If you order your supplies through the Internet, you have to pay shipping and handling charges. Also, be sure to find out how long the company takes to deliver the items to you.

If you need to order or build (which I talk more about in a minute) any of your supplies, start early so that any possible delays in getting your materials don't delay your entire project. Also have a Plan B — don't put all your specimens into one test tube, right?

Scavenge through the house

But before you grab the shopping cart (or virtual shopping cart), look around your house. If you can find some of your materials at home, you can save yourself (or your folks) some money!

A few good places to start include the kitchen, the medicine cabinet, the garage, or the garden shed. Depending on your project, you can find detergents in the laundry room; tools in the garage (great if you're building your own equipment); food, containers, and measuring cups in the kitchen; and fertilizers or weed killers in the shed.

If you build it, they will come

If you do an engineering project, you may be building a new type of device or perhaps making structural models in order to test them. In any event, you are fabricating something new instead of using existing materials.

One way of documenting items that you build is to use a diagram, as shown in Figure 9-1, which illustrates model bridges that a student built in order to test the strength of different types of bridges.

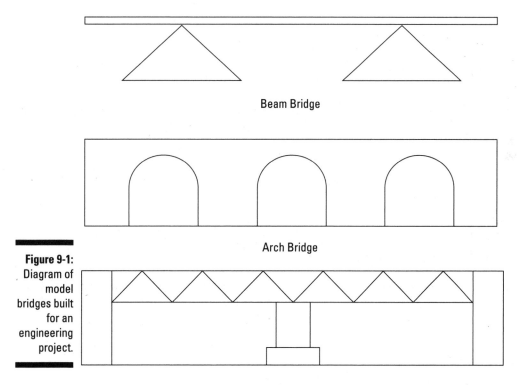

Beam Bridge

Arch Bridge

Figure 9-1:
Diagram of
model
bridges built
for an
engineering
project.

Truss Bridge

Even if you don't do an engineering project, you may need to build something in order to do your project. For example, you may have to build a model to test out your theory, or a holding device or rack in order to set up your experiment for testing. If you find it difficult to fully describe your device in words, use an illustration. Figure 9-2 shows a rack that a student built to hold soil samples and add water to them for a project to test soil erosion.

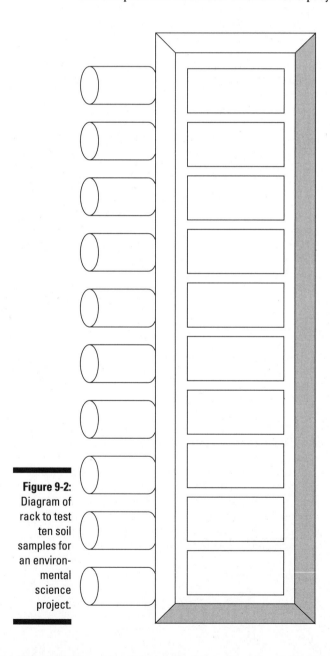

Figure 9-2:
Diagram of rack to test ten soil samples for an environmental science project.

They say that a picture's worth a thousand words, but when you build your own models or devices, you should include descriptions or procedures on how you created them. If possible, make your directions more user-friendly than the cryptic instruction sheet that comes with a bicycle in a box.

To give you an idea of how to write good instructions, Figure 9-3 contains the instructions on how to build the model bridges shown in Figure 9-1. Figure 9-4 details how the racks were built to hold the soil samples in Figure 9-2.

Figure 9-3:
Instructions
on how to
build model
bridges.

Building Model Bridges

1. Measure and cut balsa wood for roadbed span of 10" for each bridge.
2. Cut wood for beam bridge supports and glue to one roadbed.
3. Measure and cut paneling for arch bridge support and glue to second roadbed.
4. Measure and cut trusses from balsa wood and supports from paneling and glue to third roadbed.

Figure 9-4:
Instructions
on how to
build a rack
to test soil
samples.

Building a Testing Rack

1. Measure amount of 2 X 4 plank required to build a rack to hold 10 plastic trays (height and width).
2. Cut board and nail together.
3. Punch small holes into bottom of 10 juice cans and secure each can to top of rack so that water can drip into each tray.

A photograph of your model or device is also a good way to show what you built, but it doesn't replace the detailed documentation and explanation.

Sometimes, building the equipment is the lion's share of your entire project. For example, in a project that tested different types of wind turbines, the actual experiment took only one weekend (after the student spent more than a month designing and building her windmill models). One important reason is that the building process can involve a bit of trial and error. The best way that you can do is to allow yourself enough time to try and try again (if at first you don't succeed).

Building your own device is a good example of how doing a science fair project can have great benefits beyond learning science. One student who I interviewed said that building her own models was a "Power Tools 101" course. Another said that making model bridges with her dad helped them build a stronger relationship.

Taking Inventory: Listing Your Materials

After you find all the stuff you need for your project, you need to write up your materials list. Make this list precise and specific, including the brands, sizes, quantities, contents, and temperatures of all the products you use. In other words, make your list so anyone — trained monkeys included — can follow it to set up the project.

Some students' materials lists contain everything, including pencils and paper, while others include only the items used for the project itself. Which is correct? You make the call!

Materials lists can look quite different, depending on the type of project that you do. Figure 9-5 shows a materials list for a botany experiment, which includes the seeds, containers, potting medium, and measuring tools.

Materials
▪ 120 styrofoam cups
▪ 240 Cherry Belle radish seeds
▪ 1 cup measuring cup
▪ Nail set to punch drainage holes in cups
▪ Potting soil
▪ 1-foot ruler

Figure 9-5:
Materials list for a botany experiment.

The materials for a computer science project consist of hardware and software, as well as the people who are testing the program, as shown in Figure 9-6.

Materials
• One Pentium 4 computer
• C++ processor
• English/Spanish translation program
• Timing device
• Ten bilingual eighth grade students

Figure 9-6:
Materials list for a computer programming project.

For an engineering project, the materials list (see Figure 9-7) contains the things you need to build or test your device.

Materials
• Balsa wood
• Modeling glue
• Ruler
• Xacto knife
• Wood paneling
• Saw
• BBs
• Balance scale

Figure 9-7:
Materials list for an engineering project.

For a student survey project, you need very little after you've developed the survey, as shown in Figure 9-8.

Figure 9-8:
Materials list for a research project.

Materials
• 100 copies of Pet Preference Survey
• 100 student subjects to complete survey
• Computerized spreadsheet program to enter responses and tabulate results

If your list includes a "do-it-yourself" device, you can refer to the illustration and instructions that you developed. For example, if you're testing four different wind turbine models, you can refer to them as follows:

- ✔ Four-blade wind turbine with straight blades (see figure 1)
- ✔ Four-blade wind turbine with angled blades (see figure 2)
- ✔ Six-blade wind turbine with straight blades (see figure 3)
- ✔ Six-blade wind turbine with angled blades (see figure 4)

Avoiding Prohibited Materials

Whether you're entering a school fair or the International Science and Engineering Fair, follow the rules about what you can and can't use. Projects involving chemicals or animals may require extra attention to detail.

For example, experiments that use live *vertebrates* (animals with a backbone or spinal column) aren't prohibited, according to ISEF rules. However, you do need to be careful about where you get your specimens, how you take care of them, and who can formally supervise their care.

You also need to fill out some fairly official-looking forms that certify that the animals were well cared for. If you have any doubt as to whether you can take on this responsibility, change your project to use *invertebrates* (animals without a backbone or spinal column) or opt for a noninvasive animal project (such as what food do finicky cats like?).

As with vertebrates, projects involving bacteria, protozoa, chemicals, corrosive elements, or tissue samples aren't prohibited, but stringent rules govern how you must handle, use, and store the materials you use. ISEF certification forms are required for these sorts of projects, too.

If you're doing a survey, make sure that you get the subject's written permission (or the parents' permission if the subject is under 18). You also need to submit an ISEF form if you use human subjects.

Besides the ISEF rules, your local, school, or state science fair may have other regulations. Note that in some cases, the local rules are stricter than the ISEF rules. What is the moral of the story? Check the rules of whatever fair you're entering, and be sure to comply.

Writing Your Procedures

After you gather and list all your materials, you need to make a sequenced list of the exact procedures that you plan to use. Each item in the step-by-step procedure must describe only one action and be a list that anyone else can follow.

Some steps are done only once, such as the steps you take to build your equipment or set up your project. Other steps may be repetitive, such as testing your subjects and recording your data.

For example, a generic procedure list may look like this:

1. **Set up samples.**

2. **For each sample:**

    a. **Weigh sample and record weight.**

    b. **Soak in water for 1 hour.**

    c. **Weigh sample and record weight.**

Your procedure may be very short, or it may span several pages — the length of your procedures list has absolutely no relationship to the value of your project — it just relates to the type of project that you do.

Write your procedures — including measurements, time spans, and any other applicable information — so that anyone can recreate your project and get similar results.

Figure 9-9 shows the procedures for a botany experiment.

Figure 9-9:
Procedures
for a botany
experiment.

Procedures
1. Punch two holes in the bottom of 20 styrofoam cups and label Group A.
2. Punch four holes in the bottom of 20 styrofoam cups and label Group B.
3. Leave 20 styrofoam cups with no holes in bottom and label Group C.
4. Plant two radish seeds in each cup.
5. Each Tuesday and Thursday:
a) Measure and record height of each plant.
b) Water each plant with $1/4$ cup water.

To illustrate projects that aren't experiments, Figure 9-10 lists the procedures for a computer programming project.

Procedures
1. Create pseudocode to describe the logic for a program to translate commands from Spanish to English. 2. Create menus in Spanish and English so that user can select his or her language. 3. Code computer program in C++ that will allow the user to program in his or her language. 4. Test the program to make sure that program will work in both languages. 5. Time how fast the program runs in each language. 6. Have five students use the program to make sure that it is user-friendly.

Figure 9-10: Procedures for a computer programming project.

Figure 9-11 gives the steps in an engineering project and refers to the diagram and procedures for building the model bridges shown in Figure 9-1.

Procedures

1. Build model bridges according to attached diagram and instructions.
2. For each bridge:
   a) Pour water on bridge, catching water in a container until bridge breaks.
   b) Weigh and record amount of water in container.

Figure 9-11: Procedures for an engineering project.

For a research project that collects and mathematically analyzes data, check out Figure 9-12.

Procedures
1. Gather number of 6.0+ earthquakes and 7.5+ earthquakes from 1940-2000. 2. Gather statistics on solar cycles for 1940-2000. 3. Graph data comparing earthquake and solar activity data. 4. Apply correlation coefficient statistical test to see if a correlation exists.

Figure 9-12: Procedures for a research project.

Your adviser or science teacher may want to review your procedures before you begin. Looking over the list again is a good last-minute check before you begin doing the project. He or she may look at each step to make sure that you're following the scientific method (see Chapter 8).

If your teacher says that your sample is too small or that you plan to conduct too few tests, you need to enlarge your sample or add steps. If he or she says your procedure is too vague, you may need to describe your steps in more detail. Remember that your teacher can't read your mind — if you don't put a step on your list, chances are no one else can follow it.

Taking the Plunge: Doing Your Project

If you haven't done so yet, find a good spot to set up your project, post your schedule and procedures, get your measuring tools and logs handy, and prepare to begin.

Following the yellow brick road of procedures

Because you've done all the prep work, you're definitely headed toward success, but to give yourself even more of an edge, follow these guidelines:

- ✔ **Follow your list of procedures exactly.** If you improvise while doing your project, you won't know whether your results are valid. For example, in a botany experiment, if you think the plants in group B look dry, don't just give that group extra water — this action changes the procedures, and possibly the results.

- ✔ **Consistently make your observations, take your measurements, and record your findings.** (I talk more about this in the next section.)

- ✔ **If you're doing an experiment, do your tasks on a regular schedule, for example, every Saturday morning.** If you stick to a routine while doing your project, you ensure that you're not adding an unplanned variable. For example, if you're doing a project that compares water drainage and plant growth, forgetting to water the plants can affect your results.

Seeing (and measuring) is believing

While you're following the procedures, you need to stop and observe what happens. More importantly, you'll have to measure the size, weight, or amount of your samples. Both observation and measurement are essential — each adds a dimension to what your project is telling you.

As you do your project, you may make observations that you're not even expecting. For example, if you measure the height of tomato plants in your botany project, noticing that some of the plant leaves turn brown gives important information, because this information may mean that the plants are dying.

If you are taking measurements, make them as precise as possible. You can take measurements several ways:

- **If necessary, balance and calibrate your instruments.** Check your instrument by comparing it against an established standard, and then make adjustments.

- **When using scales, rulers, vessels, or other items that measure weight, size, or volume, choose the equipment that shows the smallest differences.** A ruler that shows ¹⁄₁₆ of an inch gives a more accurate measurement than one that shows only ¼ of an inch. You can't precisely compare a length that's "a little less than a millimeter" to one that's "almost a millimeter."

- **Use the same tools each time that you take measurements.** Doing so eliminates any doubt about the accuracy of your data.

- **Use metrics wherever possible.** Metrics give your work scientific credibility.

I'm going to jump ahead a little bit here, so I can talk about why measurements and observations are important. When you analyze your results and formulate your conclusions (see Chapter 10), wherever possible you want to use *quantitative analysis* (based on exact measurements). *Qualitative analysis* (based on observation only) can add valuable information, but isn't as accurate. Check Table 9-1 to compare examples of how qualitative and quantitative analyses differ.

Table 9-1	Qualitative Analysis versus Quantitative Analysis
Qualitative	*Quantitative*
The plants in Group A grew twice as tall as the plants in Group B.	Group A grew between 20 and 25 mm and Group B grew between 10 and 15 mm.
The mice kept in the dark ate less than the ones in the light.	Group A, in the dark room, ate between 4 and 6 cc per day. Group B, in the light room, ate between 8 and 10 cc per day.
The experimental group was heavier than the control group.	The average weight of the experimental group was .227 kg, and the average weight of the control group was .142 kg.

As important as quantitative analysis is to your project, I don't want to ignore the value of qualitative analysis; your observations in words or in photos can add a lot to your project.

Keeping Accurate Records

When you're doing your experiment, executing your computer program, or testing your device, immediately record your observations and measurements as soon as you make them. If you wait even a few minutes, you may forget exactly what you saw. (Funny, how the mind works, huh?) Even your recall of measurements may be inaccurate after a few minutes — you can easily think that you measured 1.625mm when you actually measured 1.652mm. If you wait a few hours, the possibility of making errors compounds.

Use your *procedural log* (see Chapter 7 for more details and some examples) to record everything that happens during your project.

Include room for a date, your measurements and observations, and your notes or comments in your procedural log. Being specific is especially useful if something unusual happens and you want to explain why. You may need a separate log for each experimental and control group in order to have enough room to record all your information.

Have your procedural log on hand while you do your project, so you don't have to go looking for after it you've measured your sample. If you have your log available, you can concentrate on doing your project, observing what happens, measuring the results, and documenting the information without worrying about how to keep track of it.

Also, don't forget to keep up your *project log.* This notebook is where you can put anything that doesn't fit in your procedural log, such as finding the right mathematical formula to use, or conversations you've had with your mentor. Include any new information that you find or surprising discoveries that you make that can add insight to your project.

Most important, if you have any problems, document exactly what they are and how you are handling them. If you have any equipment malfunctions, also make a note of them, because they may have an impact on your observations and results.

Waking Up From a Nightmare: Help, My Project Is Doomed!

Most of you have projects that go according to plan. Whether or not it looks like you're proving the hypothesis, the plants are growing, the surveys are coming back, your computer program is working, or your invention keeps chugging along. Your measurements are accurate, your logs are current, and your photos look great. Cool!

But what if you're one of the unlucky few whose experimental and control groups (see Chapter 8) are about as active as paint drying, or what if almost everyone has trashed your surveys? It's time to think about how to salvage the project.

For example, one student who had a very successful project testing different types of wind turbines ran into trouble early. Two of the models that she built were too small and light to turn the shaft and produce any electricity. In order to go on, she eliminated both models, and her project continued with four windmills instead of six.

Another student who did a project on desalinating water also had problems. Originally, he built his still out of wood, which became soaked with water. This caused the glue to melt, which caused leakage, making it impossible to measure the amount of water. To fix the leakage, he replaced the wood with transparent plastic and solved the problem. What's the moral of this story? A problem is just another opportunity. Use your imagination, get whatever help you need, and make small corrections that can save your project from extinction.

If you've lost all hope for your project as it stands, you may need to completely revamp it. This, however, is a really bad idea if the project is due next week — decisions like this need to be made early on.

However, before you consider taking drastic steps, discuss the situation with your teacher or adviser. She or he may realize that if you keep at it a little longer, you may get results. If not, your teacher may be able to give you an idea that can let you use the work you've already done. Of course, your teacher may be more willing to help if you can show (via your research, tables, and logs) that you've given it a good try.

Whatever happens, don't change your observations or measurements to fit your hypothesis. That defeats the whole objective of science — to honestly prove or disprove a hypothesis or a theory. Remember that "nothing happening" is a result, which gives valuable information. If nothing else, it may give you a topic for next year's science project!

Chapter 10

That's a Wrap: Winding Up Your Project!

. . . .

In This Chapter

▶ Checking out your results

▶ Coming up with conclusions

. . . .

*W*hen you begin your project, you probably already have a due date (oh, those deadlines!). Regardless of how you think the project is turning out, when you reach D-Day, the experiment is over. But you still have a lot of work to do.

Your next steps include looking at your results, comparing the data to your *hypothesis* (an educated guess about what your project would prove), and coming to a *conclusion,* that is, deciding whether or not you proved your hypothesis. This chapter can help you with all of that!

So just dig out the project logs and journals that you've been keeping (see Chapter 7) and get ready to see what all this information means.

Playing Detective and Examining Results

The *results* of a science project are the facts and figures that show what happened during the project. The results can include the measurements that you recorded, the notes that you made, or even the photos that you took. For more information about keeping records, have a look at Chapter 9.

However, if your project isn't an experiment, your results may be a little different. For example, if you built a device for an engineering project, your result is what you built, and if you developed software for a computer science project, your results are your program code. For a research project, the information you gathered is the result.

But, you're not quite ready to analyze or interpret the results yet. For now you simply gather, graph, and chart the data in various ways to make the results as clear and meaningful as possible.

This charting is important so you can get a clear picture of what the information is telling you. For example, when you organize the data, you may start to see trends or even some unexpected or unusual results (for example, one plant growing an extraordinary amount in one week).

In short, your results are what you see when your project is done, but before you decide to analyze or interpret what went on.

Looking at the raw data

The good news is that you don't have to do anything to get your raw data — you already have it! *Raw data* refers to the information that you collected while doing your project (not something off the sushi menu). Your raw data may be your procedural log, notes, photos, code listings, or any other data that you have. Just collect the various records that you kept over the life of the project, and you have your raw data.

The bad news is that you need to organize your data before it means anything. If you were really good about keeping a project log (see Chapter 7), you're halfway there. Remember the Girl and Boy Scouts motto, "Always be prepared!"

Figure 10-1 shows an example of a handwritten project log for the control group in an experiment that tested how the amount of drainage affects plant growth.

	Plant 1	Plant 2	Plant 3	Plant 4	Plant 5	Average
Oct 4	0	.1	.3	0	.1	.1
Oct 11	.2	.6	.3	.8	.1	.4
Oct 18	1.0	.9	1.1	.7	.9	.9
Oct 25	.8	.1	.3	.6	.2	.4
Nov 1	.4	.6	.7	.5	.3	.5
Nov 8	.7	.6	.8	.5	.9	.7
Nov 15	.8	.7	.6	.6	.8	.7
Nov 22	.2	.6	.3	.8	.1	.4
Nov 29	.5	.8	.3	.7	.2	.5

Figure 10-1: Your project log is critical in supporting your results.

I use the same information from the project log shown in Figure 10-1 in Figures 10-2 and 10-4 through 10-11 to illustrate the different methods of presenting your data.

In this experiment, three groups of identical plants were potted in the same soil in standard pots. All the plants received the same amount of water and sunlight. Before planting, one drainage hole was plugged in one third of the pots; the plants in this group were experimental group A. A second hole was drilled in one-third of the pots before planting; this group was experimental group B. The plants in the control group were in unaltered pots.

Table 10-1 displays the average growth of both experimental groups and the control group in table format. (If you need information about how to use experimental or control groups, see Chapter 8.)

Table 10-1	Plant Experiment's Project Log in Table Format (Expressed in Centimeters)		
Date Examined	*Group A*	*Group B*	*Control Group*
10/4	0.4	0.7	0.1
10/11	0.7	0.5	0.4
10/18	0.5	0.3	0.9
10/25	0.6	0.3	0.4
11/1	0.2	0.5	0.5
11/8	0.6	0.2	0.7
11/15	0.9	0.9	0,7
11/22	0.1	0.5	0.4
11/29	0.3	0.2	0.5

Graphing the project results

They say that a picture's worth a thousand words. This idea is particularly true when dealing with numeric data. You can use *graphs* (diagrams that illustrate a relationship between numbers) to represent data in a highly visual way that makes the relationships instantly apparent.

A graph generally represents these relationships on a grid, which is why graphs drawn by hand are usually done on graph paper. A graph uses two axes, the *x-axis* and *y-axis,* to express the values being compared.

If, for example, you graph the results of a survey asking eighth grade students what pets they have, the x-axis would show the different pets (birds, dogs, cats, rodents, insects, lizards, insects, younger siblings, none). The y-axis would show the range of values.

For example, if the votes for each type of pet range from 200 to 500, the y-axis must show those values so that the scale is clear and accurate without being confusing. After the x-axis and y-axis are defined, the values are plotted on the graph. You must also title the graph so that what it represents is clear to anyone who looks at it.

Figure 10-2 illustrates the parts of a graph.

Graphs come in several different types. The most common types are bar graphs and line graphs. (If you don't like those types, I give you a few more choices in the next section.)

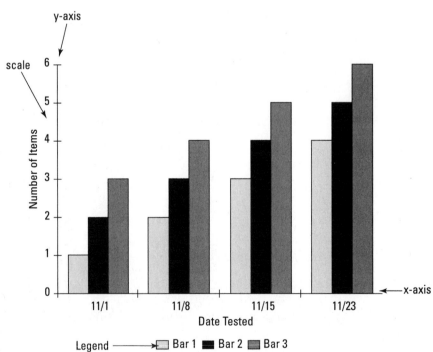

Figure 10-2:
Parts of a
graph.

Using the data shown in Figure 10-1 and Table 10-1, Figure 10-3 shows experimental group A as a horizontal bar graph.

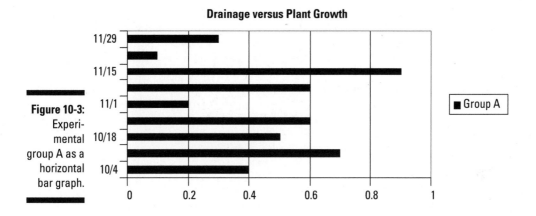

Figure 10-3:
Experimental group A as a horizontal bar graph.

Figure 10-4 shows experimental group B as a vertical bar graph.

Figure 10-5 shows the control group as a line graph.

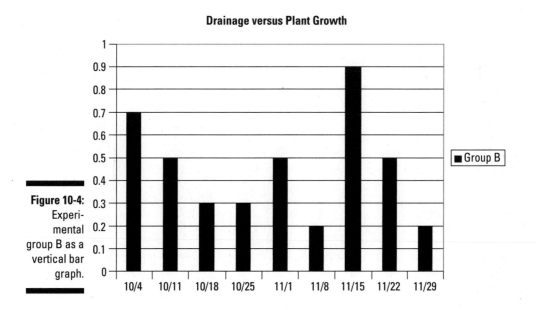

Figure 10-4:
Experimental group B as a vertical bar graph.

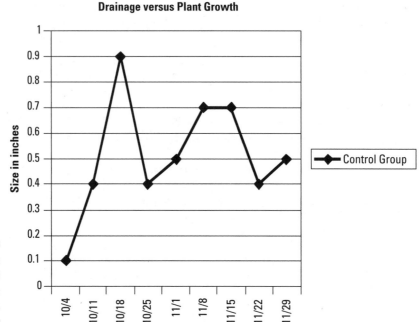

Figure 10-5:
The control
group as a
line graph.

Combining and comparing results

The next step is to combine the data from the different groups. If you didn't already see some patterns while you were doing the experiment, you'll most likely see the patterns come together when you combine the data onto one graph.

Letting your computer do the work

Your spreadsheet program can draw graphs for you, using information that you entered in the worksheet. All you need to do is show the columns and rows you want to graph, choose the graph type, and the graph appears on your screen. Don't be afraid to check out some of the different types of graphs that are available, such as 3-D bar graphs, stacked graphs, combined bar and line graphs, or 3-D line graphs. Let the image come up on your screen. If you don't like what you see, just try another!

Be sure to title each graph or chart. Also, clearly and accurately label each axis, column, or row, and specify the unit of measurement. Your software can handle all those details for you.

For more information, check out *Excel 97 for Windows For Dummies, Excel 2000 For Dummies, Microsoft Works 6 for Windows For Dummies,* or *Microsoft Works 2000 For Dummies,* (all published by Wiley Publishing). Or, if you prefer, you can refer to your software's user manual.

Figure 10-6 shows the combined data as a line graph.

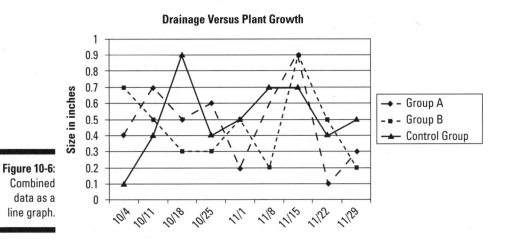

Figures 10-7 through 10-10 show examples of the other graph formats that you may want to use.

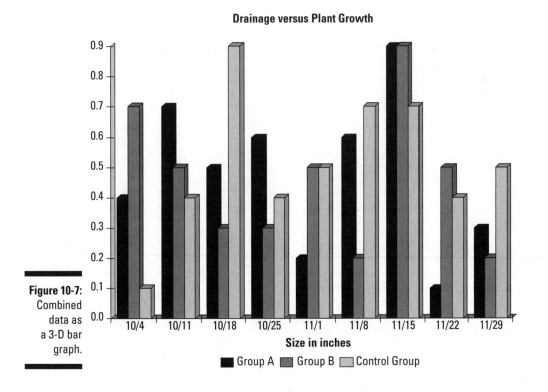

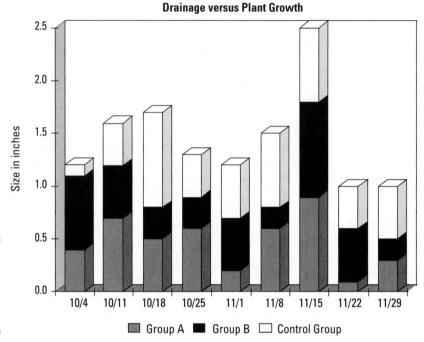

Figure 10-8:
Combined
data as
a stacked
bar graph.

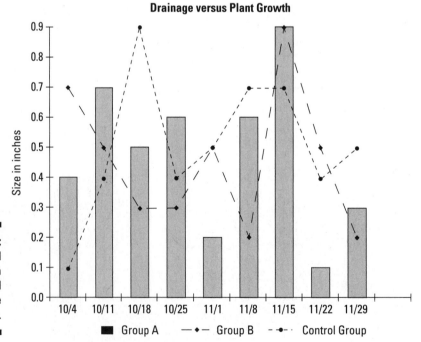

Figure 10-9:
Combined
data as a
combined
bar and line
graph.

Drainage versus Plant Growth

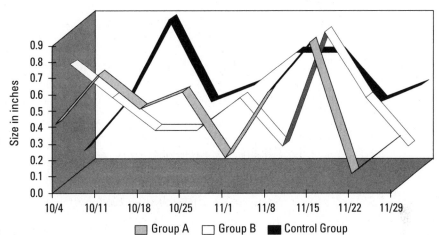

Another way to represent data is in a circle graph or pie chart, which is useful only when your information can be represented as percentages. The whole circle represents 100 percent, or the total amount, and the individual slices show parts of the whole, as you see in Figure 10-11, which illustrates how to use a pie chart.

Type	Selected
One	75
Two	67
Three	34
Four	36
Five	54

Student Choices

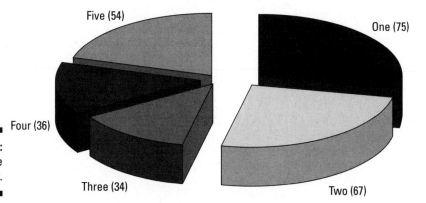

Entering calculation city

At this point, you may need to make some calculations in order to clarify your results. If you manage to stay awake during your 8:00 a.m. math class, you should understand how to handle this task. If you need help deciding what calculations you need to do (or even if you need to do any), ask your teacher. But, you'll most likely need to do calculations in a research project that mathematically compares groups of data.

As an example, in a project that correlates earthquakes of 6.0 and 7.5 magnitudes with solar activity over a 40-year period, a student used the *correlation coefficient,* a statistical test that measures how current trends follow actual past values. Incidentally, the student originally had no clue about this, but his teacher pointed him in the right direction.

Some examples of common calculations that you may need to use are:

- ✔ **Average** (also called *arithmetic mean*). A value obtained by dividing the sum of a set of items by the number of items in the set.

- ✔ **Total.** An amount obtained by adding numbers together (or, if you prefer, a common breakfast cereal).

- ✔ **Percentage.** A fraction that expresses part of a whole, which is represented by 100. For example, 98 out of 100 is 98 percent.

If it applies to your project, calculating the *standard deviation* (a statistic that measures the variation in a distribution) can give your project validity and credibility. You can also use additional statistical tests, such as the *Chi-Square* and *P-value,* to establish the validity of your conclusions. Sound a little over your head? In doubt? Just check with your science or math teacher.

Your spreadsheet software includes just about any calculation that you may need. You just have to indicate the rows and columns to use in the calculation. If you need to use an equation that's not built in, you can type in the formula and still have the spreadsheet get the results for you. If you're using Microsoft Excel and need more information, see *Excel 97 for Windows For Dummies* or *Excel 2000 For Dummies.* If you use Microsoft Works, see *Microsoft Works 6 for Windows For Dummies* or *Microsoft Works 2000 For Dummies* (all published by Wiley Publishing). For other software, check your Help menu or user manual.

Smile, your project's on Candid Camera!

Photographs are a great way to show what happened during projects that take several weeks. If you have a lot of photos (hopefully, they're all dated and labeled), choose the ones that really illustrate the project. For example, if you're performing a six-week experiment that measures plant growth, choose photos that show what the plants looked like each week. (Daily photographs are probably overkill!)

Likewise, in an engineering project, photographs may be the best way to show your progress as you built and tested a device.

Writing a results statement

Next, you need to write your results, including a brief summary of your observations and measurements. This summary can give the reader a bird's-eye view of what happened during the project.

For example, in the six-week plant growth project that I mention earlier in the chapter, you may have measured your plants every day, but in your results statement, you just need to state the overall or average growth of each group. A results statement for this project can be: "Experimental group A showed an average growth of .2cm, experimental group B showed an average growth of .4cm, and the control group showed an average growth of .3cm."

If you have strange or unexpected results, clarify them in your results statement. If possible, make your explanation sound professional. For example, what if you were growing mold on bread, and one day, halfway through the experiment, you went into your room and found your dog scarfing down experimental group B? To explain, you may say, "My results were compromised because the project area was not secured." You're not lying — just presenting the truth in different words.

Drawing Conclusions

Your *conclusion* is the relationship between your original hypothesis and your results. For example, if your hypothesis was that Brand A batteries last longest and your experiment showed that the flashlight with Brand A died first, then your conclusion is that the results didn't prove the hypothesis.

You may wonder how conclusions differ from results. Your results show what happened during the project, including any necessary mathematical or statistical calculations. To illustrate the data in your results and make it easier to understand, you create combined tables and graphs.

To draw your conclusion, then, you need to look for patterns in the data. Make sure that you review your results critically and without bias in order to reach a definitive conclusion. This process means that you look at what actually happened, even if the results aren't what you were hoping for.

Weighing results versus your hypothesis

The first step is to compare the results to your hypothesis. Closely examine your tables, graphs, and charts to see if a trend clearly emerges.

For example, consider a project whose hypothesis states that plants grow taller in composted soil. If the results show that 75 percent of the composted plants grew to 6 inches, while 90 percent of the non-composted plants grew to 4 inches, the results show a trend.

When comparing the results to your hypothesis, you have three possible outcomes:

- ✔ Proving the hypothesis
- ✔ Disproving the hypothesis
- ✔ Determining that the results are inconclusive

If the results either proved or disproved your hypothesis beyond a reasonable doubt, your results are *conclusive.* You can happily state either that you've proven your hypothesis or that the hypothesis is false. If your results don't prove anything either way or your data shows a trend but isn't strong enough to prove or disprove your hypothesis, your results are *inconclusive.*

For example, look at a research project where the hypothesis states that home teams won more games than visiting teams. If the data shows that the home team won 75 percent of the games, the results prove the hypothesis. If, however, the data shows that the visiting team won 75 percent of the games, the hypothesis is incorrect. If the data shows that the home team won only 50percent of the time, the results are inconclusive.

If your results don't support your hypothesis, don't change the hypothesis to fit the results or leave out results that disprove the hypothesis. Instead, give possible reasons why your assumption is false. Remember that your hypothesis is only an educated guess that you make before you begin your experiment, based on the information you have at the time. If it were an established fact, you wouldn't need to do an experiment. Disproving the hypothesis is as scientifically valid as proving the hypothesis.

Explaining your conclusions

Now, you need to explain your project conclusions in a paper. Ideally, you want to gauge this paper at approximately three pages long. Here, you basically state in words what your data shows — whether or not you proved the hypothesis.

The conclusion paper is not the same as your research paper (see Chapter 6).

When writing your conclusion paper, use your research (see Chapter 5) as well as your results to explain how you reached your conclusions. The clearest and easiest way is to discuss each fact or occurrence in a separate paragraph, referring to the experimentation and analysis that you did.

When explaining your conclusions, this paper should:

- ✔ Restate the original hypothesis.
- ✔ Describe and interpret your results.
- ✔ Compare your results to your original hypothesis.
- ✔ Summarize your conclusion.
- ✔ Critique your own project design, techniques, and procedures.
- ✔ Suggest possible improvements.

Be sure to check with your teacher before you begin your conclusion paper. The length may vary, depending on his or her requirements. Also, if your teacher allows, include tables and graphs to illustrate your conclusion. If you don't include tables and graphs in your paper, hold on to them. You will use them in the science project notebook (refer to Chapter 11) and the project display (see Chapter 12).

When you summarize your conclusions, briefly state whether you proved the hypothesis and why. The following example is a conclusion summary where the hypothesis was true:

> My hypothesis is that Brand A batteries will last the longest, because they are the most expensive. This hypothesis is correct, because the Brand A battery outlasted the Brand C batteries. However, when I calculated the amount of battery life per dollar spent, the Brand C battery turned out to be the best buy.

A 3-D bar graph supported the conclusion, as shown in Figure 10-12.

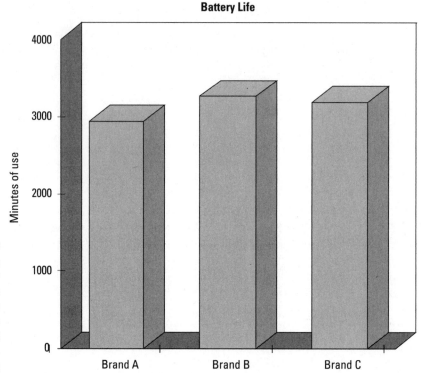

Figure 10-12:
A 3-D bar graph is one way to illustrate project conclusions.

The following conclusion summary illustrates a hypothesis that was false:

My hypothesis is that a wind turbine with more blades produces more electricity. This hypothesis is incorrect. Fewer blades on a propeller made the propeller run faster. This is because fewer blades made the propeller lighter and more aerodynamic.

I learned that the propellers have to go at a constant rate to produce energy, and also that the most aerodynamic propellers are lightweight and have either two or three blades.

My project can be improved by using the same materials in all the propellers tested. Using the same materials can give a more accurate comparison of models with different numbers of blades.

The following summary statement describes an inconclusive result:

> My hypothesis is that beverages high in sugar weaken the adhesive used for orthodontic work. My hypothesis was inconclusive because testing every day for six weeks did not weaken the bonds in the experimental groups or in the control group.

> My project may give conclusive results if the experiment can continue for a longer period.

Adding enhancements

Whether or not your project proved the hypothesis, include a brief statement that realistically discusses the strengths and weaknesses of your project procedures in light of your results and conclusions.

For example, if you gave a questionnaire to 100 subjects and only 50 people responded, your sample size was too small. The equipment you used may have been inadequate to accurately weigh or measure your sample.

Be honest; every project always has strengths and weaknesses! Finally, suggest future changes or improvements, for example, allowing more time for the experiment.

Considering follow-ups

If you're inspired to continue working in this field and bring your experiment to the next level, describe what you plan to do. Preparing this explanation can actually give you the idea for next year's project! If not, suggest further work that someone else may like to try (maybe your younger brother or sister).

Several of the big winners at the International Science and Engineering Fair work on variations of the same project for many years, refining and developing their projects. Each year, they build on the strengths and weaknesses of their prior year's experiment, until they complete a professional, top-level scientific study and experiment. For some of these students, this work has resulted in trips, scholarships, cash awards, patents, recognition, or a lifetime passion!

Considering "real life" applications

A powerful ending to your conclusions statement is a discussion of whether your project has any *practical value* (use in the real world). By applying your project to life, you show your teachers and judges that you can relate your experiment to real-life situations and other fields.

Looking at those types of relationships has brought a great deal of personal satisfaction to many students. For example, a student whose project developed computer systems for the physically challenged took great satisfaction seeing the difference that this work made for others.

Part IV
Show and Tell

In this part . . .

In this part, I talk about how to present all your hard work to the world.

Just imagine that you're launching a brand new product — you need to advertise to attract customers, right? And after they're interested, you need to give them the facts so they can understand what the product can do. In this case, the product is your science project. To attract your audience, the science fair judges, you need to grab their attention with a good-looking, informative display. The display makes them want to look at your notebook, which contains the details of what your product has to offer.

To present your project to its best advantage, both parts (notebook and display) are equally important. The best project in the world can't win any prizes if no one knows about it; however, even a display with loads of flash, dash, and pizzazz can't make up for a sloppy notebook or an inadequate project.

Chapter 11

Creating a Project Notebook

In This Chapter

▶ Preparing your final research paper

▶ Putting your notebook together and making it look good

▶ Featuring the required information

*Y*ou may have heard the expression, "The job isn't finished until the paperwork is done." The same holds true for science fair projects.

In fact, to present your project at a science fair, you need to have a *project notebook,* which includes a final version of your research paper, details about your project, and some required forms.

If you've seen other students' notebooks, you probably know that putting one together is a fairly hefty piece of work. But, the good news is that you already have most of the material. At this point in your project, you've written the research paper, posed your question and hypothesis, kept your logs, outlined your procedures, analyzed your results, and formulated your conclusions.

Now, all you need to do is edit and revise the material to get everything into an attractive, presentable form. In this chapter, I show you how to do just that.

Polishing Your Research Paper

You may have thought that you'd seen the last of your research paper (see Chapter 6). Not so fast, I'm afraid. Your research paper is a large and important part of your science project notebook. For that reason, as you assemble your project notebook, you may want to review your paper to see if you want to include new material or make some additional edits.

Because you probably wrote the paper right after you chose your topic, and now you're just about finished with the whole project, you can now look at your work with a fresh perspective.

For example, you may have seen a newspaper article or TV special that relates to your topic. Now's the time to add the information you obtained from those sources into your paper. Likewise, if you had a mentor or worked at a professional or university lab, you may have gained some new insight or discovered additional information that you want to include in your writing.

Unfortunately, adding new material has one big drawback — it gives you an opportunity to introduce more errors. To combat that, read and reread your paper to make sure that it's still organized, logical, and easy to read.

The following list explains a few other things to do before considering your paper done:

✔ Pay special attention to your introduction to see if it packs a punch, and to your summary to see that it gives a good — but brief — recap of your paper.

✔ Take one more chance to polish your prose — if the spirit moves you, that is. Check a thesaurus if you find that you've repeated the same word several times, especially in the same paragraph.

✔ Review your spelling and grammar one final time.

✔ Ask someone to take a last look through your paper before you declare, "That's a wrap!".

Getting Your Notebook Together

You can have lots of items in your science fair notebook. The following list runs down one possible sequence for those items; however, it's not the only one. Check with your teacher to see what's required for your particular project.

✔ **Required forms:** This includes your entry forms, abstract, and any certification forms that you need. See the section, "Filling Out the Required Forms" later in this chapter for more information.

✔ **Title page:** This page has the title of your project, your name, as well as your school, class, and teacher's name.

✔ **Table of Contents:** Although it goes right after the title page, you don't create it until you number your pages. The Table of Contents lists what's included in the notebook, for example, Hypothesis, Review of the Research, Variables and Controls, Materials, Procedures, Procedural Log, Results, and so on.

✔ **Research paper:** The final (finally!) version of your research paper.

✔ **Bibliography:** This is the same bibliography that you prepared for your research paper. Make sure to update it if you used any additional sources.

✔ **Question and hypothesis:** Make sure that you use your original hypothesis — don't change it to fit your results. Remember to double-check grammar and spelling.

✔ **Variables and controls, experimental and control groups:** Describe each variable and control, and each experimental and control group that you used in your project. You can describe them in table or narrative form (see Chapter 8).

✔ **Materials:** List everything that you used for your project, including items that you built. Update your list to include anything that you added while doing your project.

✔ **Procedures:** Make sure that you include everything that you did, even steps that you improvised during the course of your project. As with everything else, check your spelling and grammar.

✔ **Results:** Include all your charts, graphs, tables, photographs, and diagrams (see Chapter 10). Be sure that everything is neat and legible, as well as clearly and accurately labeled.

✔ **Conclusions:** Do a final edit and spell check on your conclusion summary (see Chapter 10). If you have graphs that illustrate your conclusions, include them, too.

✔ **Acknowledgments:** Pretend that you're accepting at the Academy Awards. "I'd like to thank my mother, my father, my aunts, uncles, and cousins, my teachers, and the salesman at the lumber yard." You get the idea! Acknowledgments are your way of thanking all the people who helped you.

Just like at the Academy Awards, though, brevity is the soul of wit (and the source of your audience's gratitude) — one paragraph is just about right for this element.

✔ **Project log:** This is the only place where neatness doesn't count. If your teacher requires you to include your log, just put it in your binder "as is" to show the detailed, day-to-day progress of your science project.

You also have to comply with the guidelines for whichever science fair you're entering. You can look at the Intel International Science and Engineering Fair (ISEF) Web site (`www.sciserv.org/isef/`), but because your science fair may be different, ask your teacher or check your science fair's Web site to get a complete list of rules.

Making a Good Impression

Appearances count, so use an attractive and appropriate cover for your notebook. Your teacher may have his or her own specific requirements for the size and type of folder. If your teacher doesn't give you any guidelines, I suggest using a three-hole folder or binder.

If you already know the colors you plan to use in your display, you may want to coordinate your notebook cover with your backboard (see Chapter 12).

Double-space all your written work, with the possible exception of tables, bibliography entries, or footnotes written in standard form, as shown in Chapter 6. Make sure that your margins are adequate (1 inch all around is a good standard to follow if you don't have any set requirements).

If your teacher allows handwritten notebooks, and you want to go that route, make sure that your handwriting is completely legible. If you have any doubts, print. Always use ink.

When you've reprinted and collected everything, review your notebook to make sure that it looks the way you want. Number the pages, and then create your Table of Contents.

Check to see that all the sections are in order, and that the pages in each section are in proper sequence. After all your hard work, you don't want to embarrass yourself by having your pages or your sections out of order.

Filling Out the Required Forms

To compete in almost any science fair (and probably in every fair that sends contestants to the ISEF) you have to have some required forms in your notebook, including both of the following:

- ✔ **An entry form.** Includes all the usual statistics, such as name, address, school, and grade. You also have to check off your project category and whether you have any certifications.

  Certifications are forms that verify you followed proper procedure when doing your project. They're usually required for projects that use *live vertebrates* (animals with a backbone or spinal cord) or hazardous chemicals.

- ✔ **An abstract.** Summarizes your project in 200 to 250 words. An abstract gives the project title, hypothesis, a summary of your procedures, and your results. The abstract and the display (see Chapter 12) give judges and other visitors a bird's-eye view of what your project is about.

  Sometimes, the abstract is a section of the entry form. Figure 11-1 shows an example of the entry form and abstract for the Greater San Diego Science and Engineering Fair.

If you wrote an awesome final paragraph for your research paper, you may already have most of your abstract.

Be sure to obtain the current year's forms for the fair that you plan on competing in. Forms change from year to year, as rules and regulations continue to change — completing an outdated form may disqualify you.

Assembling your notebook may seem tedious, especially after putting in so much time on your science project, but the work is worth it after you wow the judges!

GREATER SAN DIEGO SCIENCE AND ENGINEERING FAIR (GSDSEF)
PROJECT PROPOSAL, PROJECT DESCRIPTION AND PRE-SCREENING FORM – JUNIOR DIVISION (grades 7-8)
(GSDSEF-1, 2002 – JUNIOR)

THIS FORM MUST
- BE COMPLETED AND SIGNED PRIOR TO STARTING THE PROJECT
- BE IN THE STUDENT'S NOTEBOOK AT THE SCHOOL FAIR/SCREENING

1. STUDENT'S NAME (Last, First, Middle) _____

2. ADDRESS _____

3. CITY, ZIP _____

4. PHONE _____

5. HOW MANY PREVIOUS PROJECTS HAVE YOU HAD ACCEPTED BY THE GSDSEF? _____

6. SCHOOL _____

7. GRADE _____

8. PROPOSED PROJECT TITLE _____

9. PROPOSED CATEGORY _____

10. THIS PROJECT INVOLVES (<u>CHECK "YES" OR "NO" AFTER EACH</u>):

		YES	NO
A.	Live Vertebrate Animals	YES ___	NO ___
B.	Human/Other Vertebrate Tissue	YES ___	NO ___
C.	Bacteria/Fungi/Molds	YES ___	NO ___
D.	Chemicals	YES ___	NO ___
E.	Mutagenic Agents	YES ___	NO ___
F.	Carcinogenic Agents	YES ___	NO ___
G.	Teratogenic Agents	YES ___	NO ___
H.	Infectious Agents	YES ___	NO ___
I.	Potentially Hazardous Substances or Devices	YES ___	NO ___
J.	Human Subjects or Interviewees	YES ___	NO ___
K.	Venomous Animal	YES___	NO ___

11. THE FOLLOWING SUPPLEMENTAL FORMS HAVE BEEN COMPLETED AND ARE INCLUDED:

A. "Certification of Humane Treatment of Live Vertebrate Animals" (GSDSEF-2, 2002) -- REQUIRED for projects dealing with live vertebrate animals
YES ____ NO _____

B. "Certification of Compliance of Research Involving Humans" (GSDSEF-3, 2002) -- REQUIRED for projects involving human subjects or interviewees
YES ____ NO _____

C. "Certification of Hazards Control" (GSDSEF-4, 2002) -- REQUIRED for projects involving bacteria; protozoa, fungi or molds; chemicals; mutagenic, carcinogenic, teratogenic or infectious agents o other potentially hazardous substances or devices
YES ____ NO _____

D. "Certification of Vertebrate Tissue Source & Safety" (GSDSEF-5, 2002) -- REQUIRED for projects involving human or other vertebrate tissue (including teeth & hair roots), blood, blood parts and bodily fluids. (NOTE: if the use of hazardous organisms, substances and/or devices is part of the experimental procedures, GSDSEF Form 4 must also be completed and submitted.)
YES ____ NO _____

12. IS THIS A CONTINUATION OF A PREVIOUS PROJECT? (If "yes," attach a brief summary of your previous work) _____

13. <u>ON A SEPARATE SHEET OUTLINE THE PROPOSED EXPERIMENTAL PROCEDURE TO BE FOLLOWED</u>
(Major deviations from this plan must be approved BY THE TEACHER prior to making the changes.)

14. LOCATION WHERE EXPERIMENTAL PROCEDURES WILL TAKE PLACE _____

15. PROJECT TITLE _____

16. ABSTRACT (200-250 WORDS DESCRIBING PROBLEM, METHODS AND SIGNIFICANT FINDINGS) – <u>ADD WHEN PROJECT IS COMPLETED</u>

_____
_____
_____
_____
_____

Figure 11-1:
Your entry form and abstract gives information about you and your project.

Chapter 12

Displaying Your Project

*N*ow's the time to strut your stuff! Making an outstanding science fair project display allows your project to stand out among all the others. In a sense, when you produce your display, you create an ad for your project, inviting prospective clients (science fair judges) to look at what you have to offer. Although your prospective clients are very knowledgeable about your category, they have no idea what your particular project is about, so your display has to attract them and tell them just enough to make them want to find out more.

In this chapter, I talk about how to construct your display — what to include and what to avoid. I also give you some hints on where to get your supplies. Finally, I list some tips and tricks for making an informative and artistic display. (I promised it wasn't all about science!)

Showing Off: Organizing the Parts of Your Display

The goal of your display is to include lots of information without making it look crowded. To do that, you need to summarize the highlights of your project.

Of course, you definitely need to have the title, problem or question, hypothesis, procedures, results, and conclusions — pretty standard stuff, right? After that, it comes down to you and your creativity, so the sky's the limit! You can use all written material, or you may want to feature photos, drawings, tables, graphs, or other artwork to make your display more attractive.

All the information you choose must fit on your backboard. A *backboard* is a three-sectioned cardboard or foam board configuration that's acceptable for entry in all science fairs. (See the section, "Gathering Your Supplies" later in the chapter for more on backboards.)

Other possible topics to include on your backboard are:

- ✔ Materials
- ✔ Variables and controls
- ✔ Experimental and control groups

You may also want to put parts of your project in front of your backboard when you display your project at the science fair, as shown in Figure 12-1.

You're required to put your notebook (see Chapter 11) on the table in front of your project, so make sure to leave room for it. In addition, be sure to secure the notebook to the backboard — you don't want someone just walking off with all your hard work!

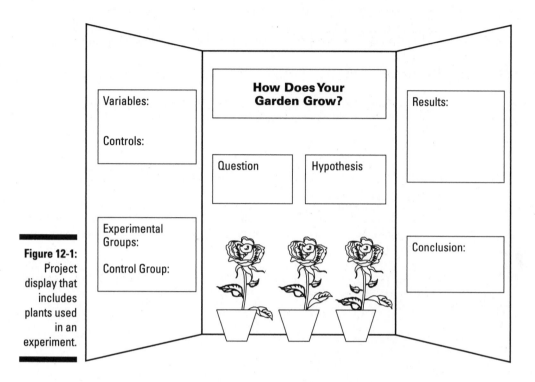

Variables:

Controls:

How Does Your Garden Grow?

Results:

Question

Hypothesis

Experimental Groups:

Control Group:

Conclusion:

Figure 12-1: Project display that includes plants used in an experiment.

Figure 12-1: Project display that includes plants used in an experiment.

Drawing a Blueprint: Laying Out Your Backboard

After you know what you want to put on your backboard, the challenge is fitting everything together in a way that's attractive and informative. Most of all, you want your display to encourage science fair judges to look at your notebook and talk to you about your project.

The key to having a great layout is planning it before you even look at paste, glue, or scissors. I recommend making several plans or blueprints for your backboard so you can choose the best way to layout your display.

When you plan your backboard, try to make it as balanced as possible. This means putting an equal amount of material on each panel and not leaving vast empty spaces (unless you want to put some of your project materials in front of the backboard).

To help you plan, Figure 12-2 shows a blank backboard. Make a few copies of the figure and use it to prepare the different blueprints for your backboard.

Here are some steps to follow when preparing your various blueprints:

1. **Draw a proportional pattern of your backboard.** For example, if the side panels are half the size of the center panel, make your drawing to that scale.

2. **Figure out what you want people to see first, and plan to make that the biggest and brightest spot on your display.** Very often, people want to read the hypothesis, and look at the attractive graphs or photos that best illustrate your project.

3. **Sketch out where the other items go.** You may want to sketch it lightly in pencil, because the object of this step is to experiment and move items around until you have the layout that looks best.

Figures 12-3 through 12-5 give you some examples of different display layouts. Check them out to get some ideas about how to plan yours.

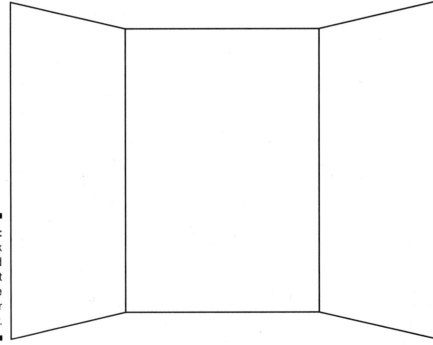

Figure 12-2:
A blank backboard layout that you can use to plan your display.

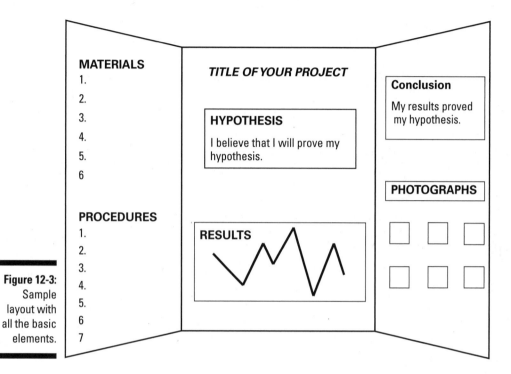

Figure 12-3:
Sample layout with all the basic elements.

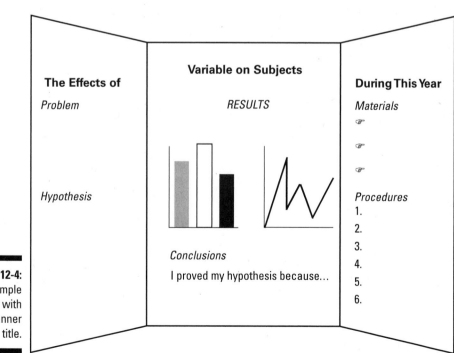

Figure 12-4:
Sample layout with a banner title.

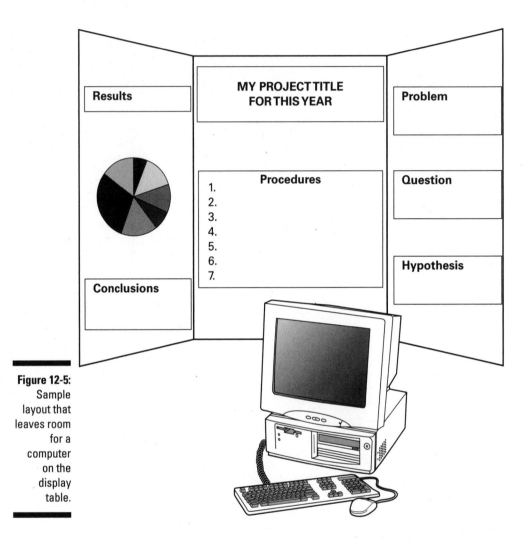

Figure 12-5:
Sample layout that leaves room for a computer on the display table.

If you have more material than you can fit on a three-panel display without crowding (the science project display cardinal sin), don't worry. You can find some creative solutions to your problem. For example, have a look at Figures 12-6 through 12-8 for some unique ways to fit more information on your science project backboard.

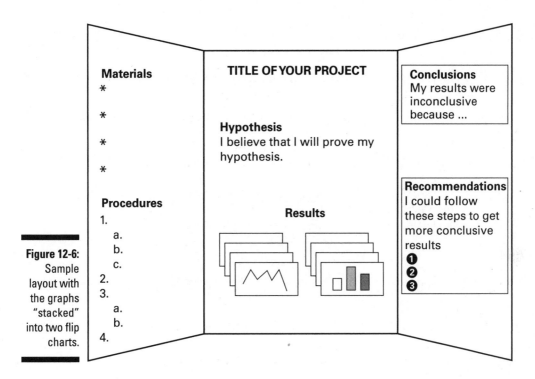

Figure 12-6:
Sample
layout with
the graphs
"stacked"
into two flip
charts.

Figure 12-7:
Sample
layout on a
five-panel
backboard.

Materials here

Results here

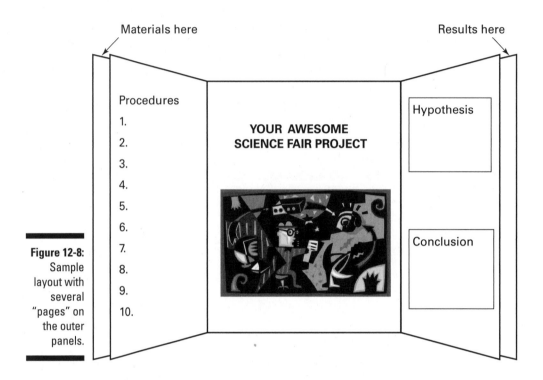

Procedures

1.

2.

YOUR AWESOME SCIENCE FAIR PROJECT

Hypothesis

3.

4.

5.

6.

Conclusion

7.

8.

9.

10.

Figure 12-8: Sample layout with several "pages" on the outer panels.

Spicing Up Your Display

When you decide on a layout, you can then choose the colors, fonts, and textures that you want to use on your backboard.

The object of the game is to create a clean, easy-to-read, professional display. After all, you want the judges to focus on your work and not be distracted by too many colors and illustrations.

Creating the display can be a really fun part of the project. Just remember how great it was to play with papers, crayons, scissors, and glue when you were small!

Showing your true colors

Using color effectively makes it easier for others to read your project from a distance.

One simple way to get the most from the colors you choose is to contrast light colors against dark ones. Another way to create a striking effect with color is to use opposite shades on the color wheel, for example, red with green, orange with blue, or yellow with violet. If you plan to put models, plants, and so on in front of your backboard, you can coordinate the color scheme of the backboard to match those items.

Another great way to choose colors is to pick something that suggests your topic, for example, green for botany or blue for oceanography. Before you get too excited, though, I suggest that you limit the number of colors you use. Keep in mind that you want to enhance, not overwhelm. Two or three colors (not counting black and white) work really well, and you can also vary your choices by using shades of the same color.

Metallic colors are very neat and attract lots of attention, but they have a downside. If the science fair area has a lot of sunlight, the metallic colors may reflect glare. However, using metallic colors is only a problem if you plan to take lots of photos of your project.

Having fun with fonts

If you've looked at your word processing software lately, you know that you have loads of fonts at your fingertips. No matter what look you want — from formal or whimsical to artistic or elaborate — you can get it. And almost every one of the available fonts comes in normal, bold, and italic, as well as in sizes from tiny to gargantuan.

All these choices make it really tempting to use a different font for each item on your backboard. But you need to try to resist that temptation.

Too many fonts cause the display to look busy and disjointed. If you use just two or three fonts that go well together, your display looks much more professional.

Some fonts look good only in the larger sizes, so make sure that the font that you love looks good in the size that you need.

Adding texture

Some students make their displays more interesting by adding texture. They put items like fabric, straw, wood, and foil on the backboard itself. For an example of using texture on a backboard, check out Chapter 18.

You can also use texture for your lettering. For example, in a project entitled "The Even-Handed Teacher" (which tested whether a right-handed teacher favors the left side of the classroom and vice-versa), the student spelled out her title with yellow pencils.

Gathering Your Supplies

Just like when you first started working on your experiment, computer program, or device, you now need to get the supplies required to create your display.

The backboard

The most important item that you need to get is your backboard, which is a stand-up display used for all science fair projects.

Buying it

You can generally find backboards in any store that sells school supplies.

They come in black and white (available everywhere) or colors, which you may have to special-order, either from your local store or via the Internet.

The good news is that when you buy your backboard, it's already the right size, and you don't need to build anything. The bad news is that it's disposable — you can't take your material off the backboard and use it for next year's project. But if that's all right with you (and lots of people think so), you may want to buy a backboard.

Building it

On the other hand, some students prefer to build their own backboards.

I suspect these children's parents had to build their own (before the pre-fab models were available). Then again, kids who are just natural builders (you know the type) likely see this task as another opportunity to have fun! One other reason for building your own is if you need a larger or more elaborate backboard than you can find at the store.

Most home-built backboards are made of foam core, wood, plastic, or fiberboard. And the items you need for the backboard (wood, screws, nails, hinges, and glue) are available in just about any home improvement store. If you decide to build your own, make sure that your backboard is light enough to carry and small enough to fit in your folks' car. Also, when you put it together, make sure that your backboard doesn't fall over.

Like store-bought backboards, home-built backboards have advantages and disadvantages. The good news is that your home-built backboard is recyclable. You can strip all your material off it and you (or your siblings or friends) can use it the following year. The bad news is that building a backboard probably is more expensive (in time and money) than a pre-fab model.

Most science fairs have restrictions on the backboard's size. If you plan to build your own, get the rules as early as possible. Also, be sure to check on what your teacher's requirements are before you start planning your backboard. You don't want to put in a lot of work only to find that you have to cut it down at the last minute.

Printed material

Of course, a lot of written material goes on your backboard. But first, I want to talk about your headings, your project's title, and subtitles, such as question, hypothesis, and so on.

The most important thing is to make sure that the lettering on your titles is large enough to stand out. Design the titles on the center panel larger than the titles on the side panels, but remember to design all the titles large enough to read without putting your nose to the backboard.

You can create your lettering in a number of different ways, including:

- ✔ Computer printout
- ✔ Hand lettering
- ✔ Stenciling or press-on letters
- ✔ Labeling machine
- ✔ Store-bought title kits that include all the required and a lot of optional titles (You can find the kits where pre-fab backboards are sold.)
- ✔ Typewritten lettering

When it comes to the rest of your written material, you need to edit and summarize *before* you put it on your backboard. For example, if your procedures are long and involved, abbreviate them as shown in Table 12-1. (The left-hand column shows the long versions; the right-hand column shows the edited versions.)

Table 12-1	Summary of Procedures for Your Backboard
Too Long	**Edited Version**
1. Punch 8 holes into each disposable foam cup.	1. Punch 8 holes into each disposable foam cup.
2. Mix equal amounts dirt and potting soil.	2. Into each cup, put 3.5 cups of soil mixture, containing equal amounts of dirt and potting soil.
3. Put 3.5 cups dirt/potting soil mixture into each cup.	3. Put a melon seed in each cup, and cover seed with .5-cup dirt/soil mix.
4. Put a melon seed in each cup.	
5. Cover seed with .5-cup dirt/soil mix.	

Too much written material makes your display too cluttered and leaves too little "real estate" for other important items. *Remember:* Make sure that all spelling and mathematical formulas are correct.

Your project notebook is on the table, right in front of your display, so if the judges want more information before they interview you, they can look it up. Therefore, you don't need to include everything on the backboard.

Illustrations

Most students include graphs, charts, and tables on their backboards.

Fortunately, you've already created them when you looked at your results and drew your conclusions (see Chapter 10). You may need larger versions to use on your backboard, however. If your printer can't accommodate larger paper, head down to your local copy shop to get some really sharp color copies.

Use graphs that summarize and combine your results. Utilize graphs that have averages or totals rather than separate measurements. Include your sample size or number of trials on the graph.

If you didn't use a computer to generate your graphs, you can still create great-looking graphs for your display. Here's how:

1. **Design a grid to create a background for your graph.** This looks a lot like store-bought graph paper, but most likely is a much larger scale.

2. **Draw the graph's lines or bars with markers, tape, string, or ribbon over the grid.**

Regardless of how you produce your graph, title it, and label your axis, keys, and legends.

Photographs are also a good addition to any display. Use either the photos that you took during your project or public domain photos that you can download from the Internet. Artwork can also enhance your display. If you're artistic, add your own drawings or paintings. If not, you can use illustrations from magazines or clip art from your software or the Internet. Just make sure that you credit the author (even if it's you!).

Everything else

Regardless of whether you buy or build your backboard, and how or where you get your lettering, you still must make a shopping list of everything else you need. The possibilities are almost endless: colored paper, glue, precision knives, scissors, rulers, hook tape, pens, pencils, or tape.

You can find almost anything you need in an office supply or art store. If you require anything unusual or exotic, you can probably find it on the Internet. However, you may need your parents' help (and credit card) to actually order merchandise online.

Before you go on a shopping trip, look around the house to see if you can scrounge any of your supplies. You may find several items just waiting to be used in your project!

Working on the Assembly Line: Putting Your Display Together

When you have all your materials, you're ready to create the final product.

Lay your backboard on a flat surface, and place all your material on it. Use a ruler to make sure that everything is level and evenly placed. When you're satisfied that everything is just as you want it, very lightly (preferably with a pencil) mark the position.

Okay, now take a deep breath and glue your lettering, graphs, and pictures onto the backboard. If you're attaching paper to a backboard made of cardboard or foam board, rubber cement is a good adhesive, because it's fairly easy to remove in case you make a mistake. (For safety's sake, follow all the manufacturer's directions.) If your backboard is made of fabric, plastic, or other materials, you can find a huge variety of adhesives in any home improvement store. You can also use staples, nails, pushpins, hook tape, or other fasteners to attach material.

Always have extra materials on hand. Running out of supplies at midnight when the project is due the next morning is the worst time to find out that you misspelled a word in your conclusion and don't have any more electric blue paper to print a new copy. Remember to save your receipts — you can always return the extras if you don't use them.

When you're finished, stand your backboard up, take a look at it, and give yourself a big hand — you deserve it!

Part V

The Finals: Knowing What to Expect at the Fair

In this part . . .

Whether your project is shown at a school gym or a major city's convention center, you need to know what happens when you display your project at a science fair. In this part, I give you some tips on getting your project from home to the science fair in one piece. I also give some hints on setting it up when you get there.

To get you through judging day with flying colors, I explain the process, tell you what the judges are looking for, and give you some tips on impressing those judges. When that's done, the fun begins — awards, prizes, and time to enjoy the fair with your friends.

Chapter 13

Entering the Construction Zone: Setting Up Your Project

. . . .

In This Chapter

▶ Preparing to transport and set up your project

▶ Complying with fair rules

▶ Getting the lay of the land

. . . .

*W*hen you go to a science fair, your first order of business is to get your project to the right place, and then set it up. Sounds simple enough, right? Well, the process may be a bit trickier than you expect.

This chapter gives you some tips about finding out where your project belongs, making sure that it follows the rules of the fair, setting it up, and if necessary, plugging it in.

Although all science fairs are similar in many ways, because of size and location, they do have their differences. In small school fairs, setup, judging, public access, and awards may all happen in one day, whereas in larger local fairs, state science fairs, and the Intel International Science and Engineering Fair (ISEF), the science fair may go on for a week, with activities spread out accordingly.

In this chapter, I try to cover all the variations, but I still recommend checking with your particular science fair for the most accurate information.

Transporting Your Project and Preparing for Setup

Before you load your project into the car to head off to the fair, be sure that everything is glued securely to your backboard.

If certain items are only lightly attached to the backboard, remove them and reattach the items when you get there. After all the time that you spent creating your display (see Chapter 12), you don't want to leave a trail of graphs and titles in the driveway. Your neighbors may appreciate the reading material, but you won't appreciate the blank spaces on your backboard.

On setup day, preparation is key! If you think you need to crawl under the table to get your project ready, wear old clothes. Of course, if your science fair has setup and judging on the same day, you may want to bring a change of clothes with you. Also, bring an "emergency first aid" kit to repair any problems with your display.

Some supplies to include in your kit (depending on what's on your display) are:

- ✔ Paste, glue, or tape
- ✔ Extra light bulbs
- ✔ Scissors, pencils, pens, touch-up paint, or markers
- ✔ Extension cord

You may want to exhibit some materials on judging day only. For example, I've seen computers, huge generators, and other devices on setup and judging day, only to be removed as soon as the judging is done. Check with your science fair management committee to see what's allowed.

If you plan to display valuable equipment, find out whether your gear is secure while on display. At some local and state fairs, display halls are locked and guarded at night to ensure that nothing is stolen. However, science fairs are free and open to the public, except for judging day.

Passing the Checkpoint: Following the Rules

In this section, I cover rules that are fairly universal. Although most local science fairs base their rules on ISEF guidelines, your local fair may have a different process, so check with your fair's management to be sure.

Many local science fairs have their own Web sites, and ISEF also has a comprehensive site (www.sciserv.org/isef/) that you can consult for help.

Most science fairs have rules that limit the size of projects, as well as how you can display projects. In addition, the rules state that you're only allowed to exhibit one project at a time. But in my personal opinion, if you have the strength and fortitude to do two projects, you should be allowed to show them both!

If your project is a continuation of a previous project, bring the prior year's notebook for the judges. If even a remote possibility exists that you want to do another project on your current topic, save your notebook. No need to start from scratch again, right?

Getting your forms in order

In Chapter 11, I discuss the various forms and certifications that you need if your project involves *live vertebrates* (animals with a backbone or spinal cord), human subjects, hazardous materials, or tissue. If your project requires such forms, make sure that you have them on hand at all times during the fair. If you don't, you risk being disqualified.

Putting safety first

At many science fairs, someone examines your project to make sure that your display is exhibit-safe.

You can't use anything that may be hazardous to the public in project displays, including highly flammable materials or decorations. You probably can't put electric lights on your backboard.

Other items that you can't display at the science fair include:

- ✔ Living organisms
- ✔ Bacteria or fungi
- ✔ Animal or human parts, except for teeth, hair, nails, and dried animal bones
- ✔ Liquids, including water
- ✔ Chemicals or their empty chemical containers, including caustics, acids, and household cleaners
- ✔ Open or concealed flames
- ✔ Syringes, pipettes, and similar devices
- ✔ Batteries with open-top cells
- ✔ Aerosol cans of household solvents
- ✔ Controlled substances, poisons, or drugs
- ✔ Sharp items, such as knives or needles
- ✔ Dry ice

Plugging into electricity rules

If you think that your display has to follow lots of general rules, just wait until you look at the electrical safety rules.

If you plan to put a plug into an outlet, make sure that your display meets these basic standards (but if you're planning to display some sophisticated equipment, be sure to check all the rules for your science fair):

- ✔ Wiring must be properly insulated and fastened.
- ✔ Wiring, switches, and the metal parts of high-voltage circuits must be located out of reach of observers and must include an adequate overload safety device.
- ✔ High-voltage equipment must be shielded with a grounded metal box or cage to prevent accidental contact.

Don't even think about trying to sneak anything in — you'll get caught!

Finding a Spot for Your Project

Most science fairs are set up pretty much the same way — the only difference is the size of the layout. You can find long tables where projects are grouped by category (see Chapter 3 for an explanation of the various categories).

Within each category, the displays are usually lined up in alphabetical order of the students' last names. See Figure 13-1 for a sample table layout of projects at a science fair.

You probably won't know where to put your project until you get to the hall. After your project and display are approved, the science fair directors may tell you where to go (in a good way, of course).

Figure 13-1:
At the science fair, long tables hold numbered science projects back to back.

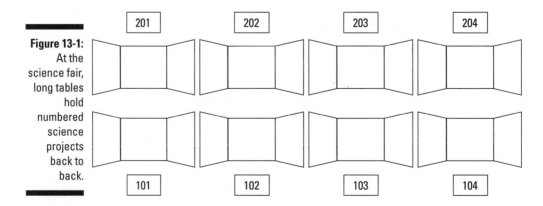

Chapter 14

Bringing On the Judges

· ·

In This Chapter

▶ Meeting the judges

▶ Surveying the criteria for judging

▶ Making a good impression

· ·

*Y*ou've probably heard from lots of people (including me) that doing a science project is good for you — you can learn a lot, build self-discipline, develop your creativity, blah, blah, blah.

However, now that you're in the game, either because you volunteered or because you've been dragged kicking and screaming, you may want to know how the judges evaluate your project. In this chapter, I let you in on everything you ever wanted to know about science fair judging, but were afraid to ask.

Who the Judges Are

First of all, who are the judges? Well, they're professionals in your community — chemists, biologists, physicians, psychologists, and engineers in various specialties who judge projects in their particular fields. Also on hand may be representatives sent by corporations and other organizations who judge projects and present special awards. These corporations and other organizations (such as hospitals, engineering firms, and software or biotech companies) are heavily involved in science.

Mostly, the judges are "just folks" who happen to be scientists. A science fair judge is interested in and committed to science education and sees you as the future of his or her field. Judges aren't interested in being critical or "dissing" your project; they're interested in encouraging and mentoring young scientists. They want to talk to you and find out what you did and how you did it. They're people you want to know if you're planning to go on in science.

What Judges Look For

To take some of the stress out of the judging process, it may help to understand what judges look for. Although local and state science fairs may be somewhat different, I can discuss the general process based on the Intel International Science and Engineering Fair (ISEF). See Chapter 4 for more on ISEF procedures.

ISEF guidelines are specific about what the judges evaluate. A representative of Science Service (the folks who run the ISEF) said, "It's no secret. We want the students to know what we're looking for so that they're better prepared."

For the science fair awards (as opposed to special corporate or association awards) the judges compare all the projects in a single category. Sometimes, if a category has many entries, they may divide it into subcategories (see Chapter 3 for information about project categories and subcategories). Judges evaluate each project, keeping in mind that students, not professional scientists or engineers, performed the work. Then, the judges rate or rank each project against other similar projects. It's somewhat like grading on a curve — no one really likes it, but it's a fact of life.

The most important thing judges look for is that your project is scientifically valid — meaning that your procedures were designed and executed in accordance with the scientific method. They also want to know that you know your project. This way, they realize that although you may have had help or worked with mentors, your project is your own work. The judges also consider whether the project is relevant — a real solution to a real problem. Outrageous inventions and gadgets aren't considered practical devices.

To make the judging process as fair as possible, judges rate projects in five areas:

- ✔ Creativity
- ✔ Scientific method
- ✔ Thoroughness
- ✔ Skill
- ✔ Clarity

Judges may have questions about your project after looking at your display. To find out what they want to know, they'll examine your notebook and then possibly ask you a few questions.

Creative ability

A unique approach to an original problem that's appropriate to your grade level can impress the judges. They aren't necessarily dazzled because you used expensive equipment, but they can be impressed by inventive use of ordinary equipment and materials.

Judges probably ask how you got your idea and whether you had any help. As long as the project is basically your own work, they don't penalize you for getting help. After all, in the "real world" professional scientists, engineers, and researchers collaborate all the time.

When evaluating creativity, the judge looks at:

✔ Originality of your question and hypothesis

✔ Approach to the problem

✔ Analysis and interpretation of the data

✔ Use of existing equipment

✔ Construction or design of new equipment

Collections and bizarre inventions aren't considered creative, just strange. Judges may find them interesting, but these types of projects don't compare favorably with others done according to the scientific method (as described in Chapter 8).

Scientific thought or engineering goals

Because experiments are so different from engineering projects, they're both evaluated using different criteria.

Experiments

For an experiment, the judges look at how you applied the scientific method to solve a problem. They check out how well you designed and followed your procedures. They also look at whether your sample size was adequate and whether you kept good records. Then, they examine how you analyzed results and whether your conclusions logically reflected your data. When they look at your work, they may ask these questions:

✔ Have you clearly stated the problem?

✔ Was the project "doable" considering your age and grade, as well as the time and resources available?

✔ Were your procedures well planned and defined?

✔ Have you recognized, defined, and correctly used the project variables and controls?

✔ Was your sample large enough?

✔ Did you do enough trials?

✔ Do your results support your conclusions?

✔ How does your project relate to other research in the field (if at all)?

✔ Is there any more work needed in the field? If so, do you plan to do it?

✔ Did you use both popular and scientific literature in your work?

Engineering and computer projects

If you did an engineering or computer programming project, the judges look at whether you identified a real need and devised a workable, achievable solution to the problem. They also check to see if you provide evidence showing that you tested your device or program to make sure that it's functional. Finally, they may want to know if you documented your project so that users can understand how it works. They may want answers to these questions:

✔ Did you have a clear objective?

✔ Did your objective satisfy potential users' needs?

✔ Did you develop a practical solution to a real problem?

✔ Did your project represent an improvement over what was previously available?

✔ Was your solution economically feasible and ecologically responsible?

✔ Did you test the solution under actual conditions?

Thoroughness

To gauge your thoroughness, the judges look at the amount of research you did, the consistency of your testing, and how faithfully you kept your records. They also check your sample size and the number of tests you conducted if that's relevant to your project. Inquiring judges want to know the following:

✔ Were you persistent in doing the project?

In other words, did you keep going (or develop an alternate plan) if your procedures weren't working?

✔ Did you spend enough time on the project to get sufficient results?

✔ Are you acquainted with other approaches to the problem?

✔ Are you acquainted with scientific literature on your topic?

✔ Did you look at various aspects of the problem?

✔ How many trials did you do before analyzing your results and drawing your conclusions?

✔ Did you keep good records?

Skill

The judges may look at how well you executed the project, in light of your available resources. For example, if you conducted your experiment in your bedroom, they don't compare you unfavorably with someone who did his experiment at a university lab.

The judges evaluate your laboratory, computational, design, and observational skills. They also consider whether you needed to design and build your own equipment. The judges want to know:

✔ Did you have the skills to get the data that you needed?

✔ Where did you do your project?

✔ Did you have help from professional scientists or engineers?

✔ Did you have adult supervision?

✔ Where did you get your equipment (or did you build it)?

Clarity

Clarity is almost a no-brainer — you need to clearly present the purpose, procedures, and conclusions of your project. Your display and notebook answer these questions for the judges:

✔ Does your research paper show that you understand the research?

✔ Is your notebook organized and orderly?

✔ Are your results presented in a meaningful way?

✔ Did you summarize your conclusions?

✔ Does your project display explain the project?

The waiting game

In larger science fairs, the judging session may take several hours. Students ask, "How can I keep occupied while waiting for the judges to come around to my project?"

Unfortunately, many students try to keep busy without thinking about the impression they're making. Having a card game on the floor isn't a good way to stay busy — you don't want to get up, grab the cards, and hurry out of the way when a judge approaches your project. Instead, you can stand near your project and read a book.

Talking to other students is also a good way to stay occupied. You can make new friends and also check out the competition! However, stay close to your project — if you have a botany project and your best friend did one in zoology (displayed in another area), don't meet to compare notes until the judging is finished.

If you need to take a break, the best time is just after the judges have visited your display. And when the boredom gets overwhelming, just remember that it's just a few hours out of one day!

Judging is a *comparative* process. That means even though your project may have won first place at the school science fair, it may take only second or third place at the state science fair. If that happens, try to figure out what the first-place winners did to get there. Maybe they did more thorough research, kept better records, or (rarely) made a more impressive presentation. Or perhaps, they just had more experience.

Knowing How to Impress the Judges

Even with some background about what science fair judging involves, you're probably still nervous. You know that your project is good and that your display is attractive. You even know what the judges are looking for. But, while you're setting up, you may see other projects that you perceive to be better than yours. Don't panic — stage fright is normal, but some simple preparation techniques may make "opening night" a little less stressful.

Ooze confidence from every pore

Probably the most important thing that you can do to get ready for judging day is to be physically and emotionally prepared. After all, if you feel good about your project and your display and know your subject matter, you'll do just fine.

But here are a few specific tips to remember:

- ✔ Be sure to get enough sleep the night before.
- ✔ Eat a good breakfast.
- ✔ Dress neatly and conservatively.
- ✔ Don't eat, chew gum, clutch a soft drink, or slouch when the judges are walking through the exhibit area. In fact, food and drink may be prohibited in some exhibit halls.

Prepare a killer notebook and display

As I explain in Chapter 12, the first thing that judges see is your display. If it attracts a judge's attention from 3 feet away, then the display has done its first job. Then, he or she should be able to quickly read some of the key information on the backboard, such as the hypothesis, procedures, results, and conclusions.

It's not necessarily flash and dash, but most judges appreciate a display that makes the most of their time!

When a judge opens your notebook, he or she looks at the basic elements, including the abstract; research paper (with bibliography); hypothesis; procedures; results (with tables, figures, and graphs); and conclusions.

He or she doesn't have enough time to read every word in your notebook, but may find out enough to know what to ask during your interview.

Ace the interview

Although lots of students dread this part, the interview is your chance to shine! Judges walk through the exhibit hall looking at displays and notebooks, and stop to interview students along the way. A lot depends on the individual judge; some talk to every student, while others interview only a few. In any event, the good news is that most interviews last only several minutes.

When the judge asks a question, don't wave your arm and say "it's all here on the backboard." The judge already knows that and now wants to hear you talk about your project. That's how he or she knows that you truly understand your work. However, you can use your backboard as a prop. Take advantage of it to point out statistics, graphs, photos, and other highlights of your project.

If English is a second language for you, speak slowly to make sure that the judge understands what you say. In fact, that's good advice for everyone — even if English is your native language. Slow down, take your time, and make sure the judge understands what you have to say.

The best preparation that you can make for an interview is to know what's in your notebook, including any formulas, terms, and acronyms that you used. The judges may very well ask you to define some scientific jargon that you have in your notebook. "Well, my teacher said . . ." just isn't a valid definition.

Don't try to memorize what's in your notebook for the following reasons.

- ✔ You don't know exactly what the judges may ask, and over-rehearsing may make you tongue-tied when trying to field an unexpected question.

- ✔ A rehearsed speech sounds exactly like a rehearsed speech, which doesn't give the judges confidence that you truly know your material.

- ✔ Although science fair judges aren't trying to trap or stump you, they do appreciate spontaneous answers that demonstrate that you understand scientific principles.

Sample questions the judges may ask

Another helpful hint that may ease pre-interview jitters is knowing some of the judges' most frequently asked questions. Just ask your folks how they'd prepare for a job interview — I bet that knowing the possible questions would make them feel much more confident and relaxed.

For example, see how you answer the following questions, which are in the guidelines for judges at the Greater San Diego Science and Engineering Fair:

- ✔ How did you get this idea?

- ✔ Is this project a continuation of an earlier year's project? If so, what did you add?

- ✔ What application does this project have to real life?

- ✔ Where was your project done?

- ✔ How is your project different from others that you researched?

- ✔ What was the most interesting background reading you did?

- ✔ How does this experiment conform to the scientific method?

- ✔ Which are your controls? Your variables? What is/are the difference(s) between your control and experimental groups(s)?

- ✔ Where did you get your animals (bacteria, plants, and so on)?

✔ Did you acquire any new skills while doing your project?

✔ What help did you receive from others (students, adults, teachers, family, and so on)?

✔ How did you determine your sample size?

✔ If you used any statistical tests, how did you choose them?

✔ Can you explain this graph to me?

✔ Can you explain your procedure to me?

✔ What does this (some project detail) mean?

✔ What do your results mean?

✔ How many times did you repeat this experiment (or test your device or program)?

✔ Did you need to change your original procedures? If so, why?

✔ Did you have any experimental errors in your project? If so, how did you correct for them?

✔ What is the most important thing you found out by doing this project?

✔ What changes can you make if you continue this project next year?

 If you don't know an answer, don't try to fake it — trust me, the judges know. Don't be afraid to admit that you're clueless; they don't expect you to know everything. You can make a better impression with your honesty.

The spirit of exploration

Besides knowledge, good use of the scientific method, and accurate record keeping, a quality that impresses scientists and engineers is a willingness to take risks and go "where no (wo)man has gone before." You can have the neatest notebook and the most beautiful display, but if you choose a project

Relax — they're on your side

I spent some time observing the judging process in 2002. Most judges were relaxed, and even casual. They were genuinely interested in talking to students and looking at their work. Practically all of them became judges because they wanted to make the science fair a positive experience for the students. So don't be intimidated when a judge approaches you. Instead try to be relaxed and upbeat, because that makes them relaxed and upbeat with you. Take advantage of the interview to discuss your work with professionals in your field (and have fun while you're doing it). Every judge that I spoke to wants you, the student, to succeed.

that you can do with a minimum amount of work, you probably won't get a high score. However, if you have a lively curiosity, a passion for finding out the truth, and the perseverance to follow good scientific procedures, the judges may like your project, even if the experiment hasn't worked out well.

Because enthusiasm is contagious, let your excitement show. The judges know that you enjoyed doing a project and being in a science fair. When your interview is over, smile, shake hands, and thank the judge. When he or she has moved on to the next backboard, you can breathe a sigh of relief. Now it's only a few more hours until you find out if you've won an award and the chance to advance to the next level.

You'll probably see the judge go off and find somewhere to make notes. Don't read too much into it — at many science fairs, judges have to fill out a form that covers the big five (creativity, scientific thought or engineering ability, thoroughness, skill, and clarity) on every project they look at.

To enjoy the science fair, realize that judges are evaluating your project, not you. Notice that they're not looking at your hair, your makeup, or your braces. They're looking at your project and how you present it in written, oral, and graphic form.

Chapter 15

Going for the Gold: Science Fair Awards

In This Chapter

▶ Getting local, regional, and professional awards

▶ Receiving ISEF awards

▶ Winning scholarships, trips, and other goodies

"It's not whether you win or lose; it's how you play the game." Yeah, right! Admit it, most everyone wants to win and not lose. But a science fair has no losers — only people who don't get awards. Actually, making and keeping the commitment to do a science project makes you an instant winner, no matter what the judges decide.

Fortunately, science fairs have quite a few prizes to go around, though! Each science fair presents first-, second-, third-, and fourth-place awards in each category. Many also give sweepstakes awards for the best projects in the fair. In addition, you can win professional society awards, given by corporations, research institutes, hospitals, scientific facilities, and military branches to projects that relate to their specific areas of interest.

A science fair awards ceremony is a completely unique experience. Where else can you see people cheering, doing the "wave," and holding school banners for academic achievement? Students, family, friends, and faculty are more enthusiastic than if they were at a homecoming game!

Winning Local and Regional Awards

In every science fair, judges can award first-, second-, third-, and fourth-place prizes in each category. The multiple awards are at the judges' discretion so that there can be many winners. Very rarely, the judges may decide not to present any awards in a given category (especially if the category has no projects).

Local science fairs can give additional awards. For example, at the Greater San Diego Science and Engineering Fair (GSDSEF), sweepstakes awards — including cash prizes ranging from $200 to 2,000 — are given to the top projects in the junior (seventh and eighth grades) and senior (ninth through twelfth grades) divisions. GSDSEF also awards some awesome trips — Intel sponsors a trip to ISEF for senior division sweepstakes winners, and the Taiwanese-American Association awards a trip to Taiwan for one winner.

Receiving Professional Awards

Corporations, professional associations and societies, universities, museums, government agencies, military branches, fraternal, environmental, and conservation organizations give professional awards. These organizations send judges to local and state science fairs, as well as the Intel International Science and Engineering Fair (ISEF), who evaluate projects in their specialties (see Chapter 14 for the lowdown on the judging process).

Often students may receive a plaque, a certificate, and an opportunity to be recognized at a future meeting. Sometimes, you may also get a trip or a cash award, which can range from a gift certificate up to the thousands of dollars. Here's just a sample of the kinds of organizations that offer professional awards:

- AARP Andrus Foundation
- Acoustical Society of America
- American Society of Mechanical Engineers
- Armed Forces Communications and Electronics Association
- Association for Women in Science
- Bureau of Reclamation/U.S. Department of the Interior
- Hewlett-Packard Company

✔ Lions Club

✔ Optical Society of America

✔ Rensselaer Polytechnic Institute

✔ San Diego Aerospace Museum

✔ Scripps Institute of Oceanography

✔ Sea World

✔ Society of Toxicology

✔ U.S. Air Force

✔ U.S. Forest Service

Getting ISEF Awards

At some of the larger science fairs, the biggest awards you can win are tickets to ISEF.

If you make it to ISEF, you notice that some of the projects are very advanced and professional. Many of these students have been working on the same topic for up to six years, and have had the advantage of working in fully equipped laboratories with professional mentors.

The grand-prize awards given for each category at the ISEF have generous cash prizes, totaling approximately $2 million. First place gets a whopping $3,000; second-place winners receive $1,500; third-place award winners collect $1,000; and fourth-place projects earn $500.

I can list only a few of the many awards at ISEF, but you can have a look at its Web site (`www.sciserv.org/isef`) to see everything that's available.

Making It Pay: Scholarships, Trips, Money, and Other Goodies

Because science and technology are so important, the awards and rewards for promising young scientists can be considerable. Besides cash, you can receive extremely valuable, enjoyable, fun, and educational prizes.

Higher education

One of the biggest sources of awards (and one that students and their parents most appreciate) is college scholarships. This list is just a partial number of scholarships available for 2002 ISEF winners:

- ✔ Asbury College (Wilmore, Kentucky) awards the Presidential Science Scholarship of $5,000 per year for four years.

- ✔ California State University at Fresno gives two four-year scholarships of $5,000 per year.

- ✔ Cornell University (Ithaca, New York) grants three four-year research awards of $5,000 per year, toward a bachelor's of science degree in specific engineering disciplines. Recipients will participate in research throughout their four years of undergraduate education.

- ✔ Drexel University (Philadelphia, Pennsylvania) awards eight scholarships for projects in behavioral and social sciences, chemistry, computer science, engineering, environmental science, mathematics, medicine and health, and physics.

- ✔ Florida Institute of Technology awards ten tuition scholarships of $10,000 per year for four years.

- ✔ Georgetown College (Georgetown, Kentucky) offers three scholarships of $5,000 per year for four years.

- ✔ Indiana University offers 12 partial tuition scholarships of $5,000 per year for projects in behavioral and social sciences, biochemistry, botany, chemistry, computer sciences, earth and space sciences, environmental sciences, mathematics, medicine and health, microbiology, physics, and zoology.

- ✔ Lehigh University (Bethlehem, Pennsylvania) gives eight scholarships of $10,000 per year to science fair participants who excel academically and have demonstrated leadership skills. Winners also take part in special trips, social events, and educational opportunities.

- ✔ Murray State University (Murray, Kentucky) awards one four-year scholarship, including housing and fees, for study leading to a bachelor's of science degree in engineering, physics, or electrical and telecommunications engineering.

- ✔ New Mexico Institute of Mining and Technology gives two four-year scholarships that cover full tuition, fees, and room and board each year.

- ✔ Northeastern University (Boston, Massachusetts) awards two five-year scholarships worth $5,000 per year.

- ✔ Polytechnic University (Brooklyn, New York) awards six partial scholarships for students with projects in chemistry, computer science, engineering, environmental science, mathematics and physics.

- The University of Kentucky College of Engineering and the Kentucky Community and Technical College System offer a joint $20,000 scholarship to a student who begins undergraduate studies at a KCTCS community college and completes a bachelor's degree in the UK College of Engineering.

- The University of Louisville has committed 28 full-tuition scholarships to finalists in behavioral and social sciences, biochemistry, botany, chemistry, computer science, earth and space science, engineering, environmental science, gerontology, mathematics, medicine and health, microbiology, physics, and zoology.

- University of the Sciences in Philadelphia awards two scholarships of $8,000 per year for four years.

- University of Southern California awards two scholarships of $5,000 per year for students pursuing undergraduate degrees in engineering or computer science.

For most of these scholarships, recipients must meet the admissions and scholarship requirements of the college to receive and maintain the award. They must also maintain a specified grade point average after they get there.

Travel

Quite a few of the top awards come with a trip, among other perks. Here are just a few examples:

- Intel Foundation Young Scientist scholarships are awarded to the top three finalists of the Intel ISEF. Each receives a $50,000 scholarship, a high-performance computer, and a visit to the Nobel Prize Award Ceremony in Stockholm, Sweden.

- The European Union Contest for Young Scientists Award is given to the Best of Category team project winners. Students earned a trip to Vienna, Austria, to represent the United States in the 14th Annual European Union Contest for Young Scientists.

- The AARP Andrus Foundation gives two students all-expenses-paid trips to present their projects at the 2002 annual meeting of the Gerontological Society of America, in Boston, Massachusetts.

- The American Committee for the Weizmann Institute of Science awards a five-week, all-expenses paid trip and a scholarship to the Bessie Lawrence International Summer Science Institute at the Weizmann Institute of Science in Rehovot, Israel.

- Axonn, L.L.C. in New Orleans, Louisiana, offers a fully paid internship (including airfare and lodging) that provides a hands-on opportunity to explore electronics in a professional engineering environment.

✔ MILSET International Expo-Sciences awards a trip to the Expo Science Europe 2002 in Bratislava, Slovakia.

✔ NASA awards 16 all expenses-paid trips to attend the U.S. Space Camp in Huntsville, Alabama.

✔ The National Taiwan Science Education Center awards two trips to attend the 2002 Taiwan International Science Fair. This prize includes a round-trip ticket, accommodations, activities, and a $300 allowance for food.

✔ The U.S. Army awards two all-expenses-paid trips to Operation Cherry Blossom in Tokyo, Japan, and one all-expenses-paid trip to the London International Youth Science Forum. Each trip winner also receives $3,000 in savings bonds, $300 from the Association of the United States Army, a gold medallion, and a Certificate of Achievement.

Money and more

Many of the awards involve recognition, prizes, and money. The following list explains some really cool prizes that you can win at ISEF. A lot of the cash awards also come with grants for the winners' school science departments.

As you can see, some of these awards are for scientific achievement, but others are for things like the project display or the use of photography.

✔ Showboard, Inc. gives a first-place award of $1,000, a second-place award of $100, and a third-place award of $50 for the best use of scientific method on a project display board.

✔ For the best projects in computer science with an artificial intelligence component, the American Association for Artificial Intelligence awards 15 prizes of $1,000.

✔ The IEEE Foundation awards a college scholarship of $10,000 for outstanding achievement in research and presentation of engineering knowledge in electrical engineering, information technology, or other IEEE fields of interest.

✔ For the best use of photography to gather data, solve a problem, or clearly explain the essence of a science project, Eastman Kodak Company presents five first-place awards of $1,000, five second-place awards of $500, and five honorable mentions worth $250.

✔ For the project that best demonstrates the use of materials-related concepts, the ASM (American Society for Metals) International Foundation awards a $5,000 scholarship and a trip to Materials Camp held in the summer. Two awards of $500 and two more of $250, plus a scholarship to Materials Camp, are also awarded.

- Intel Best Use of Personal Computer is presented to five projects that demonstrate creative use of a personal computer. Winners receive mobile computers.

- Conservation International awards prizes for projects that best advance the science of *biodiversity* (the number of species living in a specific region) conservation. The first-place award is $1,000, the second-place award is $500, and the third-place award is $250. The organization also gives three honorable mention awards.

- Given by International Amateur-Professional Photoelectric Photometry (IAPP), the Richard D. Lines Award for outstanding research in astronomy includes a scholarship of $5,000, a $1,000 grant for the school's science department, and an invitation to submit a paper on the project for its newsletter.

- The National Ground Water Association, along with its first-place award of $500, second-place award of $250, and third-place award of $200 publishes winners' abstracts in the *Journal of Ground Water.*

Basking in the Glory

Every time you win an award, you've won recognition that can be very valuable to you in the years ahead. When you apply for college, internships, or summer jobs, it certainly can't hurt to have science fair awards on your resume.

However, remember that the greatest glory was doing the project — you're a winner . . . no matter what!

Part VI
Some Superb Science Project Picks

"It's nicely done, but a bit too much like the 'Cat-in-a-Bottle' they did last year."

In this part . . .

Are you curious about projects that other students have done? In this part, I describe some great science fair projects, in a wide variety of categories. Students exhibited these actual projects at the Greater San Diego Science and Engineering Fair. Looking at these projects of varying degrees of difficulty, can give you an idea for a project of your own.

Chapter 16

Easy As Pie

● ●

In This Chapter

▶ Understanding why people do things: Human behavior projects

▶ Planting the seeds: Botany projects

▶ "If you build it, they will come": Engineering projects

▶ Making an incredible voyage: Microbiology projects

▶ Staying in motion: Physics projects

▶ Talking to the animals: Zoology projects

▶ Getting a taste of chemistry, medicine, and product testing projects

● ●

Throughout this book, I promise you that doing a science fair project can be easy, and I don't lie! Many projects don't require special tools, an equipped lab, advanced scientific knowledge, or even lots of money. You can do most of the projects in this chapter with simple household materials, a pencil and paper (and maybe a computer), and a dose of imagination and determination.

So, without further delay, I want to take you on a tour of some science fair projects that demonstrate how you can take ordinary things that you use every day and easily create a project that's out of the ordinary!

For each project, I list how the elements of the scientific method (see Chapter 8) were applied. These projects were actually displayed at the Greater San Diego Science and Engineering Fair, which mean that these projects were selected as the best projects from their school science fairs.

When you think that perhaps these projects should have had a larger sample or more trials, keep in mind that students conducted these projects under severe time constraints.

Behavioral and Social Sciences

Like me, many of you may be interested in why people think, feel, and act a certain way. (Parents, kids, and teachers especially wonder that about each other!) That's why the category of behavioral and social sciences is so popular.

Most of the projects in this category aren't experiments. To do them, you collect data from human subjects and put it together to prove the hypothesis. To get the data, you either observe people doing a certain task (or behavior) or survey a number of people to find out what they know, how they feel, or what their opinions are. When you've collected the data, you put it together and analyze the results to see whether or not they prove the hypothesis.

Your hypothesis is your educated guess about what the result of your project may show. (See Chapter 8 for more on how to come up with your hypothesis and Chapter 10 for how to relate your hypothesis to your results to come up with a conclusion.)

The next three projects show how a normal curiosity and interest in human behavior can make for a fun, interesting, and effective project.

Does age affect the ability to remember?

Bonnie Carr believed that older people had worse memory than younger people. Therefore, when considering a topic for her science fair project, she decided to test how age affects your ability to remember.

Figure 16-1 shows Bonnie's project display.

Hypothesis

I believe that age negatively impacts the ability to remember.

Experimental variables

Age groups whose memory will be tested

Measured variables

The number of correct answers that each subject gives

Controls

The memory test given to each subject

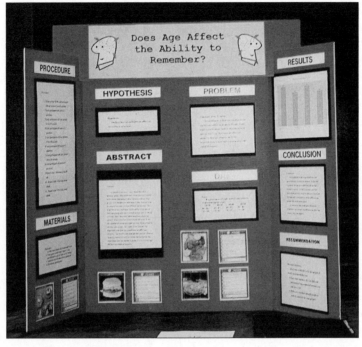

Figure 16-1:
Project
display for
"Does age
affect the
ability to
remember?"

Experimental groups

- 10-19 year olds
- 20-39 year olds
- 40-59 year olds
- 60-79 year olds

Materials

- Four game cards from Stare game
- Timer
- Four groups of five participants

Procedures

1. **Show the group a Stare card for 30 seconds.**

2. **Hide the card.**

3. **Have each participant answer five questions about the card shown.**

4. **Record the number of correct answers.**

5. **Repeat the procedure for the other groups.**

Results

- 10-19 year olds: 56 percent correct
- 20-39 year olds: 47 percent correct
- 40-59 year olds: 55 percent correct
- 60-79 year olds: 48 percent correct

Conclusions

My hypothesis that age would negatively affect memory was incorrect. I found only very slight differences in the number of correct answers by age group.

One possible reason can be that adults were more familiar with the objects that I used. Altering the age ranges may improve my project, because the first range was 10 years, and all other ranges were 20 years.

Does smell affect the way you perceive taste?

Like most people, Chia Hinchliff believed that smell affects taste. For instance, she noticed that when someone has a cold, he or she can't smell, and can't taste much either. To prove her assumption, she decided to mask the smell of certain foods, and then see if people could identify the taste of those foods.

Hypothesis

I believe that smell affects the way people perceive taste. I also believe that gender won't affect the senses of smell and taste.

Measured variables

Fruits correctly identified

Experimental groups

- Fruits with peppermint oil
- Fruits without peppermint oil

Materials

- ✔ Strawberry
- ✔ Pear
- ✔ Kiwi
- ✔ Tomato
- ✔ Banana
- ✔ Watermelon
- ✔ Orange
- ✔ Blindfold
- ✔ Peppermint essential oil
- ✔ Toothpicks

Procedures

1. Select 25 male and 25 female subjects.

2. Place pieces of fruit on toothpicks.

3. Put peppermint oil on one piece of each type of fruit to mask the fruit's real scent.

4. Blindfold subject.

5. Ask subject to taste and identify the fruit in the group with peppermint oil added.

6. Record the result.

7. Ask subject to taste and identify the fruit in the group without peppermint oil added.

8. Record the result.

Results

The subjects correctly identified the fruits as shown in Table 16-1.

Table 16-1	Number of Samples Correctly Identified			
	With Peppermint Oil Added		*No Peppermint Oil Added*	
	Male	*Female*	*Male*	*Female*
Strawberry	10	17	16	10
Pear	3	5	5	2

(continued)

Table 16-1 *(continued)*

| | With Peppermint Oil Added | | No Peppermint Oil Added | |
	Male	Female	Male	Female
Kiwi	15	15	12	15
Tomato	8	18	12	15
Banana	17	18	17	17
Watermelon	16	20	18	17
Orange	13	19	10	18

Conclusions

The hypothesis, that smell affects the perception of taste, was correct because the subjects were less frequently able to identify the fruit when the smell was masked with peppermint oil.

The results also show that gender doesn't have any real effect on the sense of smell and taste.

Obesity in 2002

In these first few years of the 21st century, an important health concern is the increase in obesity. In Charles Tafolla's project, he looked for a simple, healthy (and inexpensive) solution to the problem of being overweight in "The Fast Food Nation."

Hypothesis

I believe that drinking an 8-ounce glass of water before each meal will suppress appetite, resulting in weight loss.

Note that this project doesn't use experimental variables, controls, experimental groups, or control groups.

Measured variables

Amount of weight loss for each subject

Materials

- 30 adult subjects
- Survey forms

Procedures

1. **Select 30 subjects.**

2. **Weigh subjects; record weight.**

3. **Give each subject a survey to record whether he or she drank 0.24 liters (8 ounces) of water before each meal.**

4. **Approximately two months later, weigh subjects again; record weight.**

5. **Correlate subject log with weight results in pounds and kilograms.**

Results

The subjects, who complied by drinking 0.24 liters (8 ounces) of water before each meal, lost weight at least 50 percent of the time.

Conclusions

My hypothesis was that subjects who drank an 8-ounce glass of water before each meal would record a greater weight loss than those who did not. My results proved that my hypothesis was correct.

This project can be improved by making sure that subjects eat a specified number of calories and do the same amount of exercise.

Botany

I often joke with my friends that I have the most beautiful plants and flowers in the neighborhood, because I buy them at the craft store. Fortunately, the students who did the next four projects weren't similarly challenged.

Many students choose botany projects because they're fairly easy to set up. You can buy plants almost anywhere, pot them in just about any type of container, and easily measure their growth or observe their condition. For the most part, you won't need to work in a lab or buy any exotic or expensive equipment to do a successful botany project.

Light and mushrooms

All students learn that light is essential for green plants to grow, because they rely on the process of photosynthesis. Hanh Nguyen believed that even though mushrooms, which are fungi, do not use photosynthesis, they still grow better in light than in the dark.

Figure 16-2 shows Hanh Nguyen's project display.

Hypothesis

The mushrooms grown in the light will develop better than the mushrooms grown in the dark. Though mushrooms don't use photosynthesis, they'll grow better in the light because many living organisms obtain energy from sunlight. The amount of light would also provide heat for the mushrooms, making it easier for them to flourish.

Experimental variables

Amount of light

Measured variables

Amount of growth

Controls

✔ Amount of water given to each group

✔ Type of mushroom

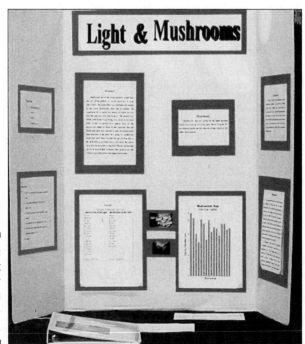

Figure 16-2: Project display for "Light and mushrooms."

Experimental groups

- ✔ Mushrooms grown in light
- ✔ Mushrooms grown in dark

Materials

- ✔ Two oyster mushroom kits
- ✔ Water
- ✔ Gloves
- ✔ Thermometer
- ✔ Two humidity tents (a *humidity tent* is a covering put over plants to keep the moisture available)

Procedures

Repeat the following procedures twice:

1. **Water both mushrooms kits generously.**
2. **Place one mushroom kit in a completely dark cabinet.**
3. **Place one mushroom kit in an area with indirect sunlight.**
4. **Cover each kit with a humidity tent.**
5. **Water both kits three times a day.**
6. **Use thermometers to keep temperature of mushrooms between 55 and 75 degrees F.**
7. **Record the growth of the oyster mushroom each day.**
8. **Use a metric ruler to measure the diameter of the mushrooms when they're full grown.**

Results

Table 16-2 shows the results of this project.

Table 16-2	Growth of Mushroom Cap Diameter (in Millimeters)	
	Mushrooms in Light	*Mushrooms in Dark*
First test	7.87	3.58
Second test	5.42	3.075

Conclusions

My hypothesis that mushrooms grown in the light will develop better than those grown in the dark was correct.

Also, I found out that the mushrooms grown in the dark get darker in color.

Effects of over-the-counter medication on cut carnations

Jana Clancy observed that many people add aspirin to the water to increase the life of their cut flowers. She figured that if aspirin were good, extra-strength pain relievers would be better, so she decided to test the effects of several over-the-counter pain medications on cut carnations.

Hypothesis

I believe that adding Extra Strength Tylenol will result in cut carnations lasting longer than those with other pain relievers (or no pain relievers) added.

Experimental variables

Medication added to water (Tylenol, Advil, generic aspirin)

Measured variables

Number of flowers that stayed alive and number of days they survived

Controls

- Tap water used
- Plastic cups
- Carnations selected

Experimental groups

- 0.95 liters (4 cups) of carnations in water with crushed aspirin added
- 0.95 liters (4 cups) of carnations in water with crushed Advil added
- 0.95 liters (4 cups) of carnations in water with crushed Extra Strength Tylenol added

Control groups

0.95 liters (4 cups) of carnations in tap water

Materials

- ✔ 16 plastic cups (4 cups each of Tylenol, Advil, and generic aspirin and 4 cups with plain tap water)
- ✔ 16 carnations
- ✔ 1 cup of tap water

Procedures

1. **Set up three experimental groups and one control group.**

2. **For 24 days, record condition of flowers and when the flowers died.**

Results

Table 16-3 shows the results for this project.

Table 16-3   Effect of Aspirin on Flowers in Various Water Solutions

Group	Average Life in Days
Aspirin	12
Advil	16
Extra Strength Tylenol	14
Tap water	24

Conclusions

My hypothesis was that Extra Strength Tylenol would result in the longest life for the carnations. The results disproved my hypothesis because the carnations in plain tap water lasted longest.

This is useful information for people who think that adding something to the water will make their flowers last longer. They can save their time and money by putting their flowers in plain tap water.

Deterring whitefly on home gardens

People spend a lot of time and effort trying to keep pests away from their gardens, and some of the things that they use to kill pests can be toxic to the environment. Mitzi Larson thought that a common household substance could kill garden pests without bad effects on the environment, so she set out to prove it with her science fair project.

Figure 16-3 shows the display for Mitzi's first-place science project.

Hypothesis
I believe that Palmolive dish soap will do the best job of deterring whitefly.

Experimental variables
Substances used to control whiteflies

Measured variables
Number of whiteflies after treatment

Controls
- ✔ Soil
- ✔ Types of plants
- ✔ Plant containers

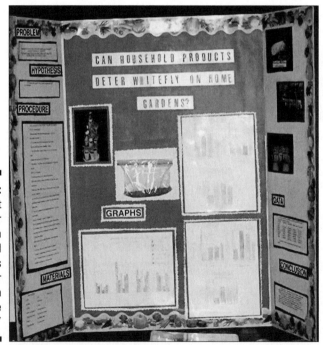

Figure 16-3: Project display for "Can household products deter whitefly on home gardens?"

Experimental groups

- ✔ Plants sprayed with acetone
- ✔ Plants sprayed with corn oil
- ✔ Plants sprayed with Palmolive soap
- ✔ Plants sprayed with WD-40
- ✔ Plants sprayed with coffee

Control groups

Plants sprayed with water

Materials

- ✔ Water
- ✔ Acetone
- ✔ Corn oil
- ✔ Palmolive soap
- ✔ WD-40
- ✔ Coffee
- ✔ 24 casaba melon seeds
- ✔ 24 disposable foam cups
- ✔ Dirt
- ✔ Potting soil
- ✔ Six spray bottles

Procedures

1. **Set up experimental and control groups as follows:**

    a. Punch eight holes into each disposable foam cup.

    b. Mix equal amounts dirt and potting soil.

    c. Put 3.5 cups dirt/potting soil mixture into each cup.

    d. Put a melon seed in each cup.

    e. Cover seed with .5-cup dirt/soil mix.

2. **Separate plants into six groups of four plants each, labeled with the name of the deterrent to be used.**

3. **Wait until plants grow and 10 to 15 whiteflies appear on each leaf.**

4. **Spray each group with equal amounts of the deterrent.**

5. **In three days, count and record the number of whiteflies.**

6. **Repeat Steps 4 and 5 three more times.**

Results

Table 16-4 shows the number of whiteflies counted every third day.

Table 16-4	Number of Whiteflies Counted			
	Check 1	*Check 2*	*Check 3*	*Check 4*
Water	10	27	23	18
Acetone	7	12	12	15
Corn oil	9	18	20	14
Palmolive	3	4	4	5
WD-40	6	16	15	17
Coffee	8	18	19	15

Conclusions

The hypothesis that Palmolive dish soap would do the best job of deterring whiteflies was correct because the group treated with Palmolive had the fewest number of whiteflies.

This project shows that pests can be controlled with a common, inexpensive substance that isn't toxic to the environment.

Effects of gibberellic acid on pea plants

Anyone who's done any gardening wants to find the perfect plant food that will make their fruits or flowers grow bigger, better, and faster. Gibberellic acid, a naturally occurring plant hormone, claims to promote increased growth, among other benefits. Brian Weddle decided to test these claims by measuring the effects of gibberellic acid on pea plants.

Figure 16-4 shows his project display.

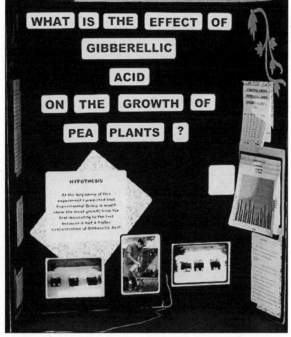

Figure 16-4:
Project
display for
"What is the
effect of
gibberellic
acid on the
growth of
pea plants?"

Hypothesis
I believe that feeding gibberellic acid to pea plants will increase their growth.

Experimental variables
Substance sprayed on plants

Measured variables
Amount of growth

Controls
Soil, water, and sunlight for plants

Experimental groups
✔ A: Pea plants sprayed with 200-ppm (parts per million) concentration of gibberellic acid

✔ B: Pea plants sprayed with 100-ppm concentration of gibberellic acid

Control groups

Pea plants that are not sprayed at all

Materials

- 27 pea plants
- Water
- Gibberellic acid

Procedures

1. **Plant 27 pea plants and divide into experimental groups A and B and control group.**
2. **Allow plants to germinate for 14 days.**
3. **Spray group A plants with 200-ppm concentration of gibberellic acid.**
4. **Spray group A plants with 200-ppm concentration of gibberellic acid.**
5. **Measure after two days.**
6. **Spray again after plants flower.**
7. **Measure after two days.**
8. **Spray again after pea pods appear.**
9. **Measure after two days.**

Results

- Experimental group A: 15.9 cm average growth (165 percent increase)
- Experimental group B: 17.7 cm average growth (165 percent increase)
- Control group: 12.1 cm average growth (142 percent increase)

Conclusions

My hypothesis that adding gibberellic acid to pea plants would increase their growth was correct.

The results also show that adding a stronger concentration of the acid resulted in no significant difference between groups A and B.

Engineering

Did you ever play with blocks? Legos? Erector sets? And what about racing radio control cars (or even Matchbox cars down the driveway)?

Answer yes to any of those questions and you may be a candidate for an engineering project.

An engineering project probably won't be an experiment. Instead, you build, test, or analyze something. With an engineering project, in one way or another you learn how things work, like the following three projects demonstrate.

Relationship of bicycle gear cogs and final height achieved

Many people want bicycles with the most gears so they can go faster, farther, and higher. Marisela Ibarra set out to show that using the smallest gear would allow a bicycle to travel farther uphill, regardless of how many more gears the bike has. (Regardless of her results and conclusions, Marisela knew that she'd get plenty of exercise doing her project.)

Hypothesis

I believe that using a smaller gear will allow a bicycle to travel farther uphill.

Experimental variables

Number of cogs in gear

Measured variables

Height achieved

Materials

- ✔ Roadmaster 10-speed bike with 28-, 38-, and 48-cog gears
- ✔ Baja 10-speed bike with 40- and 50-cog gears
- ✔ Air pressure gauge
- ✔ Air pump

Procedures

1. **Make sure that the air pressure in the Baja bike tires is 30psi.**

2. **Ride as far as possible on the Baja bike with the 40-cog gear without rising off the seat.**

3. **Record distance and recheck air pressure.**

4. **Ride as far as possible on the Baja bike with the 50-cog gear without rising off the seat.**

5. Record distance.

6. Repeat Steps 1 through 5 75 times.

7. Make sure that air pressure in the Roadmaster bike tires is 30psi.

8. Ride as far as possible on the Roadmaster bike with the 28-cog gear without rising off the seat.

9. Record distance and recheck air pressure.

10. Ride as far as possible on the Roadmaster bike with the 38-cog gear without rising off the seat.

11. Record distance and recheck air pressure.

12. Ride as far as possible on the Roadmaster bike with the 48-cog gear without rising off the seat.

13. Record distance and recheck air pressure.

14. Repeat Steps 8 through 13 75 times.

Results

Regardless of which bicycle was ridden, I could ride farthest uphill using the lowest gear.

Conclusions

My hypothesis that using a smaller gear would allow a bicycle to travel farther uphill was correct. My results show that using the lowest gear, on both types of bicycles, allowed me to ride the greatest distance without rising off the seat.

This project can be improved by resting between each ride, so that I'd have the same amount of energy each time.

Caller collar

Dogs are man's best friends. That old proverb certainly holds true for Jeff Thein and his dog, Rusty. Jeff wanted to be sure that the dog came back if he escaped from the yard. Hence, Jeff built and tested the caller collar.

Jeff's project display (featuring the now-obedient Rusty) is shown in Figure 16-5.

Hypothesis

I believe I can build a "pager" training collar that I can use to locate my dog, and also to train him to return to me when he runs away.

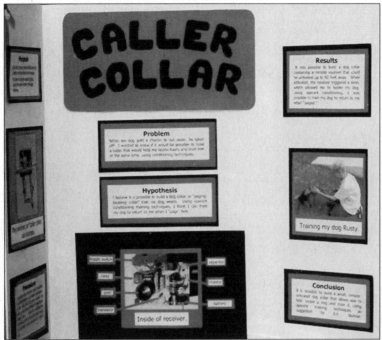

Materials

✔ Caller collar, built by modifying a garage door receiver with batteries for portability

✔ Siren

✔ Treats used as rewards for conditioning

Procedures

1. **Allow the dog to run in a specified area.**

2. **Recall him using the caller collar device (described in Materials section).**

3. **Reward the dog when he returns.**

4. **Increase the distance (up to 8 feet) that the dog can roam before recalling him.**

Results

The dog responded to the caller collar up to 8 feet away.

Conclusions

Jeff's hypothesis that he could build a "pager" training collar was correct. Using the pager and rewards, he trained Rusty to return when called.

The postscript to this project is that Jeff is waiting for his new puppy to get big enough to train with the caller collar.

Does water affect the strength of concrete?

No matter where you live, natural disasters can destroy buildings. Because concrete is used in many structures, having concrete as strong as possible is important, and Katherine Francke thought that a concrete mix with the least amount of water would be the strongest.

This project is an example of using something that isn't a common household item — but, if you can borrow it, it's yours! Katherine borrowed a *hydraulic press,* a machine that exerts a large force on a large piston via a small force applied to a smaller piston to do this project.

Hypothesis

I believe that concrete mixed with the least amount of water in it will be the strongest.

Experimental variables

Amount of water in the mixture

Measured variables

Kilometers per square inch at which concrete fails

Controls

Methods of creating, hardening, and testing concrete

Experimental groups

- Group #1: Basic cement mix
- Group #2: Basic cement mix plus 400 milliliters of water
- Group #3: Basic cement mix plus 600 milliliters of water

Materials

- ✔ 45 mailing tubes 5.1 cm wide x 10.2 cm long
- ✔ 1 bag of pea gravel
- ✔ 1 20-ton hydraulic press
- ✔ Candle wax
- ✔ 1 hot glue gun
- ✔ 45 cardboard pieces 5.1 cm x 5.1 cm
- ✔ 1 coffee can
- ✔ 1 pressure gauge attached to hydraulic press
- ✔ 1 bag of Portland cement (made by mixing substances that contain lime, aluminum, silica, and iron oxide)
- ✔ 1 bag of industrial sand

Procedures

1. **Create tubes to hold concrete as follows:**

    a. Put cardboard pieces on the bottom of the tubes using hot glue.

    b. Heat the candle wax in a coffee can halfway submerged in boiling water.

    c. Pour the hot wax into the tubes and drain immediately to coat the inside of tubes with wax.

2. **Mix experimental groups 1, 2, and 3 and pour into the tubes.**

3. **Ensure that cement is hardened.**

4. **Remove the cardboard from the hardened concrete.**

5. **Run the compression tests on the concrete as follows:**

    a. Place the gauge so that the pressure in the *hydraulic ram* (the piston on the hydraulic press) can be measured.

    b. Place the concrete test piece in the hydraulic press.

    c. Pump the pressure up noting the point at which the concrete fails.

6. **Repeat these steps for the remaining 44 pieces of concrete, while recording the data.**

Results

Table 16-5 shows the average results for the three experimental groups. The pressure is measured in kilometers per square inch.

Table 16-5	Average Pressure That Causes Concrete Failure
Group	*Average Pressure at which Concrete Fails*
1	76.0
2	65.0
3	55.0

Conclusions

The hypothesis that the mix with the least amount of water will produce the strongest concrete was correct because group 1, which was the driest, failed at a higher pressure.

Microbiology

When you look at microbiology projects, you're really looking at the world of things that you can't see — *microorganisms,* which are organisms of microscopic or submicroscopic size, such as bacteria. If you're afraid of germs, this category may not be for you. However, if you're interested in getting rid of the pesky critters, you may want to think about a microbiology project.

Be sure to check your regional or state requirements and limitations regarding the use and handling of bacteria.

What's the weakest solution of bleach that will kill bacteria?

If you've ever gone camping and had to wash your dishes without hot water, you know that washing them in diluted bleach will kill the germs. But because bleach can also have some negative effects, Jaleesa Chavez wanted to find out the least amount of bleach that was needed to still kill bacteria.

She summarized the project in her display, shown in Figure 16-6.

Hypothesis

I believe that I can find the smallest strength of bleach needed to kill E. coli bacteria.

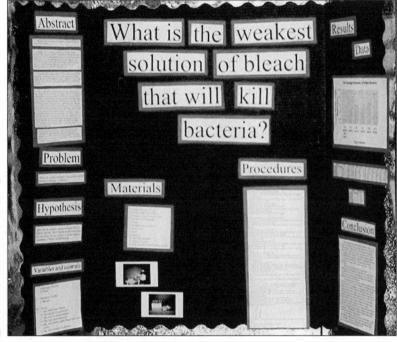

Experimental variables

Strength of bleach solution applied to E. coli bacteria

Measured variables

Percent of E. coli killed by bleach solution

Controls

Amount of solution applied to E. coli bacteria

Experimental groups

- ✔ 3 percent bleach solution
- ✔ 5 percent bleach solution
- ✔ 8 percent bleach solution
- ✔ 10 percent bleach solution
- ✔ 15 percent bleach solution

Control groups

Water

Materials

- ✔ Bleach
- ✔ Water
- ✔ 3 percent bleach solution
- ✔ 5 percent bleach solution
- ✔ 8 percent bleach solution
- ✔ 10 percent bleach solution
- ✔ 15 percent bleach solution
- ✔ E. coli bacteria

Procedures

1. **Create solutions of 3 percent, 5 percent, 8 percent, 10 percent, and 15 percent bleach in water.**

2. **Spray each solution on E. coli bacteria.**

3. **Measure amount and percentage of E. coli bacteria killed by the bleach solution.**

Results

- ✔ The 3 percent bleach solution killed 1.75 percent of the bacteria.
- ✔ The 5 percent bleach solution killed 2.4 percent of the bacteria.
- ✔ The 8 percent bleach solution killed 2.6 percent of the bacteria.
- ✔ The 10 percent bleach solution killed 2.7 percent of the bacteria.
- ✔ The 15 percent bleach solution killed 4.1 percent of the bacteria.

Conclusions

My hypothesis stated that I could find and document the smallest concentration of bleach in water that would kill E. coli bacteria. Of the solutions tested, the 3 percent solution was the smallest concentration that will kill bacteria, although the amount of germs killed went up in proportion to the concentration of bleach.

Effect of mold growth on different types of cheese

Personally, I've always called the mold growing on cheese that's been in my refrigerator for a while "my science project". But what would it be like if you purposely grew mold for your science project?

Lisa Duong decided to find out! Her project display is shown in Figure 16-7.

Hypothesis

I think that mozzarella cheese will grow mold faster in a dark place and a warm temperature. I know that because mold grows faster in dark and warm conditions. I also believe that mozzarella cheese will grow mold faster than cheddar or jack cheese because a soft cheese has a shorter life than harder cheeses.

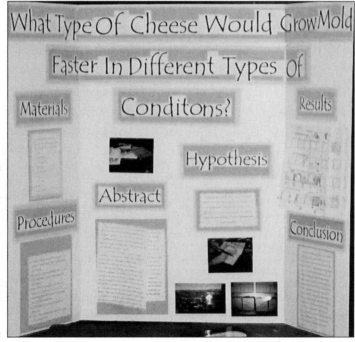

Figure 16-7: Project display for "What type of cheese would grow mold faster in different types of conditions?"

Experimental variables

- ✔ Dark and warm temperature
- ✔ Light and warm temperature
- ✔ Dark and room temperature
- ✔ Light and room temperature

Measured variables

The amount of mold that grows on the cheese

Controls

- ✔ Brand of cheese
- ✔ Size of sealable plastic bags
- ✔ Size of boxes
- ✔ Heating pad

Experimental groups

- ✔ Cheddar cheese
- ✔ Monterey Jack cheese
- ✔ Mozzarella cheese

Materials

- ✔ 8 ounces of cheddar cheese
- ✔ 8 ounces of Monterey Jack cheese
- ✔ 8 ounces of mozzarella cheese
- ✔ 1 knife
- ✔ 2 boxes with a lid
- ✔ 2 boxes without a lid
- ✔ Fluorescent light
- ✔ 36 sealable plastic bags
- ✔ 1 permanent marker
- ✔ 1 log
- ✔ 1 heating pad
- ✔ 1 ruler
- ✔ 1 pair of gloves

Procedures

For each sample:

1. **Measure and cut 16 pieces of each type of cheese, 2 x 2 centimeters.**

2. **Seal one sample in each of the 16 sealable plastic bags labeled with the type of cheese as follows:**

   - **4 labeled "dark + room temperature"**

   - **4 labeled "dark + warm"**

   - **4 labeled "light + room temperature"**

   - **4 labeled "light + warm"**

3. **Place bags labeled "light + warm" in a box with no lid and put box on a heating pad under a fluorescent light.**

4. **Place bags labeled "light + room temperature" in another box with no lid and put it near the fluorescent light.**

5. **Place bags labeled "dark + warm" in a box with a top and put it on top of a heating pad under a fluorescent light.**

6. **Place bags labeled "dark + room temperature" in a box with a lid.**

7. **Every three days, observe and record how much the mold grew.**

8. **Take pictures of all the samples and label them.**

Results

The results of this project were shown as photographs and drawings of the amount of mold grown on the cheese samples.

Conclusions

My hypothesis was that mozzarella cheese would grow mold faster in a dark place and a warm temperature because mozzarella cheese is a soft cheese and mold grows more rapidly in soft cheese than hard cheese (like cheddar).

This hypothesis was incorrect because the Monterey Jack, which is harder than mozzarella cheese, grew mold more rapidly at room temperature.

I could improve on my project the next time by using more kinds of cheese at different temperatures.

If you try a project like this, with four experimental variables and three experimental groups, you'll have an easier time if you work with one experimental group at a time.

Also, note that Lisa did this project using gloves and sealed containers. She also observed the proper handling techniques designated by the California State Education Code.

Physics Projects

Many people assume that physics projects are complicated, and totally unrelated to real life. But, from baseballs to magnets, the next two projects show that physics is down-to-earth and accessible to everyone.

Are new baseballs producing more home runs?

Does anyone besides Tyler Cochran think that more home runs are being hit now compared to two years ago? Well, he knew that the baseballs were being manufactured differently, and thought that perhaps that was the reason.

Figure 16-8 shows Tyler's project display.

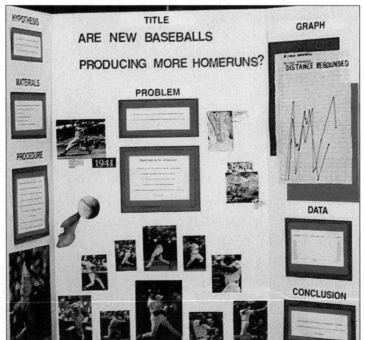

Figure 16-8:
Project display for "Are new baseballs producing more home runs?"

Hypothesis

I believe that new baseballs are producing more home runs than older baseballs, manufactured two years ago. The new baseballs are made of an inner core of rubber, wrapped in a thick layer of yarn and topped with leather. The older baseballs had a harder core, wrapped in thin yarn and then topped with leather.

Independent variables

Type of baseball

Dependent variables

Rebound of each pitch

Controls

Speed of pitch

Note: Balls were pitched by a pitching machine, and all testing was done at the same time to minimize the effects of wind, and so on.

Experimental groups

- ✔ 2-year-old baseballs
- ✔ New baseballs

Materials

- ✔ 10 2-year-old baseballs
- ✔ 10 new baseballs
- ✔ Pitching machine
- ✔ Metal sheet

Procedures

1. **From 20 yards away, pitch each baseball at metal sheet.**
2. **Measure rebound distance in centimeters.**
3. **Average total distance for each type of baseball.**

Results

On the average, the new baseballs rebounded .2 centimeters farther than the old baseballs.

Conclusions

My hypothesis that the new baseballs would go farther than the old baseballs was correct. However, the differences were insufficient to account for the greater number of home runs being hit, so other factors are possibly at work.

To improve this project, I would like to do additional research to find out what these other factors may be.

Magnets and temperature

Like me, you probably thought that the power of a magnet remained the same, no matter what. However, Colin Eldred-Cohen thought that temperature changes would change a magnet's power, and he undertook a physics project to prove it.

Hypothesis

I believe that the power of magnets is affected by temperature, regardless of magnet type.

Experimental variables

Temperature at which magnets were tested

Measured variables

Amount of material that magnets would pick up

Controls

- ✔ Variety of magnets tested
- ✔ Material to be picked up

Experimental groups

- ✔ Frozen magnets
- ✔ Magnets in dry ice
- ✔ Boiling magnets
- ✔ Baked magnets

Materials

- ✔ Iron magnet
- ✔ Cobalt magnet

✔ Alnico magnet

✔ Ceramic magnet

✔ BBs

Procedures

With each magnet type, do the following:

1. **Freeze the magnet for 10 minutes.**

2. **Place the magnet into a tray of BBs.**

3. **Record how many BBs the magnet picks up.**

4. **Place the magnet in dry ice for 10 minutes.**

5. **Place the magnet into a tray of BBs.**

6. **Record how many BBs the magnet picks up.**

7. **Place the magnet in boiling water for 10 minutes.**

8. **Place the magnet into a tray of BBs.**

9. **Record how many BBs the magnet picks up.**

10. **Place the magnet in a 350° oven for 10 minutes.**

11. **Place the magnet into a tray of BBs.**

12. **Record how many BBs the magnet picks up.**

Results

All magnets performed the best at room temperature.

Conclusions

My hypothesis was that temperature affects magnetic strength. That was true because the strength of all types of magnets changed depending on the temperature.

Zoology

I don't know anyone who doesn't like animals. Horses and dogs are popular favorites, of course. These next two projects examine an animal's sense of smell, but in very different ways.

Memory of horses

Do horses remember where to find their food? Maybe. Instead of putting the carrot on a stick, Danielle Torgeson put the carrot in a box.

Figure 16-9 shows her project display.

Hypothesis

Horses will remember the pattern on a box in which carrots are placed.

Independent variables

Boxes used to test horses' scent

Materials

- ✔ Carrots
- ✔ One box marked with triangle
- ✔ One box marked with square
- ✔ One box marked with circle
- ✔ One unmarked box.

Figure 16-9: Project display for "The memory of horses."

Procedures

Do a scent test with three horses as follows:

1. **Scent all the boxes by rubbing carrot on them.**
2. **Place the carrot under the box marked with the circle.**
3. **Allow horse to see all boxes.**
4. **Hold box with circle up to horse.**
5. **Put all boxes on the ground and allow horse to select the box with the carrot.**
6. **Record the horse's selection.**

Results

Even after the horses were shown that the carrot was in the box marked with the circle, they looked for the reward in all the boxes.

Conclusions

My hypothesis was that horses would remember the pattern on a box in which carrots are placed. This hypothesis is incorrect because the horses responded to the scent of the carrot regardless of where it was placed.

Will a dog's muzzle length affect its sense of smell?

It's amazing how many different kinds of dogs exist — big ones or little ones, longhaired or shorthaired, squished-in faces or slender, pointy snouts! A dog's sense of smell is one of its most powerful senses. Is this sensitivity to smell affected by the length of its muzzle? Ashley Wynn decided to find out.

Check out Figure 16-10 to see her project display.

Hypothesis

I believe that the length of a dog's muzzle won't affect its sense of smell.

Independent variables

25 dogs of various breeds, with different muzzle lengths

Dependent variables

Number of times that the dogs found the treat

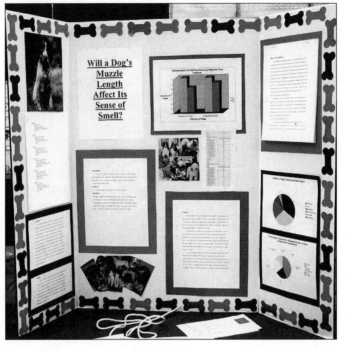

**Figure
16-10:**
Project
display for
"Will a dog's
muzzle
length affect
its sense of
smell?"

Controls

▸ Type of treat used

▸ Testing method used

Experimental groups

Each dog was a different experimental group

Materials

▸ Dog treats

▸ Plastic cups

Procedures

For each dog, do the following scent test three times:

1. **Place three cups on the ground with a treat under one cup.**

2. **Allow dog to sniff a sample of the treat in hand.**

3. **Have dog find the cup that has the hidden treat.**

Results

Short-muzzled dogs were successful at finding the hidden treat as often as long-muzzled dogs.

Conclusions

My hypothesis was that the length of a dog's muzzle wouldn't affect its sense of smell. This hypothesis was correct.

My project also showed that the sense of smell was more associated with the breed of dogs, because, for example, sporting dogs (dogs trained to detect fallen game), scent hounds (dogs that detect their prey by smell), or working dogs (dogs that do guard or rescue work) had a better sense of smell than toy dogs, who do not work at all.

Project Potpourri

When looking for a science project idea (see Chapter 3), you can find many more categories to choose from besides those mentioned in this chapter. (This chapter does give you a good representation, though.) The next three projects, for example, are from the chemistry, medicine and health, and product testing categories.

Water purification and filtration

Everyone's interested in drinking the purest water possible. In his project, Ian Boblit tested how effective different types of water filters are at eliminating chlorine from tap water.

Ian Boblit's project display is shown in Figure 16-11.

Hypothesis

I believe that carbon block filters are the most effective at blocking chlorine, and that of the carbon block filters, the carafe-style filter will be the most effective.

Experimental variables

Type of water filter used

Measured variables

Amount of chlorine in each water sample

Controls
Amount and type of water used

Experimental groups
- ✔ Faucet-mounted filtered water
- ✔ Carafe-style carbon block filter
- ✔ Refrigerator-mounted carbon block filter
- ✔ Pool water

Control groups
Plain tap water

Materials
- ✔ Kit for testing chlorine
- ✔ Plain tap water
- ✔ Faucet-mounted filtered water

✔ Carafe-style carbon block filter

✔ Refrigerator-mounted carbon block filter

✔ Pool water

Procedures

For each of three trials, do the following:

1. **Test a sample of plain tap water and record the amount of chlorine.**

2. **Test a sample of pool water and record the amount of chlorine.**

3. **Filter tap water through the three types of filters and record the amount of chlorine.**

Results

Table 16-6 shows the amount of chlorine in each different water sample.

Table 16-6	Amount of Chlorine in Different Water Samples		
	Trial 1	Trial 2	Trial 3
Tap	1.5	2.0	1.5
Faucet-mounted filter	.6	.6	1.3
Carafe-style filter	.5	.6	.9
Refrigerator-mounted filter	.1	.1	.1
Pool water	5	2.6	4.8

Figure 16-12 shows the average amount of chlorine in water samples for all three tests.

Conclusions

My hypothesis that a carbon block filter was most effective at removing chlorine was correct. However, I incorrectly stated that the carafe-style filter would be the most effective. The refrigerator-style filter actually proved to be the most effective.

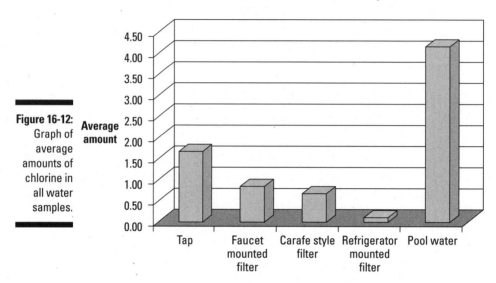

Chlorine in Filtered Water Samples

Effect of hot tubs on blood pressure

After a long, stressful day, many people like to spend some time in a hot tub, as a way of mellowing out. Robert Sagarian's project examined the effect of spending 15 minutes in a hot tub.

Hypothesis

I believe that after spending time in a hot tub, blood pressure will lower as a result of *vasodilatation* (the increase in the internal diameter of blood vessels).

Controls

All tests done in the same hot tub over period of three days

Materials

- ✔ 15 subjects ages 18 to 72
- ✔ *Sphygmomanometer,* an instrument used to measure blood pressure in millimeters

Procedures

Over a period of three days, test each subject as follows:

1. **Take and record systolic and diastolic blood pressure.**

2. **Have subject spend 15 minutes in the hot tub.**

3. **Take and record systolic and diastolic blood pressure again.**

Results

There was an average 5 percent decrease in both types of blood pressure after 15 minutes in the hot tub.

Conclusions

My hypothesis was that after spending time in a hot tub, blood pressure would lower as a result of vasodilatation. Because both types of blood pressure averaged a 5 percent decrease after 15 minutes in the hot tub, this project shows that some time in the hot tub is a good way to wind down after a particularly hectic work or school day.

Bone appetit

From soda to peanut butter, just about every manufacturer claims that its product is healthier, and many price it accordingly. With that in mind, are premium dog foods healthier than cheaper brands? Allison Sauer, a veterinarian's daughter, wanted to know.

Hypothesis

I believe that eating more expensive food doesn't make a dog healthier.

Independent variables

Dog food used

Dependent variables

Blood testing and analysis on dogs

Controls

- ✔ Age of dogs
- ✔ Number of meals
- ✔ Amount of food
- ✔ Level of exercise of dogs

Experimental groups

Different brands of dog food including:

- ✔ Eukanuba
- ✔ Purina One
- ✔ Science Diet
- ✔ Kirkland
- ✔ Iams
- ✔ Nutro
- ✔ Hunden Flocken
- ✔ Sam's Club
- ✔ Pedigree
- ✔ Natural Choice

Materials

- ✔ Ten types of dog food
- ✔ Ten dogs age 4 through 7 that ate the same food for at least three months
- ✔ Blood testing materials

Procedures

1. **Draw blood sample from each dog.**
2. **Analyze each blood sample. (Allison's mom, a veterinarian, helped with this part of the procedure.)**

Results

The values for each dog were in normal range.

Conclusions

My hypothesis was that the price of the dog food would have no effect on the health of the dog. This was correct, because for all dogs tested, the values of the analyzed blood were within normal range.

Chapter 17

Kicking It Up a Notch

• •

In This Chapter

▶ Working in the lab: Chemistry projects

▶ Building (or testing) a better mousetrap: Engineering projects

▶ Keeping it green: Environmental science projects

▶ Moving at the speed of light (and beyond): Physics projects

▶ Stirring the potpourri: Projects from other categories

• •

Maybe this isn't your first project, and you're looking forward to doing something a little more complex. Or perhaps science is your favorite subject, and you just can't wait to start your science project. Whatever the case, this chapter features several great ideas for slightly more advanced projects — ones that may use more variables or a number of experimental groups (see Chapter 8 for a quick rundown on variables and experimental groups). These projects, which come from different categories, may also require you to build your own testing apparatus (see Chapter 9 for information about how to do that).

For each project, I list how the elements of the scientific method (see Chapter 8) were applied. These projects were actually displayed at the Greater San Diego Science and Engineering Fair, which means that these projects were selected as the best projects from their school science fairs.

When you think that perhaps these projects should have had a larger sample or more trials, keep in mind that students conducted these projects under severe time constraints.

Chemistry

Okay, time to 'fess up. How many of you have played with chemistry sets? Well, doing a chemistry science project is like having your own custom-built chemistry set. Only remember, no explosions in your room.

Actually, the three projects in this section are true Californians — they deal with the chemistry of fruits and nuts.

How much potential energy do different nuts have?

It seems that at least once a year California has another energy crisis, and almost as often, someone wonders what will happen when California runs out of energy sources. Christopher Crews, knowing that all living things contain energy, set out to prove that different varieties of nuts have energy stores that can be released by burning.

Hypothesis

I believe that burning different varieties of nuts will produce energy, and that peanuts will produce the most energy.

Measured variables

Amount of heat produced

Controls

- Number of nuts tested
- Amount of water

Experimental groups

- Almonds
- Cashews
- Peanuts

Materials

- Ten each whole, raw, unshelled nuts:

    - Cashews

    - Almonds

    - Peanuts

- Lighter
- Needle
- Cork

✔ Thermometer

✔ 32-ounce coffee can

✔ Two 10-ounce soup cans

✔ Drill and bits

✔ Skewer

✔ Water

✔ Kitchen scale

Procedures

1. **Fill large coffee can with water.**

2. **Measure nut.**

3. **Weigh water on kitchen scale.**

4. **Measure and record starting water temperature.**

5. **Drill hole through nut.**

6. **Insert skewer through hole in nut.**

7. **Heat nut with lighter and let the nut burn fully.**

8. **Measure and record ending water temperature.**

9. **Calculate BTU (starting temperature minus ending temperature divided by the weight of the water).**

   BTU stands for _British Thermal Unit,_ the energy necessary to raise the temperature of one pound of water by 1° F. One BTU equals approximately 1,055 joules (or 1,055 watt-seconds).

10. **Repeat Steps 1 through 9 for each nut.**

Results

The average BTU for each type of nut is as follows:

Cashews	15.75 BTU
Almonds	13.76 BTU
Peanuts	10.77 BTU

Conclusions

The hypothesis was that burning different varieties of nuts would produce energy, with peanuts producing the most energy. That's partially correct because all the nuts produced energy. However, the hypothesis was incorrect because the cashews produced the most energy, and peanuts produced the least.

Fruit power: A study of alternative energy

The energy crisis is always on everyone's mind, including students thinking about their science projects. Laura Franke decided to find out whether the energy stored in fruits could be a possible source of electrical power.

Hypothesis

I believe that I can generate enough electric power from acid- or starch-based fruits to power a light bulb and a buzzer.

Independent variables

Type of fruit

Dependent variables

Amount of voltage produced

Controls

Wire, scale, and *voltmeter,* an instrument that measures the difference between two points, in volts

Experimental groups

- ✔ Grapefruits
- ✔ Oranges
- ✔ Limes
- ✔ Potatoes

Materials

- ✔ Three grapefruits
- ✔ Three oranges
- ✔ Three limes
- ✔ Seven lemons
- ✔ Two potatoes
- ✔ Buzzer
- ✔ Light bulbs
- ✔ Copper wire
- ✔ Zinc metal alloy wire

Procedures

1. **In each fruit, place a 2-inch piece of copper wire and zinc alloy wire.**

2. **Weigh the fruit.**

3. **Touch wire to tongue to detect current.**

4. **For 10 days, do the following two tests:**

   a. Attach Christmas tree bulb to fruit, observe whether the bulb lights, and measure current with voltmeter.

   b. Attach buzzer to fruit, observe whether the buzzer operates, and measure current with voltmeter.

Results

Each fruit sample generated enough current to power a light bulb and a buzzer.

Conclusions

My hypothesis was correct, because I was able to generate enough electric power to power a light bulb and a buzzer from acid- or starch-based fruits.

Fruit — when you're ripe, you're right

Sometimes the most common situations can spawn great project ideas. For example, did you ever wonder why fruits bought at the same time ripen at different speeds?

Well, for her science project, Shannon Gonzalez decided to find out. Her project display is shown in Figure 17-1.

Hypothesis

I believe that pears will ripen at different speeds due to their environmental conditions.

Independent variables

- ✔ Temperature
- ✔ Light

Dependent variables

- ✔ *Refractive index,* the ratio of the velocity of light in a vacuum to the velocity in a medium
- ✔ Condition of pears

Figure 17-1:
Project
display for
"Fruit, when
you are ripe,
you are
right."

Controls

- ✔ Pears used
- ✔ Process of testing

Experimental groups

- ✔ Group B: 15 pears refrigerated
- ✔ Group C: 15 pears at room temperature
- ✔ Group D: 15 pears in dark areas
- ✔ Group E: 15 pears at natural outdoor temperature

Control groups

Group A: 15 pears immediately after purchase

Materials

- ✔ 75 unripe pears
- ✔ Scalpel
- ✔ Glass test tubes
- ✔ Ohaus balance (a digital scale)

✔ Distilled water

✔ Sorvall Mc 12v (used to create centrifugal force to squeeze juice from a piece of fruit)

✔ 5–40 micro liter *finnpipette,* a device used to dispense liquid

✔ Pipette tips

✔ *Refractometer,* used to measure the turning of a light or sound wave

✔ 95 percent ethanol solution

✔ Paper

✔ Tape

✔ Permanent marker

✔ Scissors

✔ Journal/log

Procedures

1. Divide the 15 unripe pears into five groups, with each group containing three pears.

2. Label each group, for example: A1, A2, and A3 . . . E1, E2, E3.

3. Prepare fruit for testing and place in glass test tube.

4. Weigh the test tube on the Ohaus balance to determine the amount of distilled water that must be placed in the empty tube for balance.

5. Place an empty glass tube on the Ohaus balance.

6. Place both tubes on opposite holes in the Sorvall Mc machine.

7. Set the Sorvall Mc 12v at maximum speed (1200 rpm) at 2 minutes.

8. Remove tubes, extract the pear juice with a device called a finnpipette set at .10 microliter.

9. Get refractive index, using refractometer.

10. Repeat Steps 2 through 8 with all samples in group A.

11. Repeat Steps 3 through 10 with group B pears (refrigerated).

12. Repeat Steps 3 through 10 with group C pears (room temperature).

13. Repeat Steps 3 through 10 with group D pears (in dark area).

14. Place group E pears on a windowsill where they can be exposed to the natural outdoor temperature and repeat Steps 3 through 10.

15. Leave the pears in their given conditions for a week and observe the ripening process (appearance and feeling).

16. Average all the readings for groups A, B, C, D, and E.

Results

Comparing the averages for all the pears, I found that they ripened in the following sequence (fastest to slowest):

- ✔ Group E: natural outdoor temperature
- ✔ Group D: darkened area
- ✔ Group C: room temperature
- ✔ Group A: immediately after purchase (control group)
- ✔ Group B: refrigerated

Conclusions

The hypothesis was correct because all the pears ripened at a different rate due to their different environments. The refrigerated fruit had the lowest refractive index because refrigeration stopped the production of *ethylene,* a hydrocarbon gas that makes fruits ripen. The fruits that weren't placed in the refrigerator began to ripen because *hydrolases* (substances that cause the chemical reaction of a compound with water) broke down the chemicals found inside the pears.

These chemical changes also caused external evidence of ripening. When the chemicals and acids broke down, sugar was produced, which increased the juiciness of the fruit, and produced a scent. The breakdown of chlorophyll also contributed to the fruit's discoloration.

Engineering

Engineering projects not only build devices, they also test them. The next four projects analyze how some fabric insulators and synthetic oils work, and also test the strength of laminated wood and car bumpers.

Effectiveness of fabric insulation

When you're going to spend some time in the great outdoors, you probably want to know how to keep warm on cold nights. So did Michael Tran, who decided to test the heat retention of five different fabrics.

Figure 17-2 shows Michael's display.

Hypothesis

I believe that, of five samples tested, the fabric with the highest rubber content will retain the most heat.

Figure 17-2:
Project display for "Effective-ness of fabric insulation."

Independent variables
Fabric types

Dependent variables
Amount of heat retained by each sample

Controls
- ✔ Method of setting up test
- ✔ Initial heat of each sample

Experimental groups
- ✔ Rubber sheeting
- ✔ Thermo suede
- ✔ Budget blackout fabric
- ✔ Double-layered suede
- ✔ Polar fleece

Materials

- Five plastic bottles wrapped in the following:
  - Rubber sheeting
  - Thermo suede
  - Budget blackout fabric
  - Double-layered suede
  - Polar fleece
- Thermometer
- Water
- Heater

Procedures

1. Tape a fabric sample to each bottle and label it.

2. Heat water to 90° C and dispense .5 liter in each bottle.

3. Cover bottle top with a square of fabric and put thermometer through top.

4. Record drop in temperature until it reaches 82° C.

5. Record temperature every 2 minutes for 20 minutes.

6. Cool the water, and then repeat 50 times for each fabric type.

Results

The amount of heat retained by each fabric was as follows (listed from most to least):

- Polar fleece
- Double-layered suede
- Rubber sheeting
- Thermo suede
- Budget blackout

Conclusions

My hypothesis was that the fabric with the highest rubber content would retain the most heat. This hypothesis was incorrect, because the rubber sheeting, which has the highest rubber content, placed third in the amount of heat retained.

The polar fleece retained the most heat, possibly because the polar fleece was the thickest fabric.

The truth about synthetic oils

Here's yet another spin on the energy crisis: How about using synthetics instead of fossil fuels for engine oil? John Corrao tested synthetic and petroleum-based oils, hoping to show that the synthetics are just as effective.

John's project display is shown in Figure 17-3.

Hypothesis

I believe that synthetic oils are more efficient and create fewer bearing failures in an engine than petroleum-based oils.

Independent variables

Type of oil used

Dependent variables

Weight of BBs after valve springs break

Controls

Valve springs used

Figure 17-3: Project display for "The truth about synthetic oils."

Experimental groups

- ✔ Four sets of valve springs with petroleum-based oil
- ✔ Four sets of valve springs with synthetic oil

Materials

- ✔ Metal BBs
- ✔ 4 liters synthetic motor oil
- ✔ 4 liters petroleum-based motor oil
- ✔ Eight sets of valve springs
- ✔ Device to hold valve springs

Procedures

1. **Test four sets of valve springs with petroleum-based oil as follows:**

   a. Put set of valve springs into holding device.

   b. Pour BBs into fixture until the valve spring breaks.

   c. Measure the weight of the BBs after the break.

2. **Test four sets of valve springs with synthetic oil as follows:**

   a. Put set of valve springs into holding device.

   b. Pour BBs into fixture until the wood breaks.

   c. Measure the weight of the BBs after the break.

Results

- ✔ Petroleum-based oil: Inconsistent results and bearing failures
- ✔ Synthetic oil: No bearing failures recorded

Conclusions

My hypothesis was correct, because the results showed that only the synthetic oil produced no bearing failures. The petroleum-based product gave more inconsistent results and more failures.

In the future, I believe that I could improve on this project by doing additional tests.

Strength in numbers

Anyone who's visited a home improvement superstore knows that laminated wood products are as popular as natural wood. But how strong are they?

Jonathan Davis used his science fair project, as shown in Figure 17-4, to find out.

Hypothesis

I believe that using more layers in laminated wood creates a stronger and more durable product.

Independent variables

Number of layers in laminated boards

Dependent variables

Weight of BBs required to break the board

Controls

✔ Type of wood used

✔ Type of BBs used

✔ Test fixture used

Figure 17-4:
Project display for "Strength in numbers."

Experimental groups

- ✔ 1-layer laminate
- ✔ 2-layer laminate
- ✔ 4-layer laminate
- ✔ 6-layer laminate
- ✔ 8-layer laminate

Materials

- ✔ Balsa wood boards
- ✔ Metal BBs
- ✔ Slide to test boards
- ✔ Vegetable oil to grease the slide

Procedures

For each experimental group:

1. **Put test board in fixture.**
2. **Pour BBs into fixture until the wood breaks.**
3. **Measure the weight of the BBs after the break.**

Results

Weight of BBs required to break boards:

- ✔ 1-layer laminate: 12.6 lbs.
- ✔ 2-layer laminate: 7.8 lbs.
- ✔ 4-layer laminate: 9.8 lbs.
- ✔ 6-layer laminate: 11 lbs.
- ✔ 8 layer laminate: Didn't break

Conclusions

My hypothesis was that using more layers would strengthen a laminated wood board. This hypothesis was correct, even though the 1-layer laminate required 12.6 pounds to break. This was because for the first trial, the slide wasn't lubricated enough.

Fender bender bumper damage resistance

From looking at television commercials you may think that just about every automobile bumper can protect you in a crash. So, is that idea built on fact or fiction? Steven Steckbeck built and tested a few models to find out what bumper material was most effective.

Check out his project display in Figure 17-5.

Hypothesis

I believe that titanium is the best material for a car bumper because of its strength and flexibility.

Independent variables

Composition of bumper

Dependent variables

Measurement of dent

Controls

- Weight dropped on bumper
- Cradle used to hold bumper

Experimental groups

- Titanium bumper
- Steel bumper
- Aluminum bumper
- Weather-resistant thermoplastic bumper

Materials

- Model bumpers of titanium, steel, aluminum, and weather-resistant thermoplastic (these were built in a machine shop, with the help of a family friend)
- Cradle to hold model bumper

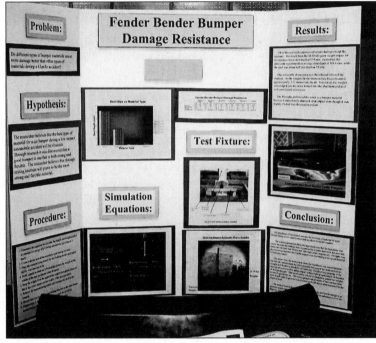

Figure 17-5:
Project display for "Fender bender bumper damage resistance."

Procedures

1. **Determine the height and weight needed to simulate the crash of an automobile weighing 1,364 lbs. going 4 mph.**

2. **Drop weight on bumper.**

3. **Measure dent in bumper.**

Results

✔ Titanium: 2.4 mm dent

✔ Steel: 50 mm dent

✔ Aluminum: 104.6 mm dent

✔ Weather-resistant thermoplastic: shattered on impact

Conclusions

My hypothesis that titanium is the best bumper material is correct, because it resulted in the smallest dent.

Environmental Science

Today, many people are interested in the environment. The next two projects explore alternate energy sources and a way to protect the environment from toxic substances.

Ants be gone

For many years, the use of chemical pesticides has been bugging environmentalists. But if you've ever faced a line of ants marching across your kitchen counter, you know that you'll try almost any debugger. Therefore, the search for nontoxic pest control is ongoing. Amy Achille tested natural substances to find out if they're effective in getting rid of ants.

Her project display is shown in Figure 17-6.

Hypothesis

I believe that I can find an organic ant repellant.

Independent variables

Ant repellant used

Dependent variables

Number of ants before and after the repellant is applied

Controls

Feeding station and bait

Experimental groups

- Peppermint
- Catnip
- Pennyroyal, an aromatic mint
- Red and green chili
- Society garlic, a blooming evergreen plant with a garlic odor
- Ammonia
- Pyracantha, an evergreen shrub

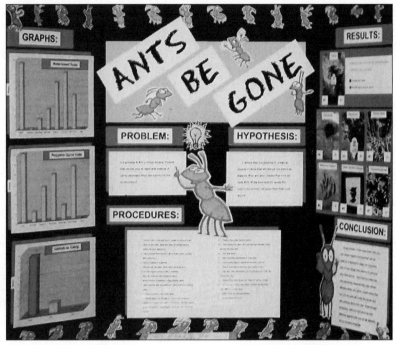

Control groups
Chemical pesticide

Materials
- Peppermint
- Catnip
- Pennyroyal
- Red and green chili peppers
- Society garlic
- Ammonia
- Pyracantha
- Chemical pesticide

Procedures
1. Create feeding station for ants with first repellent material.
2. Bait feeding station with honey.
3. Surround feeding station with repellent materials.

4. Count the number of ants that came through to the feeding station.

5. Record results and repeat steps 3 through 5 with the next repellent.

6. Score repellents on scale of 1 to 10, according to number of ants killed and how long the repellent was effective.

Results

Table 17-1 shows how the different repellents performed in terms of the number of ants killed and how long the repellent was effective.

Table 17-1	Kill and Persistence Scores of Nine Repellants	
Substance	**Killing**	**Persistence**
Ammonia	2	4
Catnip	6	8
Green peppers	5	5
Red peppers	3	3
Pesticide	10	10
Pennyroyal	0	6
Peppermint	3	7
Pyracantha	0	1
Society garlic	6	6

My results show that all the repellants killed ants. Of the natural repellants, catnip and society garlic had the highest kill rate, and catnip lasted longest. However, the chemical repellant killed more ants and lasted longer than any natural repellant.

Conclusions

My hypothesis that I could create an organic ant repellent was correct, because all the natural repellents were effective, with catnip being the most effective. However, the chemical pesticide was the most effective of all.

Is horse manure a possible energy source in a crisis?

Pioneers used organic waste for fuel. Why can't modern men and women? Garrett Rueda decided to see how effective an energy source organic waste would be.

Hypothesis

I believe that horse manure can be a possible energy source in an emergency, because I know that the pioneers used different types of animal waste for fuel.

Independent variables

Type of fuel used

Dependent variables

Average temperature of heated water

Controls

- Amount of water heated
- Fire pit and fire starter used

Experimental groups

- Avocado wood
- Buffalo chips
- Horse manure
- Charcoal

Materials

- Home-built fire pit (instructions documented in student's project notebook)
- Horse manure
- Buffalo chips
- Avocado wood
- Charcoal
- Fire starter

Procedures

1. Make fire pit.

2. Line up two bricks in the fire pit, leaving a space large enough for the soup can.

3. Fill soup can with 112 grams of water, and place between the bricks in fire pit

4. **Light fuel with fire starter.**

5. **Check temperature of water.**

Results

The average peak temperature of the water samples was as follows:

✔ Charcoal: 66° C

✔ Buffalo chips: 61° C

✔ Horse manure: 48° C

✔ Avocado wood: 43° C

Figure 17-7 shows a graph of the average peak temperature of the four samples.

Conclusions

My hypothesis was that horse manure would be an effective alternate energy source in an emergency. My hypothesis was correct. Even though the horse manure didn't create the most energy, it can be used in an emergency.

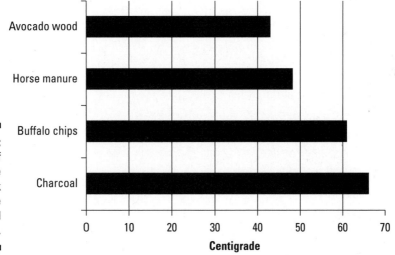

Average Peak Temperature of Four Fuel Sources

Figure 17-7:
Graph of average peak temperature of four fuel sources.

Physics

Physics is the study of light, sound, and motion. But it's not just light years, sound waves, and supersonic travel — it's electricity, golf, cosmetics, and e-ticket rides, as the next four projects demonstrate.

Temperature's effect on rebound of a golf ball

Temperature can have a great effect on the properties of different objects. Can it change the rebound of golf balls? Kelly Buckingham boiled and froze some golf balls to find out.

Hypothesis

I believe that the temperature of a golf ball will affect the amount of its rebound.

Independent variables

Temperature of golf balls

Dependent variables

Amount of rebound

Controls

- ✔ Type of golf ball used
- ✔ Height from which ball is dropped

Experimental groups

- ✔ Boiled golf balls
- ✔ Frozen golf balls

Control groups

Golf balls at normal temperature

Materials

42 golf balls

Procedures

1. Divide golf balls into three equal groups of 14 balls each.

2. Freeze one group of golf balls.

3. Drop each frozen golf ball from 7 feet and record its rebound.

4. Boil one group of golf balls.

5. Drop each boiled golf ball from 7 feet and record rebound.

6. Leave the last group of golf balls at normal temperature.

7. Drop each unchanged golf ball from 7 feet and record rebound.

Results

The recorded rebound of the golf balls, from highest to lowest is:

> Normal temperature
>
> Boiled
>
> Frozen

Conclusions

My hypothesis was that temperature would affect the rebound of golf balls. My results proved that the hypothesis was true. Both boiling and freezing reduced the amount of rebound in the golf balls. The golf balls had the greatest rebound at normal temperature.

Does my makeup look right?

Though many people may not think so, physics projects can also relate to common, everyday situations in the lives of teenagers. Case in point, Paula Besa used her project to examine how lighting can make makeup look right.

Hypothesis

I believe that colors under a warm light bulb most closely resemble colors under true sunlight. I also believe 40-watt light bulbs, used in my bathroom, distort the colors farthest from their appearance in sunlight.

Independent variables

Type of light bulb used

Dependent variables

Color observed under different light

Controls

- ✔ Color box (described in the Materials section)
- ✔ Photograph

Materials

- ✔ Sunlight
- ✔ A big piece of cardboard with color stripes on one side and picture of a lady wearing makeup on the other side
- ✔ *Color box,* a cardboard box, lined with colored cloth.

  When a light is shined in the box, the reflected light, which bounces off the surface of the cloth, determines the colors that you see.
- ✔ Warm light bulb
- ✔ Cool light bulb
- ✔ 40-watt light bulb
- ✔ SPX35 light bulb
- ✔ SPX41 light bulb
- ✔ SP35 light bulb
- ✔ SP41 light bulb
- ✔ Incandescent light bulb

Procedures

For each light source, do the following:

1. **Take the cardboard outside and observe what the color stripes and makeup look like under the sun.**

2. **Record your observations.**

3. **Indoors, test each type of light bulb using the color box.**

4. **Observe the color stripes and write down your observations.**

Results

The results for each light source are as follows:

Sunlight

The red stripe was pink.

The orange stripe was orange-yellow.

The yellow stripe was yellow.

The green stripe was yellow-green.

The blue stripe was blue.

The purple stripe was purple.

The lipstick was pink.

The blush was red-orange.

The eye shadow was green-black.

Warm white light bulb

The red stripe was dark red.

The orange stripe was yellow-orange.

The yellow stripe was bright yellow.

The green stripe was dark green.

The blue was dark blue.

The purple was dark purple.

The lipstick was reddish pink.

The blush was light brown.

The eye shadow was dark green.

SP41 light bulb

The red stripe was pinkish red.

The orange stripe was dark orange.

The yellow stripe was yellow.

The green stripe was green.

The blue stripe was blue.

The purple stripe was dark purple.

The lipstick was pink.

The blush was dark red.

The eye shadow was dark green.

SP35 light bulb

The red stripe was pink.

The orange stripe was bright orange.

The yellow stripe was bright yellow.

The green stripe was green.

The blue stripe was blue.

The purple stripe was dark purple.

The lipstick was red.

The blush was pink.

The eye shadow was dark green.

Incandescent light bulb

The red stripe was pink.

The orange stripe was yellow-orange.

The yellow stripe was yellow.

The green stripe was green.

The blue stripe was green-blue.

The purple stripe was purple.

The lipstick was pink.

The blush was red-orange.

The eye shadow was brown.

Cool white light bulb

The red stripe was dark red.

The orange stripe was yellow-orange.

The yellow stripe was green-yellow.

The green stripe was green.

The blue stripe was blue-green.

The purple stripe was purple.

The lipstick was red.

The blush was orange.

The eye shadow was blue.

SPX41 light bulb

The red stripe was pink.

The orange stripe was dark orange.

The yellow stripe was yellow-green.

The green stripe was green.

The blue stripe was blue-green.

The purple stripe was purple.

The lipstick was red.

The blush was pink.

The eye shadow was gray.

40-watt light bulb

The red stripe was dark pink.

The orange stripe was yellow-orange.

The yellow stripe was yellow-green.

The green stripe was light green.

The blue stripe was blue-green.

The purple stripe was purple.

The lipstick was orange.

The blush was pink.

The eye shadow was gray, almost black.

Conclusions

My hypothesis was that the warm light bulb would show colors and makeup closest to sunlight, and that the 40-watt light bulb was the farthest from natural sunlight. The hypothesis was partially correct because the closest to natural was the SPX30 light bulb, but the 40-watt light bulb was the farthest from sunlight. Therefore, the best bulb to use for putting on makeup is the SPX30 light bulb.

My recommendations for future experiments include measuring the *footcandles* (the light on a surface, equal to one lumen per square foot) and *lumens* (the amount of light given out through a solid angle) of each light bulb. Another improvement would be using more types of bulbs, and observing the difference in sunlight at different times of day.

How slow can you go until centrifugal force has no effect?

Did you ever go on one of those rides where you spun around so fast that you seemed to stick to the wall? That's *centrifugal force* making you feel like that, and Alexis Alvarez wanted to know the minimum speed you need to cause centrifugal force to occur.

Alexis's project display is shown in Figure 17-8.

Hypothesis

I believe that the force created by rotation must be greater than the force of gravity for centrifugal force to occur.

Dependent variables

For each trial, the number of seconds until the water spills

Controls

Amount of water in each bucket before performing each trial

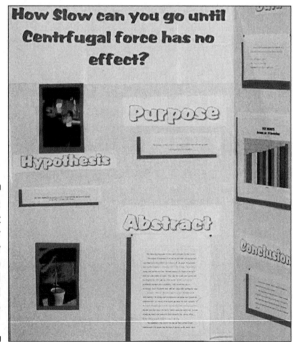

Figure 17-8:
Project display for "How slow can you go until centrifugal force has no effect?"

Materials

- ✔ Bucket
- ✔ Measuring tape
- ✔ 1 liter of water
- ✔ Spring scale
- ✔ Stopwatch
- ✔ 40 cm rope

Procedures

1. **Fill bucket with 1 liter of water.**
2. **Attach rope to bucket.**
3. **Spin bucket until water spills.**
4. **Repeat for 15 trials.**

Results

Table 17-2 displays the number of seconds until centrifugal force has no effect.

Table 17-2	Time Until Centrifugal Force Has No Effect
Test	*Number of Seconds*
1	11.25
2	11.55
3	11.68
4	12.44
5	14.84
6	15.65
7	11.96
8	12.25
9	12.74
10	13.11
11	13.54
12	13.73

(continued)

Table 17-2 *(continued)*	
Test	**Number of Seconds**
13	14.05
14	14.29
15	15.10

Conclusions

My hypothesis that centrifugal force increases at higher rotational speed was correct.

I'll have the volts, please — oh, and hold the resistance

Electricity must move through a conductor in order to be harnessed. Frank Barrack was curious about how to use temperature to change the resistance (or block) a conductor. In his project, Frank used string as a conductor and tested the resistance at different temperatures.

Hypothesis

I believe that freezing a conductor will lower its resistance.

Independent variables

Temperature of the conductor

Dependent variables

Number of ohms of resistance

Controls

Test setup of each experimental or control group

Experimental groups

- String soaked in water (group A)
- String soaked in water and frozen (group B)

Control groups

Dry string at room temperature

Materials

- ✔ 20 cm of string
- ✔ Wood
- ✔ 12 hooks
- ✔ 12 screws
- ✔ Cookie sheet
- ✔ Metric ruler
- ✔ *Ohmmeter,* an instrument that measures the resistance of a conductor

Procedures

1. **Prepare the experiment as follows:**

   a. Cut a piece of wood 23 cm long.

   b. Screw 12 hooks into wood, 2½ cm apart and 4 cm across.

   c. Tightly tie piece of string between each pair of hooks.

2. **Test the control group (dry string at room temperature) as follows:**

   a. Set up ohmmeter.

   b. Touch the electrodes on the ohmmeter to each string and record data in logbook.

3. **Test group A (string soaked in water) as follows:**

   a. Pour water onto the cookie sheet and soak block with string by turning the block upside down in water for 5 minutes.

   b. Follow procedure in Step 2.

4. **Test group B (string soaked in water and frozen) as follows:**

   a. Soak string as described in Step 3a.

   b. Place the wood block in the freezer for 1½ hours.

   c. Follow procedure in Step 2.

5. **Repeat Steps 2 through 4 two more times.**

Results

Table 17-3 shows how the changes in temperature changed the resistance of the string.

Table 17-3   Test Results of Conductor at Different Temperatures (Measured in Ohms of Resistance)

	Test 1	Test 2	Test 3	Average
Room temperature	2,000,000+	1,200,000-2,000,000+	1,200,000-2,000,000+	1,988,888
Soaked string	150,000-310,000	380,000-2,000,000	180,000-1,030,000	969,666
Frozen string	1,400,000-2,000,000	620,000-1,900,000	620,000-1,900,000	1,626,111

Conclusions

My hypothesis that freezing the conductor would result in the lowest resistance was incorrect, because the soaked string resulted in the lowest resistance.

Project Potpourri

The next five projects take a look at a few different categories, including behavioral and social science, botany, computer science, product testing, and zoology.

The even-handed teacher

Are teachers fair? Who knows? Are they even-handed?

That can be tested, and Lea Cohen did just that, as shown in her project display in Figure 17-9.

Hypothesis

I believe that a right-handed teacher pays more attention to the left side of the room, so that he or she can pay attention to the class while writing on the board.

Independent variables

Left- and right-handed teachers

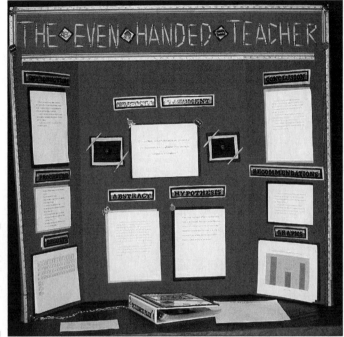

Figure 17-9:
Project
display for
"The even-
handed
teacher."

Dependent variables

Classroom location of students called on

Experimental groups

Fourteen classrooms, between fourth and eighth grades

Procedures

Visit 14 classrooms 4 times, for 10 minutes each and observe the following:

- ✔ Whether the teacher is left- or right-handed
- ✔ The arrangement of the classroom (in rows, in a semi-circle, and so on)
- ✔ The location and frequency of the students called on

Results

On average, the right-handed teachers called on students as follows:

On left side of room: 3.17 times

In center of room: 1.69 times

On right side of room: 2.88 times

Note: Only one left-handed teacher was in the sample.

Conclusions

My hypothesis was that a right-handed teacher would pay attention to the left side of the room, so that he or she can pay attention to the class while writing on the board. The results proved that my hypothesis was correct.

A possible improvement in my project would be to include more left-handed teachers in the test.

Arundo Donax: Cockroach of the plant kingdom

Cockroaches are some of the oldest life forms, and they reproduce like crazy! Their equivalent in the plant world is called *Arundo Donax* (a common weed). Most gardeners want to get rid of the pesky weed, and Kristine Creveling wanted to find out if there's a nontoxic way to do just that.

Her project display is shown in Figure 17-10.

Hypothesis

I believe that the manual removal method will work better than chemical weed removers when trying to eradicate the weed, Arundo Donax.

Independent variables

Weed removal method used

Dependent variables

Number of plants left alive

Experimental groups

- Chemical weed killer
- Manual weed removal

Materials

- 50 Arundo Donax plants
- Concentrated chemical weed killer

Figure 17-10:
Project
display for
"Arundo
Donax: The
cockroach
of the plant
kingdom."

Procedures

1. Locate and pull up 50 Arundo Donax plants of the same size.

2. Divide the plants into two groups of 25 each.

3. Manually extract the plants in one group.

4. To the second group, apply chemical weed killer, and wait two weeks.

5. Count and record the number of plants in each group that are still alive.

Results

There were more Arundo Donax plants left alive in the group that was manually removed.

Conclusions

My hypothesis was that the manual removal method works better than chemical weed removers when trying to eradicate the weed, Arundo Donax. The experiment proved my hypothesis to be incorrect, because the chemical weed killer removed more plants. However, I feel that the manual method can work better if the manual removal was thorough and ensured that all roots were removed.

Which upgrade is best for your computer?

Memory or megahertz — which gives you the most bang for your buck? Sean Locko tested different computer upgrades to find out which is best.

Note: Sean's project is unique — it's a computer science project that looks a lot like an experiment, because it uses variables and controls.

Hypothesis

I believe that adding a faster CPU results in more improved system performance than adding more memory.

Independent variables

- ✔ Memory chips
- ✔ Processors

Dependent variables

- ✔ Processing speed
- ✔ Software load time

Controls

- ✔ Computer system
- ✔ Computer game
- ✔ Benchmarking software, which compares performance to specified standards

Materials

- ✔ One computer
- ✔ Three memory chips:
  - 32MB (megabytes)
  - 64MB
  - 96MB
- ✔ Two AMD K6-2 processors:
  - 350 MHz (megahertz) — A *megahertz* represents how many million cycles the computer processes per second.
  - 550 MHz
- ✔ Benchmarking software

Procedures

1. **Modify computer as follows:**

    a. Replace current processor with 350 MHz processor and put on proper jumper settings.

    b. Replace current processor with 550 MHz processor and put on proper jumper settings.

    c. Replace memory chip with 32MB chip.

    d. Replace memory chip with 64MB chip.

    e. Replace memory chip with 96MB chip.

    f. Combine the 96MB and the 32MB chips to equal memory size of 128MB.

2. **For each modification, perform the following test:**

    a. Record how long it takes to load computer game.

    b. Run benchmark software to determine processing time.

    c. Restore computer to original configuration before running next test.

Results

My results show that the computer performed better by installing a higher MHz CPU, rather than by adding more memory. The tests measured the computer's speed and time to load programs. The results showed the computer actually slowed down and took longer to load with additional memory added.

Conclusions

My hypothesis that adding a higher MHz CPU would create a faster computer than adding more memory was correct.

If you can't (or don't want to) buy a new computer, the best way to improve performance is to install a faster CPU, rather than increase the amount of memory.

Antibacterial hand sanitizers: Hype or help?

Lately, it seems that people have become more conscious of cleanliness. And in response, many soaps and cleansers claim to be antibacterial. Is it true?

Steven Paletz wondered whether ethanol is the only effective waterless antibacterial agent and decided to check it out.

His project display is shown in Figure 17-11.

Hypothesis

I believe that waterless hand sanitizers and generic ethanol are equally effective in killing bacteria. I also believe that AloeGuard, which contains chloroxylenol, will be just as effective as ethanol products, because it is used in hospitals.

Independent variables

Antibacterial cleaners

Dependent variables

Number of bacteria colonies

Figure 17-11:
Project
display for
"Anti-
bacterial
hand
sanitizers:
Hype or
help?"

Controls

- Bacteria tested
- Incubation type and period
- Measurement methods

Experimental groups

- Purell
- AloeGuard
- Alcare Plus
- Bath & Body Works antibacterial hand sanitizer
- 62 percent solution of ethyl alcohol
- 6.2 percent solution of ethyl alcohol

Control groups

No cleaner used

Materials

- One 8 oz. bottle of Purell waterless hand sanitizer with aloe
- One 8 oz. bottle of Bath & Body Works waterless hand sanitizer
- One 9 oz. can of Alcare Plus waterless hand wash foam
- One 4 oz. bottle of AloeGuard waterless hand cleansing lotion
- 40 petri dishes with nutrient *agar* (a seaweed product used as a medium for growing cultures)
- Ethyl alcohol
- Rotating plate
- Bunsen burner
- Glass rod
- XL1 blue strain of E. coli bacteria
- 40 test tubes
- Eyedropper
- Vortex
- Incubator
- Gloves

✔ Distilled water

✔ Tape

✔ Pipette

Procedures

1. **Put on gloves and other protection.**

2. **Dilute the different hand sanitizers in the bacteria (using the testing tube) as follows:**

   a. For the 1:1 dilution, 100 ml of bacteria to 100 ml of the cleanser

   b. For the 2:1 dilution, 50 ml of bacteria to 100 ml of the cleanser

3. **Shake the tubes that contain bacteria and hand sanitizers and let them sit for 15 minutes.**

4. **Place 50 ml of each dilution onto a petri dish.**

5. **Place the bacteria in the incubator for 24 hours at 37° Celsius.**

6. **After incubation period, count the bacteria colonies and record the results.**

7. **Seal the petri dishes with tape and dispose of them properly.**

8. **Repeat for trials 2 and 3.**

Results

Table 17-4 shows the number of colonies remaining after 24 hours, for both the 1:1 and the 2:1 concentration of each antibacterial.

Table 17-4		Bacteria Remaining after Application of Test Substances for Each Trial					
Trial	*Purell*	*AloeGuard*	*Alcare Plus*	*Bath & Body Works*	*6.2% Ethyl Alcohol*	*Control*	*62% Ethyl Alcohol*
Trial 1 1:1	>1,000	0	>1,000	>1,000	>1,000	>1,000	0
Trial 1 2:1	250	0	250	340	355	360	0
Trial 2 1:1	>1,000	0	>1,000	>1,000	>1,000	>1,000	1
Trial 2 2:1	460	0	240	300	250	380	0
Trial 3 1:1	>1,000	0	>1,000	>1,000	>1,000	>1,000	0
Trial 3 2:1	400	0	255	370	490	240	0

Table 17-5 shows the average number of colonies, for both the 1:1 and the 2:1 concentrations of each antibacterial.

Table 17-5	Average Amount of Bacteria Remaining for Each Concentration						
	Purell	*AloeGuard*	*Alcare Plus*	*Bath & Body Works*	*6.2% Ethyl Alcohol*	*Control*	*62% Ethyl Alcohol*
1:1	>1000	0	>1,000	>1,000	>1,000	>1,000	0.33
2:1	370	0	248	337	365	327	0.00

Figure 17-12 shows the average amount of bacteria remaining as a 3-D graph.

Conclusions

My hypothesis that waterless hand sanitizers, generic ethanol, and AloeGuard are equally effective at killing bacteria wasn't correct. Testing showed that the antibacterial hand sanitizers didn't live up to their claims. However, the chloroxylenol found in AloeGuard, was very effective, killing 100 percent of the bacteria colonies tested after 24 hours.

Also, it appears that when products are diluted with perfumes, lotions, and other additives, they become less effective.

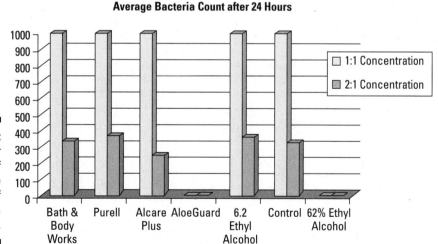

Average Bacteria Count after 24 Hours

Figure 17-12: 3-D bar graph of average amount of bacteria remaining.

Effects of an electromagnetic field on mealworms

People are exposed to electromagnetic fields daily, when they walk through metal detectors, stand under power lines, ring an electric doorbell, or use computers.

Although the effects of electromagnetism on organic material aren't yet completely known, some studies suggest an association between exposure and cancer. With his project, Robert Knight tested the effects of an electromagnetic field on 100 mealworms.

His display is shown in Figure 17-13.

Hypothesis

I believe that mealworms exposed to an electromagnetic field will develop faster than those that are not exposed to electromagnetism.

Independent variables

Electromagnetic field

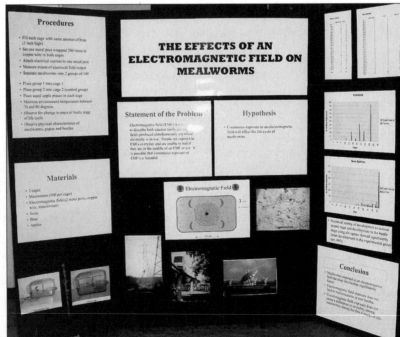

Figure 17-13: Project display for "The effects of an electromagnetic field on mealworms."

Dependent variables

Rate of change through developmental stages

Controls

✔ Types of mealworms used

✔ Conditions in cages, including food given to each group

Experimental groups

One hundred mealworms are continuously exposed to an electromagnetic field using copper wire coiled around a steel pole and attached to a transformer

Control groups

One hundred mealworms exposed to all the same conditions but with no electric current attached to the copper wire

Materials

✔ Two cages

✔ Mealworms (100 per cage)

✔ Electromagnetic field (two metal posts, copper wire, transformer)

✔ Electronic scale

✔ Bran

✔ Apples

Procedures

1. **Fill each cage with same amount of bran (1 inch high) and add pieces of apple.**

2. **Set one metal post wrapped 200 times in copper wire in both cages.**

3. **Attach electrical current to one metal post.**

4. **Measure extent of electrical field output.**

5. **Separate mealworms into 2 groups of 100, and place each group into labeled cage (groups 1 and 2).**

6. **Maintain environment temperature between 70 and 80 degrees.**

7. **Observe for change to cocoon and beetles.**

Results

Table 17-6 shows my observed mealworm development in the experimental and control groups.

Table 17-6	Observed Weekly Development of Mealworms			
	Pupa		Beetles	
Week	Experimental	Control	Experimental	Control
1	1	0	0	0
2	6	0	0	0
3	27	12	11	0
4	60	51	20	14
5	0	20	50	61

The results obtained showed significantly faster development to pupa and beetle stages in the experimental group. There were no differences in the physical characteristics and no difference in mortality up to the first month of life.

Conclusions

My hypothesis was that mealworms exposed to an electromagnetic field would develop into beetles significantly faster. My results proved that my hypothesis was correct.

An improvement to this project would be to repeat testing with additional groups of mealworms to validate the results of this experiment.

Chapter 18

Taking the Challenge

· ·

In This Chapter

▶ Working with wings (and more): Engineering projects

▶ Saving the planet: Environmental science projects

▶ Seeing the unseen: Microbiology projects

▶ Understanding matter and energy: Physics projects

▶ Bringing up the rear: Math, medicine, and more projects

· ·

*I*f you've had some previous experience with science or science fair projects, you may want to try something that's a little more challenging.

Exactly what does "more challenging" mean? Think multiple variables or experimental groups, complex mathematical calculations, or procedures with a number of steps. But, just as with easier projects, these more challenging undertakings can be from just about any science project category. This chapter gives you sample projects, and hopefully some ideas and inspiration.

For each project, I list how the elements of the scientific method (see Chapter 8) were applied. These projects were actually displayed at the Greater San Diego Science and Engineering Fair, which means that these projects were selected as the best projects from their school science fairs.

When you think that perhaps these projects should have had a larger sample or more trials, keep in mind that students conducted these projects under severe time constraints.

Engineering

Engineering projects cover a broad spectrum of ideas. Two of the projects in this section use engineering principles to conserve resources, and the others explore ways to fly higher!

Alternative fuels

Fossil fuels are often in the news — either because there's a shortage of them or because the United States is dependent on other countries for fuel. Therefore, countries always have an interest in developing nonfossil fuels. With help from his teacher/mentor, Chris Tiu created a project that tests whether nonfossil fuels are as effective as fossil fuel.

Hypothesis

I believe that it's feasible to run a diesel engine on fuels derived from vegetable oils, with emissions, power, and economy equal to or better than that of fossil fuels.

Independent variables

Type of fuel used

Dependent variables

- Horsepower
- RPMs (rotations per minute)
- Run time
- Carbon dioxide (CO_2), carbon monoxide (CO), and hydrocarbon emissions
- Cylinder head, exhaust, and oil temperatures
- Fuel consumption

Controls

- Sample density
- Amount of fuel tested

Experimental groups

- Diesel fuel
- Vegetable oil
- Waste vegetable oil

Materials

- Diesel engine
- Diesel fuel

✔ Vegetable oil

✔ Waste vegetable oil (saved after cooking)

Procedures

1. **Process vegetable oil and waste vegetable oil into biodiesel fuels. (A science teacher helped out with this step, and the explanation is detailed in the student's project notebook.)**

2. **Measure density of all samples.**

3. **Run 50 ml of each fuel in diesel engine.**

4. **Measure and record the following:**

   a. Horsepower

   b. RPMs

   c. Run time

   d. Carbon dioxide (CO_2), carbon monoxide (CO), and hydrocarbon emissions

   e. Cylinder head, exhaust, and oil temperatures

   f. Fuel consumption

Results

The vegetable oil was the most effective nonfossil fuel. On the average, it was 29 percent more effective, with 21 percent fewer emissions, 3.7 percent less fuel consumption, and 2.8 percent higher temperature.

Conclusions

My hypothesis that it's feasible to run a diesel engine on fuels derived from vegetable oils, with comparable emissions, power, and economy was correct.

Insulation value: Straw bale versus conventional methods

In times of rising energy costs, everyone wants to find insulation that can keep a home cool in the summer and warm in the winter.

During the pioneer days of the 1800s, settlers in Nebraska used straw bale to insulate their houses — in fact, straw bale is still used today in many areas. Athena Merica wanted to know how this method compares to conventional methods.

Check out Figure 18-1 to see her project display.

Hypothesis

I believe that if I test three structures — straw bale, concrete insulated with fiberglass, and drywall over a stud frame insulated with fiberglass — the straw bale structure will provide the best insulation.

Controls

✔ Size and volume of each structure

✔ Times that temperature was recorded for each structure

Experimental groups

✔ Straw bale structure

✔ Concrete structure

✔ Drywall over stud frame structure

Figure 18-1:
Project display for "Insulation value: Straw bale versus conventional methods."

Materials

✔ Four thermometers (Celsius)

✔ Pair of working gloves

✔ Three small metal hooks

✔ Four bales of straw

✔ 16 concrete building blocks

✔ 2 x 4 studs of wood

✔ One sheet of dry wall (cut into 16 inches on center)

✔ One roll of R-13 fiberglass insulation (3 inches thick)

✔ Bale needle

✔ 5 gallons of clay slip mixture (clay and water)

✔ Scissors

✔ Two rolls of polypropylene string

✔ One small straw bale

✔ Two larger 30-inch straw bales

✔ Three whole straw bales (one for base of structure, two bales for roof)

Procedures

1. **Build three structures, one of straw bales, one of concrete insulated with fiberglass, and one of drywall over a stud frame insulated with fiberglass.** (The student who did the project included instructions on how to build each structure in the project notebook.)

2. **Hook one thermometer inside each structure, 5 inches from the top of the structure.**

3. **Place the last thermometer outside all the structures, to measure outside temperature.**

4. **Note the temperature inside and outside the structures at 7 a.m., 3 p.m., and 8 p.m.**

5. **Repeat Step 4 for 10 days.**

Results

Table 18-1 shows the average range of temperatures that each insulation type kept the structure warmer (in the mornings and evenings) or cooler (in the afternoon).

Table 18-1	Average Temperature Ranges for Each Insulation Type		
Time	Straw Bale	Concrete	Drywall/Stud Frame
7 a.m.	4–9° C	1–4° C	0–4° C
3 p.m.	4–14° C	0–4° C	0–7° C
8 p.m.	4–12° C	1–5° C	0–4° C

Conclusions

My hypothesis that straw was the best insulator was correct, because the hay structure retained the most warmth over the ten-day test. It's also excellent for keeping a building cool in the heat of the afternoon. Therefore, using straw is an excellent alternative to fiberglass insulation.

5 . . . 4 . . . 3 . . . 2 . . . liter — Blast off

If you've ever shot off a bottle rocket, you'd probably like to know how to make it go even higher. So did Daniel Stenavich, so he made it the main topic of his science project.

Figure 18-2 shows his project display.

Hypothesis

I believe that the rocket, when launched, will reach its highest altitude when 50 percent of the bottle's capacity is filled with water.

Materials

- Bottle rocket (built according to instructions included in the project notebook)
- Rocket launcher (built according to instructions included in the project notebook)
- Measuring cup
- Water
- Angle finder
- Tape measure

Figure 18-2:
Project
display for
"5 . . . 4 . . .
3 . . . 2 . . .
liter —
Blast off."

Procedures

The following procedures explain how to fill the bottle rocket, launch it using the specified amount of water pressure, and measure the angle formed by the altitude that the rocket reaches.

1. **Make bottle rocket.** (The instructions for this were explained in the Materials section of the student's project notebook.)

2. **Make bottle rocket launcher.** (The instructions for this were explained in the Materials section of the student's project notebook.)

3. **Launch an empty bottle rocket five times.** Measure the angle of height with angle finder and record the height in feet.

4. **Add 200 ml of water to the bottle rocket and launch it five times.** Measure the angle of height with angle finder and record the height in feet.

5. **Add 200 ml of water every 5 launches until the bottle rocket is at full capacity (2,000 ml).** Measure the angle of height with angle finder and record the height in feet.

Results

Table 18-2 shows the results for this project.

Table 18-2 Height (in Feet) of Bottle Rocket Launches for Each Trial						
Amounts of Water	*Trial 1*	*Trial 2*	*Trial 3*	*Trial 4*	*Trial 5*	*Average*
0 ml	21.1	29.1	29.1	26.4	26.4	26.42
100 ml	48.7	54.5	83.1	60.6	63.6	62.1
200 ml	105	90.1	83.1	113	90.1	96.26
300 ml	97.4	117.1	105	117.1	105	108.32
400 ml	101.1	93.7	83.1	86.6	93.7	91.64
500 ml	93.7	105	86.6	90.1	83.1	91.7
600 ml	105	121.4	101.1	113	108.9	109.88
700 ml	121.4	105	113	113	108.9	112.26
800 ml	144.8	121.4	113	121.4	108.9	121.9
900 ml	125.8	103.3	105	125.8	121.4	116.26
1,000 ml	121.4	121.4	121.4	125.8	125.8	123.16
1,100 ml	113	105	113	113	101.1	109.02
1,150 ml	117.1	117.1	121.4	113	125.8	118.88
1,200 ml	144.8	130.3	125.8	121.4	117.1	127.88
1,250 ml	125.8	125.8	130.3	135	125.8	128.54
1,300 ml	113	97.4	101.1	93.7	121.4	105.32
1,400 ml	86.6	108.9	69.9	66.7	101.1	86.64
1,500 ml	45.8	48.7	51.6	45.8	48.7	48.12
1,600 ml	37.3	26.4	66.7	43	18.4	38.36
1,700 ml	21	18.4	23.7	13.1	18.4	18.92
1,800 ml	7.8	10.4	5.2	7.8	13.1	8.86
1,900 ml	2.6	5.2	2.6	5.2	5.2	4.16
2,000 ml	0	2.6	0	0	2.6	1.04
Average	82.6	80.8	79.8	80.5	79.8	80.7

Conclusions

In most of the launches, the rocket reached the highest altitude when filled with 1200–1250 ml of water. That's just more than half full.

In conclusion, the hypothesis of filling the bottle with 50 percent water was incorrect. The rocket reached the highest altitude when it was 60 percent full.

Shape versus lift and drag

Why are there so many different wing shapes? John Hawkins thought that the shape would affect the amount of lift, so he decided to test his theory.

Hypothesis

I believe that the wing with the most curvature will produce the greatest lift.

Independent variables

Wing angle of attack (0°, 5°, 10°, 15°, 20°)

Controls

- ✔ Wood used for wings
- ✔ Wind tunnel

Experimental groups

Five wing shapes, as follows:

- ✔ A: Square
- ✔ B: Equilateral triangle (least curvature)
- ✔ C: Right triangle
- ✔ D: Square with rounded corner
- ✔ E: Square with rounded corners but with greater curve than D

Materials

- ✔ Wood
- ✔ Home-built wind tunnel (Plans for this wind tunnel were included in the project notebook and on the project display.)

Procedures

1. **Build wind tunnel.**
2. **Cut five wings of different shapes.**

3. For each wing, test at each angle of attack (0°, 5°, 10°, 15°, 20°):

    a. Mount wing inside wind tunnel at specified angle of attack.

    b. Energize the wind tunnel.

    c. Record the measured force in *Newtons*. According to Tufts University Center for Engineering Educational Outreach, a Newton is a basic unit of force, and is the metric equivalent of a pound (for example, 1 Newton = .224 lbs.).

    d. Calculate *lift* (the force that makes an object rise) and *drag* (a force that slows motion through the air).

Results

Table 18-3 shows the average lift, in Newtons, compared to the angle of attack.

Table 18-3	Average Lift Versus Angle of Attack				
Angle of Attack	*0°*	*5°*	*10°*	*15°*	*20°*
Wing A	0.025	0.188	0.225	0.28	0.355
Wing B	0	0.02	0.05	0.11	0.19
Wing C	0	0.0275	0.05	0.0938	0.12
Wing D	0.01875	0.125	0.2	0.295	0.386
Wing E	0	0.0875	0.195	0.24	0.3

Figure 18-3 shows a line graph with the average lift of the five wing samples.

Table 18-4 shows the average drag, in Newtons, compared to the angle of attack.

Table 18-4	Average Drag Versus Angle of Attack				
Angle of Attack	*0°*	*5°*	*10°*	*15°*	*20°*
Wing A	0	0.005	0.035	0.075	0.13
Wing B	0	0.002	0.01	0.0325	0.07
Wing C	0	0.002	0.01	0.0275	0.04
Wing D	0	0.01	0.035	0.08	0.14
Wing E	0	0.01	0.035	0.06	0.1075

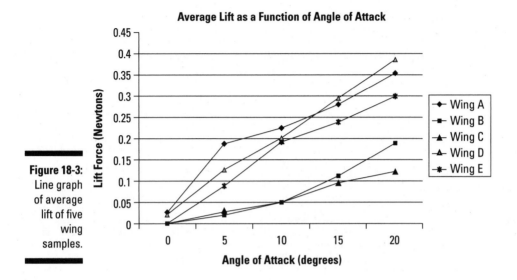

Figure 18-3:
Line graph
of average
lift of five
wing
samples.

Figure 18-4 shows a line graph with the average drag of the five wing samples.

Conclusions

My hypothesis that the wing with the most curvature would produce the greatest lift was partially correct. Wing E had the greatest curve, but wing D had more lift, possibly because it was lighter than wing E.

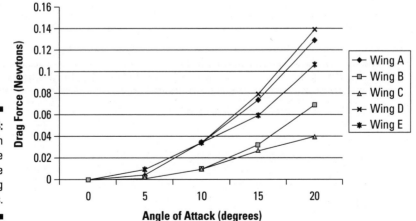

Figure 18-4:
Line graph
of average
drag of five
wing
samples.

Environmental Sciences

Environmental issues are among the most popular science fair project ideas. In fact, environmental concerns show up in almost all project categories. But the "third rock from the sun" actually has a category all its own — environmental sciences, with projects dealing with the purity of our natural resources.

Estimating future NO_2 concentrations

NO_2 (nitrogen dioxide) is one of the common components of automobile exhaust, which in high concentrations, can be a potential health hazard. Because a new freeway is being built immediately adjacent to Mt. Miguel High School (MMHS), Nicole Francisco decided to do a project to estimate the future NO_2 levels at MMHS to see if they would be safe.

Hypothesis

I believe that by collecting and testing air samples at freeway locations similar to the distance between MMHS and the new freeway, I can estimate the NO_2 levels when the freeway is completed.

Dependent variables

- ✔ Percentage of transmittance
- ✔ Absorbance
- ✔ Concentration in mol/L(molecules per liter)
- ✔ Concentration in ppb (parts per billion)

Controls

Sampling and testing equipment

Experimental groups

Six samples taken at four different freeways

Materials

- ✔ Sampler tubes 71 mm (length) x 11 mm (diameter)
- ✔ Stainless steel meshes

> ✔ *Spectrophotometer,* an instrument that measures the intensity of wavelengths in a spectrum of light
>
> ✔ TEA (a chemical compound that absorbs NO_2)

Procedures

Test NO_2 at four freeway sites as follows:

1. **Prepare passive diffusion sampler tubes by placing two stainless steel meshes in one cap at the closed end.**

2. **Coat tubes with TEA, which will absorb NO_2 during the exposure period.**

3. **Place samples at freeway locations at distances from the freeway similar to MMHS and the new freeway under construction.**

4. **Expose samples for three days.**

5. **Apply color development solutions to sampler tubes.**

6. **Analyze results of color development solutions with a spectrophotometer at 540 normal magnification.**

7. **Use nitrite standards to create a standard curve.**

Results

Results showed that the concentrations were just below the World Health Organization's issued guidelines for human exposure to NO_2 (1987). Results were calculated as shown:

> ✔ Absorbance = -log (percent transmittance/100)
>
> ✔ Concentration NO_2(mol/L) = in sample collected
>
> ✔ ppb = concentration in air sampled

Table 18-5 shows the results from January 18 through January 21. The asterisk (*) denotes concentrations below detectable levels.

Table 18-5	**NO_2 Levels from Six Samples, January 18–21**			
Sample	*% Transmittance*	*Absorbance*	*Concentration (mol/L)*	*Concentration (ppb)*
1	90.5	0.043	-0.0098	*
2	88.2	0.055	0.00	*

(continued)

Table 18-5 *(continued)*

Sample	% Transmittance	Absorbance	Concentration (mol/L)	Concentration (ppb)
3	87.1	0.060	0.0030	6.4
4	89.0	0.051	-0.0038	*
5	85.0	0.071	0.011	23
6	86.2	0.064	0.0061	13
Average	87.7	0.057	0.0011	7.1

Table 18-6 shows the results from January 21 through January 24. Again, the asterisk denotes concentrations below detectable levels.

Table 18-6   NO$_2$ Levels from Six Samples, January 21–24

Sample (mol/L)	% Transmittance Concentration (ppb)	Absorbance	Concentration	
1	88.9	0.051	-0.0038	*
2	87.9	0.056	0.00	*
3	89.0	0.051	-0.0038	*
4	88.9	0.051	-0.0038	*
5	89.0	0.051	-0.0038	*
6	89.0	0.051	-0.0038	*
Average	88.8	0.053	-0.0025	*

Conclusions

My hypothesis was that I could simulate the conditions that will occur when a new freeway is built near Mt. Miguel High School, and this hypothesis was correct. I was able to estimate NO$_2$ levels when the freeway is completed.

Because the estimated levels were just below published guidelines, there's reason to carefully monitor nitrogen dioxide concentrations after freeway construction is complete. Warmer weather and greater traffic concentration increase NO$_2$ concentrations. Surrounding vegetation could also affect NO$_2$ concentrations.

Regular long-term exposure to these levels may cause preventable respiratory problems in the future. When trying to solve traffic congestion by putting a freeway where people spend a lot of time, possible health hazards should be considered.

Does temperature affect oil spill cleanup

Because oil spills are a constant environmental concern, environmentalists are always looking for effective ways to clean up the pollution. You can find several good products on the market, but does water temperature affect how they work? Rebecca Marcus wanted to know.

Check out her display in Figure 18-5.

Hypothesis

I believe that of five absorbents tested, Enviro-Bond 403 will work better than other substances in absorbing oil at 21° C (70° F) and 6.6° C (44° F).

Figure 18-5: Project display for "Does temperature affect oil spill cleanup?"

Absorbents such as Sea Sweep and Spill Magic will work better at warmer temperatures, and absorbents such as peat moss and sawdust will work better at colder temperatures.

Independent variables

- ✔ Temperature of water
- ✔ Oil cleanup substance used

Dependent variables

Amount of oil and water absorbed by each absorbent at both temperatures.

Controls

- ✔ Amount of water and oil used for each test
- ✔ Time allowed for each test

Experimental groups

- ✔ At 70° F and 44° F:

    - Enviro-Bond 403

    - Sea Sweep

    - Sawdust

    - Spill Magic

    - Peat moss

Materials

- ✔ Enviro-Bond 403 polymer (a natural or synthetic compound of high molecular weight)
- ✔ Sea Sweep
- ✔ Sawdust
- ✔ Spill Magic
- ✔ Peat moss
- ✔ 250 ml and 50 ml beakers (2 each)
- ✔ One gallon crude oil or Marvel Mystery oil
- ✔ Bowl or tub of water
- ✔ Mixing and measuring bowls, spoons
- ✔ Thermometer

✔ Scale

✔ Timer

✔ Disposal containers

✔ Clean-up materials

Procedures

1. **Prepare water at the proper temperatures (70° F and 44° F) for absorption tests with each absorbent.**

2. **For each absorbent at each temperature, do the following:**

    a. Pour 200 ml water into glass bowl.

    b. Pour 50 ml oil into small beaker.

    c. Add oil to glass bowl with water.

    d. Add 50 ml absorbent and wait 10 minutes.

    e. Strain contents of glass bowl into clean beaker.

    f. Wait 10 minutes for oil and water to settle, and let strainer drip into beaker.

    g. Tape the side of the beaker and mark the levels of oil and water to determine amount of oil remaining.

3. **Clean beakers and bowl between each test.**

Results

Table 18-7 shows the results for volumes of 50 milliliters at 21° C (70° F).

Table 18-7	Absorption Levels of Five Substances at 21° C		
Absorbent	**Weight (in grams)**	**Oil Absorption (in milliliters)**	**Water Absorption**
Sea Sweep	10	10	0
Enviro-Bond 403	12	25	0
Spill Magic	8	10	25
Sawdust	5	10	25
Peat Moss	7	18	6

Table 18-8 shows the results for volumes of 50 milliliters at 6.6° C (44° F).

Table 18-8	Absorption Levels of Five Substances at 6.6° C		
Absorbent	**Weight (in grams)**	**Oil Absorption (in milliliters)**	**Water Absorption**
Sea Sweep	10	25	0
Enviro-Bond 403	12	35	0
Spill Magic	8	0	19
Sawdust	6	10	6
Peat Moss	8	20	10

Conclusions

My hypothesis was correct because the Enviro-Bond 403 worked better than the Sea Sweep, sawdust, Spill Magic or peat moss at both temperatures.

Testing San Diego's water for purity and safety

More and more people are drinking bottled water instead of water from local lakes and reservoirs. Guatam Wilkins wanted to know if people received any benefits from drinking bottled water, so he compared lake water to bottled water.

Hypothesis

I believe that the water from San Diego lakes is as pure as bottled water, in terms of pH level, nitrates, turbidity (amount of sediment suspended in the water), total-dissolved solids, phosphates, dissolved oxygen, and biochemical oxygen demand.

Independent variables

Water source

Dependent variables

- ✔ pH level
- ✔ Nitrates
- ✔ Turbidity

✔ Total dissolved solids

✔ Phosphates

✔ Dissolved oxygen

✔ Biochemical oxygen demand

Controls

Testing methods used on each sample

Experimental groups

✔ Water sample from Lake Jennings

✔ Water sample from Lake Murray

✔ Bottled water sample

Materials

The following materials were obtained from water testing kits:

✔ Demineralizer bottle, which is used to remove mineral salts from a liquid

✔ Eyedropper with a .5 ml mark

✔ Graduated cylinder that can hold 50 ml

✔ Two graduated cylinders with black dots on the bottom of the cylinders

✔ Standard turbidity reagent (a substance used to produce, measure, or detect a chemical reaction)

✔ TDS electronic tester

✔ Two glass vials that have a 5-ml line marked on them

✔ Wide range indicator

✔ Color slides

✔ Nitra Ver 5 (brand name) reagent

✔ Four glass vials with a 5-ml line marked on them

✔ pH neutralizer

✔ One water-sampling bottle (for dissolved oxygen)

✔ One titration bottle (*Titration* is a process of adding a reagent to a substance until a change in the substance is detected.)

✔ Starch indicator solution

✔ Alkaline potassium iodide azide (a reagent)

- Sulfuric acid
- Manganous sulfate solution
- Sodium thiosulfate
- Titrator
- Phos Ver 3, an acid
- Color wheels

Procedures

For each water sample, do the following:

1. Determine pH using the following steps:

   a. Fill one test tube to the 5-ml mark.

   b. Add ten drops of the wide range indicator to the test tube.

   c. Cap the tube and shake solution gently until the color is the same.

   d. While looking at a light source, match the color in the test tube to the color in the color slide.

2. Determine dissolved oxygen using the following steps:

   a. Fill dissolved oxygen water sampling bottle to overflowing.

   b. Cap the bottle to remove a small bit of water to leave room for chemicals.

   c. Add eight drops of manganous sulfate and eight drops of alkaline potassium iodide azide.

   d. Cap bottle and gently mix for about 30 seconds; let bottle sit for a few minutes.

   e. Add eight drops of sulfuric acid.

   f. Gently mix bottle by inverting until precipitate is gone.

   g. Fill the titration tube to the 20-ml line with the sample.

   h. Add eight drops of the starch indicator.

   i. Cap the titration tube and swirl gently.

   j. Fill the titrator to the "0" mark with sodium thiosulfate.

   k. Add the thiosulfate to the solution until it's clear.

   l. Note the location of the marker, which shows the dissolved oxygen level.

   m. Add 20 drops of the pH neutralizer before disposing.

3. **Determine biochemical oxygen demand using the following steps:**

    a. Fill two dissolved oxygen samples.

    b. Perform the dissolved oxygen test on one bottle and leave the other one in darkness at $20°$ C for five days.

    c. After five days, conduct the dissolved oxygen test.

    d. Subtract the five-day results from the initial results to get the biochemical oxygen demand.

4. **Determine nitrates using the following steps:**

    a. Fill one test tube to the 5-ml mark with sample water.

    b. Fill the other tube with tap water to the 5-ml line.

    c. Add the Nitra Ver reagent to the sample water.

    d. Mix for one minute.

    e. Match the color of the sample to the color of the wheel.

5. **Determine turbidity using the following steps:**

    a. Fill one turbidity tube to the 50-ml line with tap or bottled water.

    b. Fill the other with the sample water.

    c. Add the turbidity reagent by .5-ml increments until the cloudiness of the water is the same.

    d. Check results; every .5-ml is equal to 5 turbidity units.

6. **Determine the total dissolved solids using the following steps:**

    a. Put the TDS electronic tester into a 250-ml beaker of the sample water.

    b. Multiply the reading on the digital display by .65 to determine the water's TDS level.

7. **Determine phosphates using the following steps:**

    a. Fill one test tube to the 5-ml mark with sample water.

    b. Fill the other tube with tap water to the 5-ml line.

    c. Add the Phos Ver reagent to the sample water.

    d. Mix for one minute.

    e. Match the color of the sample to the color of the wheel.

Results

Table 18-9 shows the results of this experiment.

Table 18-9	Levels of Substances in Water Tested		
	Lake Murray	*Lake Jennings*	*Bottled Water*
Average pH	8.0917	8.025	7
Average nitrate	6.1601	6.6733	0
Average turbidity	4.75	5.25	0
Total dissolved solids	348.68	291.5	65
Average phosphate	0.39	0.26	0
Dissolved oxygen	7	5.52	6
Biochemical oxygen demand	2.42	2.38	0

Conclusions

My hypothesis was mostly correct. All the pH levels of the water were from six to eight, except one, meaning that the water was fairly close to the having a neutral pH level, which is ideal.

The dissolved oxygen level of the water never dropped below five except once (on December 22) in both Lake Murray and Lake Jennings. This shows that in most instances, the amount of oxygen in the water was sufficient for most species of fish to survive. The biochemical oxygen demand never rose above five, but with the bottled water the level was zero. This also shows that the water had little organic decay.

The nitrates level rose above eight in a few instances, but overall was stable, meaning that the level of nitrates was very healthy. The phosphate level never rose above three, meaning the level of phosphates in the water was also healthy.

The turbidity rose above five only one time in a shallow water sample of Lake Murray, and dropped below five in a few other cases. This shows that it maintained a normal level of turbidity. The total dissolved solids never rose above 1,000, but instead maintained a level of around 350 parts per million (ppm), giving it a very good quality for fresh water.

In summary, the water from the two lakes tested was as clean and safe as bottled water.

Microbiology

Germs are everywhere, and most people are concerned about keeping them from contaminating the world.

This section takes a closer look at microbiology projects that explore the hidden world of bacteria.

Garlic and bacteria inhibition

Does garlic keep vampires away? You can't prove it scientifically, but many people do believe that garlic is good for what ails you — among other things it helps to ward off infection.

Emily Koch noticed that her mom, who eats garlic, has fewer colds than other family members, so she decided to see if the stories about garlic are true.

You can get a look at her project display in Figure 18-6.

Figure 18-6:
Project display for "Garlic and bacteria inhibition."

Hypothesis

I believe that garlic will inhibit the growth of the bacillus subtilis bacteria, but not as effectively as antibiotics and disinfectants.

Independent variables

Bacteria-inhibiting agents

Dependent variables

Amount of bacteria incubated

Controls

- ✔ Bacteria used
- ✔ Technique and time of incubation

Experimental groups

- ✔ Penicillin
- ✔ Streptomycin
- ✔ Tetracycline
- ✔ Glutaraldehyde
- ✔ 5 percent phenol alcohol
- ✔ Garlic

Materials

- ✔ 30 petri dishes
- ✔ Nutrient agar (a culture containing agar used to grow bacteria)
- ✔ Sterile paper disks
- ✔ Bacillus subtilis broth
- ✔ Home-built incubator (a sealed box with a heat pad underneath)
- ✔ Light box
- ✔ Penicillin
- ✔ Streptomycin
- ✔ Tetracycline
- ✔ Glutaraldehyde
- ✔ 5 percent phenol alcohol
- ✔ Fresh garlic extract

Procedures

1. **Divide petri dishes into six groups of five.**

2. **With adult supervision, melt the agar medium.**

3. **When liquid agar cools, pour an equal amount into each dish.**

4. **Press 25 cloves of garlic to make garlic juice.**

5. **Saturate one group of paper disks in the following:**

   a. Penicillin

   b. Streptomycin

   c. Tetracycline

   d. Glutaraldehyde

   e. 5 percent phenol alcohol

   f. Fresh garlic extract

6. **Put all petri dishes into incubator. The temperature in the incubator is 35° C (95° F).**

7. **After 24 hours, observe petri dishes, and use light box to take pictures of each dish. Repeat again after 24 hours.**

8. **Calculate *zones of inhibition* (the areas where no bacteria grow) to determine the area where each agent inhibited bacterial growth.**

Results

Table 18-10 shows the results for this experiment. The zone of incubation was calculated by placing the photograph of the petri dish on a sheet of graph paper, counting the number of squares with bacteria, and then calculating the percentage of squares where bacteria was inhibited from incubating.

Table 18-10	Zone of Inhibition for Each Inhibiting Agent
Bacteria Inhibitor	*Average Zone of Inhibition*
Penicillin	22.14
Streptomycin	67.84
Tetracycline	65.30
Glutaraldehyde	18.09
5 percent phenol alcohol	14.94
Garlic	42.68

Conclusions

My hypothesis was that garlic would inhibit the growth of bacillus subtilis, but not as effectively as antibiotics and disinfectants. This hypothesis was partially correct; the garlic was effective. It incubated more bacteria than the antibiotics, but less bacteria than the disinfectants.

Generic versus name-brand acne cleansers

You hear plenty of myths and old wives' tales about acne, most of which are easily disproved by looking at the facts.

Consumers have plenty of acne medications to choose from. Luis Montoya thought that the most famous and most expensive product would be most effective, but he wanted to see if the facts supported that idea.

Hypothesis

I believe that in three tests, a brand-name acne medication will work more effectively than a generic acne medication.

Independent variables

- ✔ Brand of acne cleanser used
- ✔ Types of bacteria

Dependent variables

Amount of bacteria killed

Controls

Amount of bacteria incubated in each petri dish

Experimental groups

Generic and brand-name acne cleaners incubated with:

- ✔ E. coli bacteria
- ✔ Mutans
- ✔ B.subtilis
- ✔ B.cereus
- ✔ Cercererisiae

Materials

- ✔ Five different bacteria:
    - E. coli bacteria, strain B
    - Mutans
    - B.subtilis
    - B.cereus
    - Cercererisiae
- ✔ Brand-name acne-cleanser pads
- ✔ Generic acne-cleanser pads
- ✔ Mueller Hunton media to sterilize petri dishes
- ✔ 30 petri dishes
- ✔ Sterile cotton swabs
- ✔ Bunsen burners
- ✔ *Autoclave*, a pressurized steam-heated vessel used for sterilization
- ✔ Sterile scissors

Procedures

1. **Label petri dishes with name and date.**

2. **Completely cover petri dish with bacteria, and label with bacteria type.**

3. **Mix the Mueller Hunton media as follows:**

    a. Thoroughly mix 39 grams powder and 1 liter water.

    b. Heat for approximately 1 minute, until boiling.

    c. Sterilize in the autoclave at 121° C for 15 minutes.

4. **Spread media on the petri dishes and sterilize each dish with the Bunsen burner.**

5. **Using sterile scissors, cut acne-cleanser pads into 4 mm squares.**

6. **Using a cotton swab, spread bacteria samples over the cleanser pads in the petri dishes.**

7. **Sterilize forceps as follows:**

    a. Dip into 70 percent alcohol solution.

    b. Pass through Bunsen burner flame until forceps are red.

    c. Let cool for 2 to 3 seconds.

8. **With sterile forceps, lift square of acne-cleanser pad onto petri dish.**

9. **Incubate petri dish for one day.**

10. **Measure and record amount of bacteria killed.**

Results

Tables 18-11 and 18-12 show the results for this experiment.

Table 18-11	Amount of Bacteria Killed (in Millimeters) by Brand-Name Cleanser				
Experiment number	*E. coli*	*B. subtilis*	*B. cereus*	*Cercererisiae*	*Mutans*
1	10	6	7	2	7
2	7	8	9	3	9
3	8	4	5	7	11
Total	25	18	21	12	27
Average	8.3	6	7	4	9

Table 18-12	Amount of Bacteria Killed (in Millimeters) by Generic Cleanser				
Experiment Number	*E. coli*	*B. subtilis*	*B. cereus*	*Cercererisiae*	*Mutans*
1	13	25	29	39	24
2	11	22	28	35	31
3	15	29	33	42	33
Total	39	76	90	116	88
Average	13	25.3	30	38.6	29.3

Conclusions

My hypothesis that the brand-name acne medication would work best was incorrect. The results show that the generic medication killed more bacteria. This result shows that the better-known and more expensive product doesn't necessarily work the best.

Physics

The *first law of motion* states: "A body at rest tends to remain at rest, while a body in motion tends to remain in motion in a straight line unless subjected to an outside force." The students who did the next three projects exerted considerable force and stayed in motion too while doing their experiments.

What is the effect of binders on adobe brick strength?

Since prehistoric times, people all over the world have been using *adobe*, bricks made of clay soil and unbaked earth as a cheap and plentiful building material. However, adobe erodes over time.

Alex Niles wanted to find out what kinds of binders will strengthen adobe bricks. See his project display in Figure 18-7.

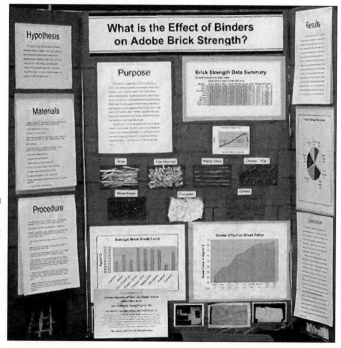

Figure 18-7: Project display for "What is the effect of binders on adobe brick strength?"

Hypothesis

I believe that adding various binders, such as straw, pine shavings, chicken wire, metal sheets, Fiberglass, plastic strips, asphalt emulsion, or Portland cement to adobe bricks will strengthen them.

Independent variables

Binders added to adobe bricks

Dependent variables

Amount of pressure required to break bricks

Controls

- Basic materials and methods for making bricks
- Method of testing strength of bricks

Experimental groups

Adobe bricks with the following binders:

- Straw
- Pine shavings
- Chicken wire
- Metal sheets
- Fiberglass
- Plastic strips
- Asphalt emulsion
- Portland cement

Control groups

Adobe bricks with no binders added

Materials

Note: All linear dimensions in the following list are in centimeters (cm).

- Adobe kit consisting of adobe soil and a small plastic mold ($\frac{1}{16}$ scale of traditional adobe bricks)
- 25 kilograms of adobe soil

- One wooden mold made out of pine, measuring 10 L x 5 W x 2.5 H on the inside (¼ scale of traditional adobe bricks)
- Four small nails
- Wood glue
- Clear spray
- Large flat board
- Water
- 90 plastic strips cut from the flat portion of 3.78-liter water containers measuring ½ cm x 10 cm
- 12 galvanized metal sheets with holes, called corner beams, measuring 5 cm x 10 cm
- 18 strips of galvanized chicken wire measuring 5 cm x 10 cm
- 18 pieces of Fiberglass cloth, measuring, 5 cm x 10 cm
- 30 g straw
- 60 g natural pine shavings
- 5 ml asphalt emulsion (tar)
- 225 g Portland cement (made by mixing substances that contain lime, aluminum, silica, and iron oxide)
- Sieve for removing rocks and debris
- Scale
- Measuring cup
- Teaspoon
- Ruler
- Glass jar with a lid
- Large buckets
- Large plastic bag
- Paper towels
- Band saw
- Scissors
- Wire cutters
- Shovel

Procedures

1. **Make test bricks as follows:**

   a. Dig up about 25 kg of adobe soil and place in two large buckets.

   b. Mix equal quantities of soil and water.

   c. Make eight small test bricks, and make sure they don't crumble or crack.

2. **Make six bricks for control group as follows:**

   a. Mix 340 g of soil, cleared of rocks and debris, with 15 ml of water.

   b. Knead the mud in a plastic bag until it's sticky enough to form a small ball.

   c. On a large flat board, pack mud tightly into the mold, level it, release the brick from the mold, and then rinse the mold before starting another brick.

3. **Make six bricks for each experimental group by modifying Step 2 as follows:**

   a. Add 5 g of straw to the mud mixture.

   b. Add 10 g of pine shavings to the mud mixture.

   c. Add three layers of five plastic strips to each brick.

   d. Add three layers of chicken wire to each brick.

   e. Add three layers of Fiberglass to each brick.

   f. Add three layers metal sheets to each brick.

   g. Mix 5 ml of asphalt emulsion, 115 ml of water and 2 kg of soil.

   h. Mix 3.2 kg Portland cement, 1 kg soil, and 60 ml of water to make 3 bricks, and then repeat.

4. **Let the bricks dry on the board at room temperature for one week and turn them over; let them dry for five to seven days or until they're very hard.**

5. **Place a 1.3-cm round magnet on a hydraulic jack to use as the pressure point.**

6. **Place the bathroom scale on the hydraulic jack, and then put each brick on top of the bathroom scale.**

7. **While one person pushes the lever on the hydraulic jack to exert pressure on the brick, have a second person read the kilograms on the scale until the brick breaks, and a third person record the kilograms every five seconds.**

Results

Table 18-13 shows the percentage that bricks with binders are stronger than the control group with no binder.

Table 18-13		Average Additional Strength of Each Binder					
Straw	Pine Shavings	Chicken Wire	Metal Sheets	Fiberglass	Plastic Strips	Asphalt Emulsion	Portland Cement
10%	1.5%	19%	19%	17%	21%	-6%	13%

Conclusions

My hypothesis was that adding various materials to adobe bricks would strengthen the bricks. The hypothesis was correct for all the binders except for the bricks made with asphalt emulsion.

Making efficient use of solar panels

All life on earth depends on the sun for heat, warmth, and energy. Solar panels allow people to capture the sun's rays to create electricity. But are solar panels operating at top efficiency?

Koa Tran's project (see Figure 18-8) tested how solar panels could be improved.

Hypothesis

I believe that using *bi-convex lenses,* which concentrate a beam of light, will improve the efficiency of a solar panel.

Independent variables

Lenses used on solar panels

Dependent variables

Amount of voltage, current, and resistance

Controls

- ✔ Time of tests
- ✔ Angle of solar panels
- ✔ Measurement tools

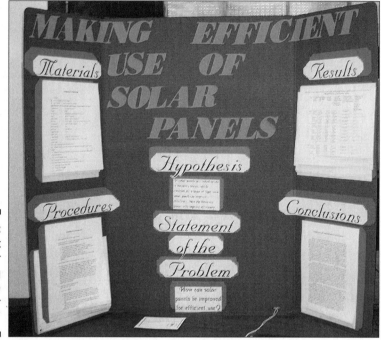

Figure 18-8:
Project display for "Making efficient use of solar panels."

Experimental groups

One 12-volt (v) solar panel with three bi-convex lenses connected in a clockwise pattern on three sides of the test solar panel

Control groups

One 12v solar panel

Materials

- ✔ Sunlight
- ✔ Three bi-convex lenses, measuring 5 cm in diameter
- ✔ Two 12v/15.24 cm x 17.78 cm x 2.54 cm solar panels
- ✔ Two built-in blocking diodes for solar panels
- ✔ Two 220-ohm resistors
- ✔ Two 60.96 cm x 60.96 cm x 0.7 cm wooden boards
- ✔ Two Radio Shack digital multimeters (voltage/ohmmeters)

✔ Three 68-cm wire hangers

✔ Three lens holders

✔ Four 357A 1.5 v button-cell batteries

✔ 500-cm tape ruler, 30.5-cm ruler, and protractor

✔ Solar calculator

✔ Connectors

✔ Brackets

✔ Adhesives

✔ Tape

✔ Marker

✔ Tools

Procedures

1. Set up experimental and control groups.

2. Place both groups outside at 8:50 a.m., when the sun's rays are striking the groups' location, at optimal angles to the sun.

3. For both groups, record the amount of voltages, without the resistors attached.

4. For both groups, remove the test leads and reset each voltage/ohmmeter.

5. For each solar panel, make contact between red and black test lead with the end wires of the 220-ohm resistor.

6. Record amount of resistance (in ohms) for both groups.

7. Take both groups indoors at 3:26 p.m., when the sun's rays are still strongly contacting with the solar panels and the bi-convex lenses.

8. Measure and record voltage, resistance, and current from each group; round the current and the voltage of each solar panel with the internal and external resistance to the nearest hundredths place.

9. Repeat experiment for the next two weeks, adjusting the times that the experimental and control groups are set out, after calculating the time for optimal sunlight.

Results

Table 18-14 shows the average volts and milliamps for each test.

Table 18-14	Average Volts and Milliamps for Each Solar Panel			
	Control Group		Test Group	
	Volts	Milliamps	Volts	Milliamps
Test 1	16.14286	5.85714	15.42857	5.15714
Test 2	17.00000	18.80000	16.85714	13.38571
Test 3	17.14286	31.84286	17.42857	20.51429

Conclusions

My hypothesis was that solar panels using bi-convex lenses are more efficient than standard solar panels. My hypothesis was incorrect, because the experimental group with the bi-convex lenses actually reduced the amount of milliamps, voltages, and current that the solar panel received.

A future experiment would use mirrors in front of the solar panel rather than bi-convex lenses, which would increase the amount of sunlight coming into contact with the photovoltaic cells.

Which slope best allows an object to complete a loop?

How to make things go faster? Does it depend on the angle of the slope or the size and weight of the object? Christine Robles built a few models to determine which slope angle allows a marble to quickly and safely complete a loop.

Check out Christine's project display in Figure 18-9.

Hypothesis

I believe that both the small and large object will best complete the loop on the most vertical slope, and will perform most poorly on the most slanted slope.

Independent variables

 ✔ Slope angles

 ✔ Size of marbles

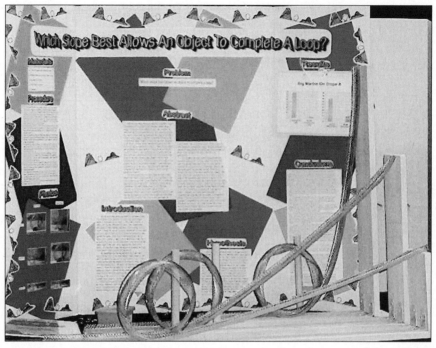

Figure 18-9:
Project
display for
"Which
slope best
allows an
object to
complete a
loop?"

Dependent variables

Time for marble to complete each loop

Controls

- ✔ Type of marbles used
- ✔ Material used to construct loops
- ✔ Stopwatch used to time tests

Materials

- ✔ 15 feet of braided plastic tubing for loops
- ✔ Wooden boards
- ✔ Screws to support loops
- ✔ Big marble (21 g)
- ✔ Small marble (6 g)
- ✔ Stopwatch

Procedures

1. **Build three loop models as follows:**

   a. Cut the plastic tubing in half

   b. Shape the tubes into the loops, each with a diameter of 19.05 centimeters.

   Slope A has a starting point of 71.12 cm high and a slope angle of 80°.

   Slope B has a starting point of 45.72 cm high and an angle of 35°.

   Slope C has a starting point of 20.32 cm high and an angle of 10°.

   c. Cut the boards to fit the loops and screw them together.

2. **For slopes A, B, and C, test large marble on slope by releasing it onto the slope. Test 50 times; time and record each observation.**

3. **For slopes A, B, and C, test small marble on slope by releasing it onto the slope. Test 50 times; time and record each observation.**

Results

Table 18-15 shows how many times the slope was completed out of 50 trials; the number in parenthesis shows the number of smooth completions.

Table 18-15   Number of Completions and Average Speed for Each Slope

	Large Marble		Small Marble	
	Completions	Average Speed (in Seconds)	Completions	Average Speed (in Seconds)
Slope A	48 (40)	0.88	50 (50)	0.75
Slope B	44 (34)	0.99	50 (50)	0.88
Slope C	0 (0)	1.10	50 (0)	1.09

Conclusions

My hypothesis for the big marble was correct. The bigger and heavier object best completed the loop using Slope A. It did complete the loop using Slope B, but the results were not as accurate. The big marble did not complete the loop on Slope C due to lack of force and acceleration.

On Slope A, the small marble is more accurate and completed the loop more times than the big marble. With Slope C, both marbles are equally accurate. In view of this experiment, Slope C is unacceptable. Therefore, this project shows that a more vertical slope and lighter object produce better performance.

And Many More . . .

No one category is harder than another when it comes to science fair projects.

You can do an easy project in any category, and you can create a challenging project in any category — it all depends how you use the scientific method (see Chapter 8). The next three projects come from the mathematics, medicine and health, and zoology categories.

Statistical frequency of red light running — a comparative study

Does it seem to you as though people are always running red lights? Mark Kramer thought so too, and decided to prove it in his mathematics project.

See Figure 18-10 for a look at Mark's display.

Hypothesis

I believe that I can mathematically demonstrate a high incidence of drivers running through red and yellow lights.

Procedures

This project observed and recorded the occurrences of vehicles running red and yellow lights according to these definitions:

✔ Red lights:

- Police definition. A car that crosses the intersection or crosswalk line *after* the light has turned red.

- Observational definition. A vehicle that had time to stop, entered the intersection on yellow, and was *less* than halfway through the intersection when the light turned red.

✔ Yellow lights:

- Observational definition. A vehicle that had time to stop, entered the intersection on yellow, and was *more* than halfway through the intersection when the light turned red.

What follows are some additional details about the experiment:

✔ All types of vehicles, including cars, trucks, sport utility vehicles, vans, recreational vehicles, motorcycles, and in rare cases, buses and a police car, were observed.

✔ The observations were performed at the intersection of College Boulevard and Oceanside Boulevard in 2000 and at El Camino Real and College Boulevard in 2001.

✔ A total of 28 observations, done from a parked car, were performed in half-hour shifts, for a total of 14 hours.

✔ At each intersection, observed seven left-turn lanes and seven straight lanes, two lanes at a time (either two straight or two left lanes going in the same direction).

✔ All runners of red and yellow lights were marked down on a pre-made tally chart, noting the type of vehicle, day of the week, time, weather conditions, total number of vehicles passing through intersection, number of light changes, and observed traffic pattern.

Figure 18-10:
Project display for "Frequency of red light running."

Results

Using *statistical extrapolation* (which just means estimating unknown information by projecting known information) and the combined statistics from 2000 and 2001, it was discovered that a red light is run every 5.6 minutes at these two intersections.

Conclusions

My hypothesis that a high incidence of drivers run through red and yellow lights is correct, according to the tests done.

Although I ran the tests at only two of the busiest intersections in the city, I think caution when entering an intersection is always a wise choice considering how often people run red lights.

To clean or not to clean

Did you ever wonder if your ready-to-eat packaged lettuce is really free from bacteria? Does the brand of packaged lettuce really matter? Or if bacteria are present, how can you wash the lettuce to get ride of bacteria? Jane Alejandro really wanted to know those answers.

Check out Jane's project display in Figure 18-11.

Hypothesis

I believe that washing pre-washed lettuce with a vinegar and water solution will remove more bacteria than washing with water only.

Independent variables

Type of wash used for lettuce

Dependent variables

Amount of bacteria on samples after three-day test

Controls

- ✔ Lettuce samples
- ✔ Sterilization techniques

Experimental groups

- ✔ Lettuce washed with plain tap water
- ✔ Lettuce washed with mixture of vinegar and water

Figure 18-11:
Project
display for
"To clean or
not to
clean."

Control groups
Lettuce that wasn't washed

Materials

- ✔ 37 nutrient agar plates (which contain a culture to grow bacteria)
- ✔ 40 sterile plates
- ✔ Six packages prewashed lettuce
- ✔ 70 percent ethanol
- ✔ De-ionized water
- ✔ Two sets of tweezers
- ✔ Two 100-ml beakers
- ✔ One 200-ml beaker
- ✔ One Bunsen burner
- ✔ 45 sterile cotton balls
- ✔ One liter of tap water

✔ One liter of vinegar (bottled)

✔ Three stirring rods

Procedures

To perform this experiment, I took a piece of lettuce from each package, swiped it with a cotton swab and streaked the swab on the nutrient agar plate. I then placed the agar plates in an incubator set at 37° C.

When bacterial growth was evident, I took the same pieces of lettuce and put them through either a tap water or vinegar/water wash. Note that on each day, the workstation, tweezers, and stirring rods are cleaned and sterilized with 70 percent ethanol.

The following is a closer look at the procedures.

✔ **Day 1: Incubate bacterial growth:**

1. Mark each lettuce sample as XI, XII, YI, YII, ZI and ZII.

2. Label one nutrient agar plate the control plate and streak with de-ionized water.

3. Divide the remaining 18 nutrient agar plates, into six groups of three. Label the first group XI, and assign a number to each plate (for example, XI 1, XI 2, and XI 3). Repeat with remaining groups (XII, YI, and so on).

4. Dampen the cotton ball with the de-ionized water and streak it twice across the agar on the control plate.

5. Place a piece of lettuce on each labeled sterile nutrient agar plate.

6. Incubate nutrient agar plates overnight at 37° C.

7. Refrigerate sterile plate with lettuce piece at 4° C.

✔ **Day 2: Wash lettuce with tap water or vinegar and water:**

1. Observe, note, illustrate, and photograph the agar plates.

2. Divide the 18 nutrient agar plates into six groups of three. In each group label one as the control plate, the second PW (plain water) and the third group VW (vinegar/water mix).

3. Group each sterile plate with its corresponding nutrient agar plate containing a lettuce sample.

4. Bathe PW samples in tap water using stirring rod.

5. Bathe VW samples in vinegar-water mix using stirring rod.

6. Incubate the nutrient agar plates overnight at 37° C.

> ✔ **Day 3: Observe and record bacterial growth:**
>
>   1. Remove agar plates from incubator.
>
>   2. Observe, note, illustrate, and photograph the agar plates.

Results

All samples washed with tap water grew bacteria, while only one sample washed with vinegar mix grew bacteria.

On day 2, after incubating the bacteria overnight, each plate had bacterial growth except for the control plate. Many distinct colonies formed, with two massive colonies in one of every group. All brands had relatively equal bacterial growth.

On day 3, all the control plates had bacterial growth. Only one of the VW plates had bacterial colonies formed, but all the PW plates had evident bacterial growth.

None of the plates were clear of bacterial growth.

Conclusions

My hypothesis was that re-washing pre-washed lettuce with a vinegar and water solution removes more bacteria than re-washing with water. The results show that this hypothesis is correct.

The significance of my findings is that bacteria does exist in packaged, ready-to-eat lettuce despite its label, "no washing needed." The best way to get rid of the bacteria is to wash the lettuce with a mixture of vinegar and water.

Solitary and social problem-solving behavior in Mus musculus

Many zoology projects about animal learning and behavior are done using mice. In this project, Hazel Villasin wanted to know what mice — when trained alone — carried over when they were paired with other mice.

Check out her project display in Figure 18-12.

Hypothesis

I believe that mice with a high-performance rate in solitary tests will be dominant when paired with mice with low-performance rates.

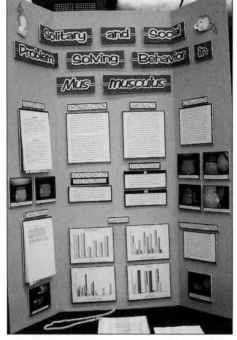

Figure 18-12:
Project display for "Solitary and social problem-solving behavior in Mus musculus."

Dependent variables
Rates of response

Controls
Types of mice

Materials
- Six male albino mice (*Mus musculus*) that were full siblings and raised together
- Plastic aquaria measuring 36 x 21.5 x 24 cm
- Balsa-wood food trays, fitted with balsa-wood lever that can deliver food pellet when lever was pressed

Procedures
1. **Tag each mouse on the tail with identifying color.**
2. **Before the experiment, handle and weigh each mouse and familiarize it with the isolation box.**

3. Train each mouse to get a food pellet by pressing a lever. Each mouse was trained three times over the period of nine days with each session lasting 30 minutes.

4. Record the mean number of reinforcements and average rate of response.

5. Place each mouse in the isolation box for 30 minutes.

6. Classify the mice into two groups: the three mice with the highest rate of response (H), and the three mice with the lowest rate of response (L).

7. Pair the highest scoring mouse from group H with the highest scoring mouse in group L, next highest H with next highest L, and so on.

8. Move lever to the opposite side of the aquarium (34.5 cm from the food chute), so that the mouse had to run across the box to get the food pellet.

9. Place one pair of mice in the aquarium for 30 minutes.

10. Record each time that a mouse presses the lever.

11. Repeat Steps 9 and 10 for the other two pairs of mice.

Results

Table 18-16 shows the average rates of response for the solitary test sessions, as well as the placement of each mouse into the high or low performing group.

Table 18-16		Average Results of Solitary Test Sessions		
Group	*Color*	*Average Rate*	*H/L Rating*	*Average Rate of Response*
High	Brown	4.00	H1	
	Green	3.67	H2	
	Pink	3.33	H3	
				3.67
Low	Yellow	2.67	L1	
	Blue	2.33	L2	
	Orange	1.67	L3	
				2.22

Table 18-17 shows the average results of each paired test sessions, as well as the average results of all paired test sessions. Note that mice that pressed the lever significantly more times than their partners exhibited dominant behavior, and mice that pressed the lever fewer times exhibited dependent behavior.

Table 18-17			Results for Paired Test Sessions			
	Pairs			**Number of Presses**		
			2/4	**2/5**	**2/6**	**Average**
1	H1	Dominant	12	14	15	13.7
	L1	Dependent	7	5	5	5.7
2	H2	Dominant	2	11	10	7.7
	L2	Dependent	3	2	2	2.3
3	H3	Dominant	9	13	*	7.5
	L3	Dependent	2	3	*	2.5

Conclusions

My hypothesis was correct because the results show that in paired sessions, mice that had high-pressing rates in solitary learning sessions assume the dominant role, and those who achieved low-pressing rates maintain the dependent role.

I, therefore, conclude that certain types of solitary training do influence social behavior.

Part VII
The Part of Tens

The 5th Wave — By Rich Tennant

"It's little Alan Mendle from next door. He wants to know if Wendy's flame retardant science project is finished yet."

In this part . . .

A lot of great science fair project information either doesn't fit in anywhere or belongs everywhere. In true Dummies tradition, all this good stuff finds a home in the Part of Tens.

To help you come up with a great project idea, I give you a list of bad project ideas, which can keep you off the wrong track. I also give you a number of Web sites that can help you get information, write your paper, or design your display. (In most cases, each Web site points you to even more sites to check out.)

You'll also get a look at how to claim your reward for finishing a great science project — having fun at the science fair. To all you parents out there, I provide a list of ten survival tips to make sure that you survive and enjoy science fair time. Last but not least, you get a list of ten things that you absolutely, positively can't live without.

Chapter 19

Ten Bad Project Ideas and Why You Should Avoid Them

. . . .

In This Chapter

▶ Identifying "non-projects"

▶ Retiring stale project ideas

▶ Adhering to established science fair rules

. . . .

Some projects have been done so many times that teachers and judges can't stand looking at them anymore. Likewise, some projects can't give scientifically reliable results with the time and resources that you have to do them.

If you checked out Chapter 4 (which talks about how to get project ideas), but still haven't found one, you may want to look at what sorts of ideas not to use. In this chapter, I describe some projects that aren't really projects. I also list projects that violate the rules of just about any official science fair.

Making Models

Okay, models were great for your third-grade science project. But model volcanoes, solar systems, solar collectors, or tidal waves just don't qualify as a bona fide science project when you get older. Why? They don't use the scientific method to prove a hypothesis.

This doesn't rule out an engineering project where you're building models in order to conduct performance tests, or where you're creating a new device to solve a specific problem.

Going Against the Law

Each year, science fair committees outlaw more projects because they're considered harmful to the subjects, the student, or the visitors to the fair.

For example, several years ago, students could do projects that measured the amounts of tar in cigarette smoke or that evaluated how cigarette smoke affects plants. Now, however, these projects are prohibited. Even though the smoke was produced using a smoking machine, the secondhand smoke can still pose a serious health hazard.

In many science fairs, you're allowed to have projects that involve *live vertebrates* (animals with a backbone or spinal column such as reptiles, birds, and mammals). However, you can't have a project that intends to kill or cause unnecessary pain or discomfort to animals. You also can't conduct alcohol, acid rain, insecticide, herbicide, or heavy metal toxicity studies on live vertebrates.

Some science fairs prohibit all live vertebrate projects, so make sure to check before you start. Some other illegal projects are those that include DNA requiring *containment* (a system designed to prevent the accidental release of materials) and black powder, explosives, or firearms.

Speaking Unscientifically

You may be interested in *graphology* (handwriting analysis), astrology, extrasensory perception (ESP), pyramid power, and other aspects of the occult, but unless you have a really scientific approach where you can produce specific, measurable results, judges typically don't look favorably on those types of projects. Why? The judges are scientists, and most of them are rather skeptical about what they consider pseudoscience, even if you think it's the real deal.

Making the Judges Count Sheep

You don't get any brownie points for putting teachers and judges to sleep. Here are a few ideas guaranteed to bore them to tears:

- The effects of almost anything on blood pressure
- The effect of music or talking on plants

> ✔ The effect of cola, coffee, candy, gum, and so on on teeth
> ✔ Growing molds, crystals, or planaria
> ✔ Sleep learning

However, if you can put a new spin on an old idea (and do it scientifically), give it a try.

Expressing It with Music and Art

Many students look at the effect of color or music on plants, memory, emotion, mood, taste, strength, grades, or manual dexterity. Unless you have a way of doing it originally, accurately, and objectively, go on to the next idea.

Making a Personal Choice

Projects that survey and tabulate preferences or opinions don't always produce reliable results. For example, doing the cola taste challenge or finding out which fries are fabulous doesn't exactly follow the scientific method.

Measuring taste, color choices, or paw preferences of cats, dogs, goldfish, or other pets is also a no-no (unless you can apply the scientific method).

Deciding What's Best

You can find lots of great consumer science and product testing projects, but teachers and judges like to see a good use of the scientific method and effective statistical analysis of results.

So if you plan this type of project, set up an experiment with specific variables and controls and adequate experimental and control groups (see Chapter 8 for information about using the scientific method).

Make sure you do a sufficient number of tests to ensure that your results are valid.

Testing, 1, 2, 3

A common mistake that students make when doing their first physics or engineering project is testing something without considering all the factors that can affect the outcome. Here are some examples:

✔ Acid rain tests without doing an accurate simulation of acid rain composition

✔ Basic flight tests of planes, rockets, and so on without considering factors, such as design or fuel

Ask your science teacher to review your procedures (described in Chapter 9) to make sure that you've covered all the bases.

Guesstimating the Numbers

If you can't take accurate measurements, you can't get accurate project results.

For example, it may be impossible to measure exactly how high a ball bounces, because you don't have adequate equipment, and you can't evaluate how fluoride affects teeth, because you don't have enough time to evaluate the results in a meaningful way.

Proving (Like Breaking Up) Is Hard to Do

In some projects you can test something or survey groups of subjects, but your results will be inconclusive no matter what the data shows. This usually happens because different uncontrolled variables can affect the outcome. Some examples of these types of projects are:

✔ Optical illusions

✔ Reaction times

✔ Basic flower preservation techniques (how healthy were the flowers to begin with?)

✔ Basic maze running

✔ Male/female comparisons (keeping these bias-free is almost impossible!)

Chapter 20

Ten Great Web Sites (Okay, 23 Actually)

In This Chapter

▶ Getting and giving information

▶ Checking out official sites

I'm certainly not suggesting that you use the Internet instead of reading *Science Fair Projects For Dummies,* but I do want you to know about some excellent Web sites that are available.

I've limited this list to 23 sites, arranged by the type of information they offer. Of course, many more exist — but finding them is half the fun, right?

Just about every Web site that I list in this chapter has several links to other Web sites, so as soon as you start exploring, you're off and running!

Information, Please

When you're looking for information, encyclopedias are great places to start. Not only do they give you a good overview of whatever subject you're looking up, but they also point you to other resources that you can check out.

But why go through huge volumes when you can let your fingers do the walking on the Web? The following are some particularly good sites to hit.

> ✔ **Encyclopedia Britannica** (www.britannica.com/): You can browse just about any subject, narrowing it until you get to exactly what you need. For example, you can ask to browse by subject, and then, from the science category, select what you want, for example, biological sciences. At that point, you get a list breaking the subject down further. Pick one of

the choices given, for example, zoology, and you get another list. Eventually, you arrive at where you want to go, and with a bibliography, too.

✓ **Bartleby.com** (www.bartleby.com): Not only does this link give you the *Columbia Encyclopedia,* but also other fabulous references, such as a dictionary, thesaurus, quotations, English usage (rules of grammar), and more.

✓ **U.S. Government Printing Office (GPO)** (www.access.gpo.gov/su_docs/index.html): If you think you need information from a federal government agency, check out this Web site. You can search by subject, and the site directs you to the department or agency that publishes the information. Then, if the document is online, the site takes you there directly. You can also search the GPO online bookstore, where you can order what you need.

Asking Questions (and Getting Answers)

Some really cool sites allow you to ask a question and get an answer. One of the first and foremost Q&A sites is Ask Jeeves at www.askjeeves.com/index.asp. This site isn't just for science questions — you can ask a question about almost anything, from the sublime to the ridiculous. You can also browse by subject, or ask other people. Another feature on this site is Ask Jeeves for Kids, which supplies information specifically directed toward children.

Some question-and-answer sites deal exclusively with science. The following list takes a look at three of them.

✓ **MadSci Network** (www.madsci.org): This site delivers the meat (solid scientific knowledge) on wry (with a touch of humor).

✓ **Ask Discover** (www.discover.com/ask/): Sponsored by *Discover* magazine, this site can answer your specific questions. You can also check out previous questions and answers or look up a specific topic. For example, a search on "evolution" turned up 40 replies. Also, someone who asked a specific question about animal and human evolution received a detailed reply from a biology professor.

✓ **Ask Dr. Universe** (www.wsu.edu/DrUniverse/Contents.html): Based at Washington State University, this site provides another place to get your questions answered. This site is geared toward the layperson — in other words, even if you're uncomfortable with science, you can feel comfortable with Dr. Universe.

Consulting an Online Writing Lab

This site is fabulous! **Purdue University's Online Writing Lab (OWL)** at `owl.english.purdue.edu/` tells you everything you ever wanted to know about all types of writing.

You can find out how to do research, organize your information, write your paper, and credit your sources. You probably can't use even a tenth of what's available while you're working on your science project. But you may want to remember this site when you need help with any type of writing in the future.

Understanding the Science Project Game

Because science fairs have become a mainstay of the American educational experience, Web sites directed at students at various levels, seem to pop up regularly. Here are some worth checking out:

- **Cyber-Fair** (`www.isd77.k12.mn.us/resources/cf/steps.html`): A virtual science fair site aimed at third- through sixth-grade students, this site is sponsored by the Mankato, Minnesota, Area Public Schools. Mankato State University also has a site for introductory projects at `www.isd77.k12.mn.us/resources/cf/SciProjIntro.html` and another for intermediate projects at `www.isd77.k12.mn.us/resources/cf/SciProjInter.html`.

- **The Kids' Guide to Science Projects** (`edweb.tusd.k12.az.us/jtindell/`): This site explains how to do a science project, illustrated by a sample science project.

- **The Kennedy Space Center** (`bioscience.ksc.nasa.gov/education/general/scifair1.html`): The space center has a Web site to help science fair participants. It offers very concise and complete information.

- **Successful Science Fair Projects** (`faculty.washington.edu/chudler/fair.html`): Hosted by a teacher and science fair organizer, this site provides another short and sweet summary of the science project process.

- **Science Fair Central, part of the Discovery Channel site** (`school.discovery.com/sciencefaircentral/scifairstudio/index.html`): This site offers a science project handbook, a catalog of project ideas, and a list of links and resources. The site also has sections specifically aimed at teachers and parents.

Manufacturers and suppliers of project backboards operate a few sites. Along with general info on science projects, you can find the stuff you need for your display. **Showboard** is at www.showboard.com, and **Science Hunt** is at www.sciencehunt.com.

Finding Science Fairs

You can find loads of international, regional, local, and virtual science fair sites. To get a comprehensive list of them, visit the World Wide Web Virtual Library of Science Fairs at physics.usc.edu/~gould/ScienceFairs/.

However, I also want to list a few individual sites that I particularly like, because they can give you a good feel for what a science fair is all about and what's required.

If you can visit only one site, go to the Intel International Science and Engineering Fair (ISEF) site (www.sciserv.org/isef/). Because many local and regional fairs send their top projects to ISEF, other fairs have adopted the ISEF requirements.

Some other outstanding local and regional sites are:

✔ **Greater San Diego Science and Engineering Fair** (www.gsdsef.org)

✔ **Chicago Student Science Fair** (www.chicagostudentscience fair.org/)

✔ **The Junior Academy of the Nebraska Academy of Science** (www.unl.edu/stc-95/njas.htm)

✔ **Florida's Orange County Regional Science and Engineering Fair** (www.awesomeguides.com/OCRSEF_orange_county_regional_science_and_engineering_fair.htm)

Chapter 21

Ten Fun Things to Do at the Science Fair

In This Chapter

▶ Seeing new people and projects

▶ Getting freebies

▶ Walking proud

*I*f you make it beyond your school science fair, you're going to the big leagues, a whole new ball game, the show! The next level may mean a city-wide, regional, or state science fair.

Besides the prestige and recognition of getting there (and the stress of competing), you can find lots of fun things to see and do at the fair. This chapter explores just a few of your options.

Nabbing a "Get Out of Jail (er, School) Free" Card

Doing a science project is definitely about discovery, discipline, and plenty of other stuff that's good for you. So, here's one more perk: If you're chosen to go to a regional, city, state, or international science fair, you have an automatic excused absence from school (unless, of course, the fair is on a weekend).

Depending on the fair, this absence may be just for judging day, or it may be for up to a week if you're going to the Intel International Science and Engineering Fair (or ISEF; see Chapter 4). The bad news? You'll probably have a whole bunch of assignments to make up.

Meeting New People

You know all about what's going on at your school, academically and socially, and you probably know lots of people. But when you go to a large regional or state science fair, you get to meet people from many other schools. And if you get to go to ISEF, you'll meet people from all over the world (and exchange pins from their hometowns, a time-honored ISEF tradition).

Take advantage of any scheduled events when you have the opportunity to meet and talk to people from different schools, many of whom likely have different backgrounds and different ideas from your own.

Perusing Other Projects

You're probably well acquainted with your classmates' science projects, but when you go to a regional fair, you get to see what other people have done. Use your time to look at the award-winning projects in your category. It may give you an idea of how the judges made their decisions.

This extra peek can be interesting and fun, but it can also be a great source of ideas for next year.

Taking Tours

At some of the larger science fairs, participants can take tours. Various organizations donate the many tours, which are usually free to students. Others carry a nominal cost.

For example, at the Greater San Diego Science and Engineering Fair, you can get free admission to all the area museums for the duration of the science fair, and at the Orange County (Florida) Regional Science Fair, you can visit the Orlando Science Center.

At some fairs, you can also sign up for some fun and educational field trips to local science-related sites.

Meeting Scientists

When you meet the science fair judges, you have the chance to talk to professional scientists and engineers working in the same field that your project covers.

During judging, the judges ask you questions, but why not take the opportunity to ask them questions as well? Don't be shy; they don't bite. Also, if the fair features any seminars or career days where students can talk to the scientists, sign up and find out if you want to go further in the field.

Playing Tourist

If you're at a science fair that's quite a distance from home, you have the chance to sample the attractions of a whole new place.

Even at a regional fair, you can play tourist in a new city. Before you go, get a guidebook or surf the Web to find out all you can about your destination. See the sights, meet the people, taste the food, and have a great time.

Getting a Free Lunch

If the fair is big enough, the judging sessions go on long enough, and supporters donate enough, you may get a free lunch on judging day. If you're lucky, the lunch may include pizza (or whatever your favorite food happens to be)!

Winning Awards

If you read Chapter 15, you know all about the awards you can win at a science fair. Go to the awards ceremony and share the winners' excitement. If you get an award, fabulous — be proud. If you don't win an award, be proud anyway — after all, you made it this far.

Showing Off

After the judging and awards ceremony are over, you can show off your achievements. Invite friends, family, neighbors, and whoever else may be interested, to come and see your project.

If you're at a rather large science fair, you may accidentally meet someone you know. Isn't it a great feeling to say, "Yes, my project is over there! Do you want me to show it to you?"

Having Fun

'Nuff said.

Chapter 22

Ten Science Project Survival Tips for Parents

. . . .

In This Chapter

▶ Supporting your student through a science project

▶ Having fun

▶ Remembering whose project it really is

▶ Taking care of yourself

. . . .

*V*ery often, I hear that parents are just as stressed as their sons and daughters at science project time, if not more so. Believe me, I understand your concern. While your child is working on a science project, you have demands on your time and knowledge (I've been there — I was a liberal arts student), wear and tear on your car, and the ever-present guilty feeling that you should be doing more.

Despite all that, I'd like to try to make this experience as easy and enjoyable as possible for you, so this chapter takes a look at ten ways to make the science project journey pleasant and fun.

Supporting Versus Nagging

If you've ever had a nagging parent, spouse, or boss, you know the difference between supporting and nagging. However, you can sometimes forget this distinction pretty quickly when you're trying to help your child be successful.

Instead of getting both you and your child worked up, try the following steps when tempers look like they're going to flare.

- ✔ **Make it easy for your student to remember his or her assignments and deadlines so you don't have to be the bad guy.** Give your child a convenient, visible place to post a calendar or schedule (perhaps on the refrigerator door).

- ✔ **Allow your child to make a mistake or two.** Think of yourself as a coach, but not a supervisor or a drill sergeant.

- ✔ **No matter how close the deadline or how much still needs to be done, allow your child some "down time".** A well-timed break or breather from the work can give your child the energy to get going again. Remember, sometimes, being a little lazy is okay.

Discovering New Things

If you haven't studied much science over the years, you may be intimidated by the thought of helping your kids with their science projects. However, this can be a great opportunity to find out about some things you were always curious about. Or possibly, the project can give you an idea of something you didn't even know existed.

For example, while cruising through a science fair, I saw a project about how police use cyanoacrylate (a fast-bonding adhesive used in industry and medicine) to lift fingerprints from various surfaces.

Making Friends with Your Child

Doing a science project can give you something in common with your son or daughter, at a time when understanding between parents and children (particularly teenagers) is sometimes rare. In fact, both students and parents have often told me that one of the best things about doing a science project is the opportunity to spend some quality time together and develop common interests.

For example, some parents and teens have bonded while building equipment out in the family garage. In another instance, a child began a project based on a parent's profession or hobby, and the two developed a lifelong interest.

Living Your Second Childhood

You still can't run with scissors, but if you enjoyed arts and crafts as a kid, you can really have fun when it's time to build the project display (see Chapter 12 for more information).

Personally, when my son was doing his project, I had so much fun lining up the letters that he had to beg me to get my hands off his backboard!

Your child's science project may be a great opportunity to shoot off a bottle rocket, play with a chemistry set, or watch insects reproduce. How many other times do you get to do that just for fun?

Knowing When to Say No

How much help you can and will give is entirely up to you.

For example, getting on the Internet to help your child order supplies may be perfectly reasonable. However, running out to the store at 9 p.m. when you're already in your pajamas (and your child knew what she needed three days ago) may be over the line.

My best advice is to feel free to set reasonable limits. You have the right to

- ✔ Refuse to respond to any request at any time.
- ✔ Set a spending limit for your child.
- ✔ Object to a colony of earthworms in your bathroom sink or a container of mold in the refrigerator.

Probably the best way to deal with conflict is to prevent it. Simply make your expectations clear at the beginning of the project. Then, stick to your guns and "just say no!"

Taking Time for Yourself

No matter what your child needs, remember that his or her science project is no reason to put your life on hold.

You don't need to call off your golf game, stop going to yoga class, or cancel an evening out with friends. You do a lot for your family, and probably more while your child is working on a science project.

Just as your car won't run without fuel, you can't keep giving if you don't keep getting. So, explain to your child that you want to help him, but that he needs to remember that this project is his to do — not yours.

Staying Centered

Take a minute to get calm and quiet, and the confusion that a project can often bring won't seem so overwhelming.

If you're still feeling confused, guilty, or out of control, try confiding in a friend or writing your feelings down in a journal.

Getting a Self-Checkup

Ask yourself how your life is going (and not just as a parent, either).

On a scale of 1 to 10, rate yourself in the following areas:

- Relationships
- Friends and family
- Home environment
- Career
- Personal growth and fulfillment

Compare your results each week. If things are going downhill during science project time, it may be time to adjust your priorities (and check out the two previous points I discussed).

Letting It Go

Whose science project is it anyway?

As concerned parents who are interested and involved with your children's lives, you can easily get so preoccupied that the project becomes more important to you than to your child. Keep reminding yourself that her grades or awards belong to her and not to you.

You can help, but don't do the project yourself — you're not doing your child any favors. Besides, teachers and judges usually know when a child didn't do the work.

Asking for Help

You (and your child) don't have to do it alone — help is available.

If you need assistance with the project itself, check out one of the great science project Web sites (see Chapter 20) where you can find some expert advice. Another source of information are the folks who run the science fair. At the local level, a committee usually manages the science fair. You may be able to phone or e-mail one of them for help.

You can also ask your child's science teacher for advice, or make a quick call to any friends who are scientists, engineers, or computer gurus. If you're really lucky, you may have an older son or daughter who's already done a science project.

Chapter 23

Ten MVPS (Most Valuable Project Supplies)

In This Chapter

▶ Getting supplies for reading, writing, and drawing

▶ Finding tools to use when building, computing, and experimenting

▶ Staying safe

▶ Cleaning up

*N*o matter what your project is about, having certain supplies close at hand can definitely make your life easier.

In this chapter, I explain what those supplies are and when you need to have them ready to ensure smooth sailing to the finish.

Going to the Library

Before you go to the library to do your research, get your supplies ready.

By supplies, I mean that you need to have enough paper or index cards to record all the information that you find for your project research. In addition, you'll want to take along plenty of pens and pencils so you don't run dry, and plenty of coins for the copy machines. Chapter 5 runs down all the information you need about doing library research.

Doing Interviews

Of course, you want to bring plenty of pencils and paper to any interviews you plan to do (Chapter 5 also offers information about doing interviews).

But, what's even better is if you have a small tape recorder (you can buy a microcassette recorder for $10 to $50). A microcassette recorder can really help you "remember" your subject's answers.

Don't be caught short in the middle of an interview. If you're using a tape recorder, be sure to take along extra batteries and a spare tape. Also, remember to keep an eye on the recorder — you don't want to get home and find out that you have only half the interview on tape.

Staying Organized

I suggest that you get a good calendar or organizer to keep track of your deadlines. You may also find it helpful to get a bulletin board to pin up your important papers, such as addresses, phone numbers, and shopping lists.

If you like to write notes and reminders for yourself, a whiteboard or chalk-board can come in handy. See Chapter 7 for detailed information about the best ways to organize your project.

Staying Current with Computing Supplies

Having a computer at home can be a real timesaver on your project, but only if you're prepared.

Internet access can make a big difference when doing research, and working with word processing or spreadsheet software can simplify your writing and calculating tasks immensely.

If you don't have a computer at home, don't worry. You can always use the ones at your school or local library, or even a family member's. However, if you think a computer will be helpful for more than just your science project (in other words, you'll use it for many other school assignments too), perhaps this may be a good time to consider getting one. These days, you can get a refurbished computer for less than $300, and a brand-new one for $500 (with rebates).

No matter who's computer you may be using, don't wait until the night before your research paper is due to realize that you've run out of paper or that your print cartridge has run dry. Keep an eye on both as you progress through your project to make sure that you don't have any surprises at the end.

Also, you may want to consider using a zip drive or diskettes to back up your project data.

Avoiding Accidents

Depending on your project, you may want to wear plastic gloves to protect your hands, goggles to shield your eyes, or a mask to cover your nose and mouth (you can buy these items at most home improvement stores).

If you use anything flammable, have a fire extinguisher handy or better yet, ask an adult for some help. See Chapter 4 for a list of ways to keep your project safe.

Measuring Up

While you're doing your project, have your measuring tools handy.

These tools may include rulers, scales, or meters. Preferably, your tools should be metric (because globally, science uses the metric system), and in the smallest possible unit of measure in order to achieve the most accurate results.

Observing and Recording Results

Your eyes and ears are the best tools you have when compiling your results, but a good notebook for your project log and some pre-made forms to write down your measurements can make this part of the project a lot simpler. Chapter 10 tells you everything you need to know about results and conclusions.

Photos are another great way to document your project (they're worth a thousand words, right?). Just keep a loaded camera and extra film handy, so you're ready to capture that "a-ha" moment.

If you have a digital camera, you can choose your best shots, download them to your computer, and enlarge or crop them — they'll come in handy when working on your backboard (see Chapter 12).

While you're at it, why not ask your Mom or Dad to snap some photos of you, working hard on your project. It'll be fun to look at them later, when you're all done.

Drawing and Painting

Before you begin working on your backboard, I recommend gathering everything you think you'll need in one central place.

Markers, paint, construction paper, scissors, a straight edge, and glue are just a few of the things that you'll need. You may also want to choose your favorite photos and graphs to put on the backboard before you get started.

Having everything in one place makes it easier to sketch out some sample backboards to see what works best for your project. See Chapter 12 for the whole story on science project displays.

Putting Everything Away

If you need to stow things while you're working, just gather up your boxes, bottles, plastic containers, and sealable plastic bags and keep them close to the work area.

Just be sure that you choose the right container for the right substance, and label each one with their contents. You don't want to confuse the motor oil and the salad oil.

Mopping Up

Cleaning up is easier and faster when you have the right tools, so keep the paper towels, soap, detergent, and water close at hand.

Also, remember to clean as you go. When you clean as you go, you have less to clean up when you complete your work (your mess won't be as big, and you get done sooner).

No doubt the rest of your family will appreciate your diligence in this area too. (The less time they have to look at your bacteria cultures, the better, right?)

Index

• F •